VOLTAIRE'S

PHILOSOPHICAL
DICTIONARY

1924

This book has been published by:

Contact: sales@nuvisionpublications.com

URL: http://www.nuvisionpublications.com

Publishing Date: 2008

ISBN# 1-59547-637-7

Please see our website for several books created for
education, research and entertainment.

Specializing in rare, out-of-print books still in demand.

NuVision Publications, LLC is dedicated to bringing new life to rare, historic, and formerly out-of-print books. Most re-print publishers simply photocopy, or scan and print the pages from the original book, which can make the book hard to read as most re-print books are 100+ years old. It is our policy to take the time to convert the original faded, sometimes blotched text into crisp, clear digital text. All of our printed books have been completely reformatted to be easy to read and enjoy.

Please note that we do not correct out-of-date facts or grammar-type errors that were in the original book. We do our best to retain the original composition of the text, the way the author intended it.

NuVision Publications, LLC
Sioux Falls, SD USA

CONTENTS

PREFACE...9

ADULTERY 11
ADVOCATE...14
ANCIENTS AND MODERNS.................................14
ANIMALS 17
ANTIQUITY 19
ARTS 21
ASTROLOGY...22
ATHEISM..23
AUTHORITY 33
AUTHORS...34

BANISHMENT 35
BANKRUPTCY...36
BEAUTY..37
BISHOP 39
BOOKS 40
BOULEVERD OR BOULEVART.........................42
BOURGES 43
BRAHMINS 43

CHARACTER..45
CHARLATAN 47
CIVIL LAWS 51
CLIMATE 51
COMMON SENSE 53
CONCATENATION OF EVENTS 55
CONTRADICTIONS...57
CORN 58
CROMWELL...59
CUSTOMS..63

DEMOCRACY...65
DESTINY..65
DEVOUT 68

ECCLESIASTICAL MINISTRY 69
EMBLEM 70
ENGLISH THEATRE 73
ENVY 74
EQUALITY 76
EXPIATION 78
EXTREME 81
EZOURVEIDAM 83

FAITH 84
FALSE MINDS 85
FATHERLAND 87
FINAL CAUSES 88
FRAUD 90
FREE-WILL 94
FRENCH 96
FRIENDSHIP 98

GOD 99

HELVETIA 102
HISTORY 103

IGNORANCE 107
THE IMPIOUS 109

JOAN OF ARC 109

KISSING 113

LANGUAGES 116
LAWS 121
LIBERTY 123
LIBRARY 126
LIMITS OF THE HUMAN MIND 128
LOCAL CRIMES 128
LOVE 129
LUXURY 131

GENERAL REFLECTION ON MAN 134

MAN IN THE IRON MASK 134
MARRIAGE 138
MASTER 139
MEN OF LETTERS 141
METAMORPHOSIS, METEMPSYCHOSIS 142
MILTON, ON THE REPROACH OF PLAGIARISM AGAINST ... 143
MOHAMMEDANS 145

MOUNTAIN 146

NAKEDNESS.. 146
NATURAL LAW.. 147
NATURE 149
NECESSARY 152
NEW NOVELTIES... 155

PHILOSOPHER 156
POWER, OMNIPOTENCE... 158
PRAYERS... 161
PRÉCIS OF ANCIENT PHILOSOPHY 162
PREJUDICES... 165

RARE.. 168
REASON 169
RELIGION 171

SECT 176
SELF-ESTEEM... 179
SOUL.. 180
STATES, GOVERNMENTS 195
SUPERSTITION 198

TEARS 199
THEIST 200
TOLERANCE 201
TRUTH... 203
TYRANNY.. 205

VIRTUE.. 206

WHY?.. 209

DECLARATION OF THE ADMIRERS, QUESTIONERS AND DOUBTERS
WHO HAVE AMUSED THEMSELVES BY PROPOUNDING TO THE
SCHOLARS THE ABOVE QUESTIONS IN NINE VOLUMES.................... 210

PREFACE

This book does not demand continuous reading; but at whatever place one opens it, one will find matter for reflection. The most useful books are those of which readers themselves compose half; they extend the thoughts of which the germ is presented to them; they correct what seems defective to them, and they fortify by their reflections what seems to them weak.

It is only really by enlightened people that this book can be read; the ordinary man is not made for such knowledge; philosophy will never be his lot. Those who say that there are truths which must be hidden from the people, need not be alarmed; the people do not read; they work six days of the week, and on the seventh go to the inn. In a word, philosophical works are made only for philosophers, and every honest man must try to be a philosopher, without pluming himself on being one.

This alphabet is extracted from the most estimable works which are not commonly within the reach of the many; and if the author does not always mention the sources of his information, as being well enough known to the learned, he must not be suspected of wishing to take the credit for other people's work, because he himself preserves anonymity, according to this word of the Gospel: "Let not thy left hand know what thy right hand doeth."

ADULTERY

Note on a Magistrate Written about 1764

A senior magistrate of a French town had the misfortune to have a wife who was debauched by a priest before her marriage, and who since covered herself with disgrace by public scandals: he was so moderate as to leave her without noise. This man, about forty years old, vigorous and of agreeable appearance, needs a woman; he is too scrupulous to seek to seduce another man's wife, he fears intercourse with a public woman or with a widow who would serve him as concubine. In this disquieting and sad state, he addresses to his Church a plea of which the following is a précis:

My wife is criminal, and it is I who am punished. Another woman is necessary as a comfort to my life, to my virtue even; and the sect of which I am a member refuses her to me; it forbids me to marry an honest girl. The civil laws of to-day, unfortunately founded on canon law, deprive me of the rights of humanity. The Church reduces me to seeking either the pleasures it reproves, or the shameful compensations it condemns; it tries to force me to be criminal.

I cast my eyes over all the peoples of the earth; there is not a single one except the Roman Catholic people among whom divorce and a new marriage are not natural rights.

What upheaval of the rule has therefore made among the Catholics a virtue of undergoing adultery, and a duty of lacking a wife when one has been infamously outraged by one's own?

Why is a bond that has rotted indissoluble in spite of the great law adopted by the code, *quidquid ligatur dissolubile est*? I am allowed a separation *a mensa et thoro*, and I am not allowed divorce. The law can deprive me of my wife, and it leaves me a name called "sacrament"! What a contradiction! what slavery! and under what laws did we receive birth!

What is still more strange is that this law of my Church is directly contrary to the words which this Church itself believes to have been uttered by Jesus Christ: "Whosoever shall put away his wife, except it be for fornication, and shall marry another, committeth adultery" (Matt. xix. 9).

11

I do not examine whether the pontiffs of Rome are in the right to violate at their pleasure the law of him they regard as their master; whether when a state has need of an heir, it is permissible to repudiate her who can give it one. I do not inquire if a turbulent woman, demented, homicidal, a poisoner, should not be repudiated equally with an adulteress: I limit myself to the sad state which concerns me: God permits me to remarry, and the Bishop of Rome does not permit me.

Divorce was a practice among Catholics under all the emperors; it was also in all the dismembered states of the Roman Empire. The kings of France, those called "of the first line," almost all repudiated their wives in order to take new ones. At last came Gregory IX., enemy of the emperors and kings, who by a decree made marriage an unshakeable yoke; his decretal became the law of Europe. When the kings wanted to repudiate a wife who was an adulteress according to Jesus Christ's law, they could not succeed; it was necessary to find ridiculous pretexts. Louis the younger was obliged, to accomplish his unfortunate divorce from Eleanor of Guienne, to allege a relationship which did not exist. Henry IV., to repudiate Marguerite de Valois, pretexted a still more false cause, a refusal of consent. One had to lie to obtain a divorce legitimately.

What! a king can abdicate his crown, and without the Pope's permission he cannot abdicate his wife! Is it possible that otherwise enlightened men have wallowed so long in this absurd servitude!

That our priests, that our monks renounce wives, to that I consent; it is an outrage against population, it is a misfortune for them, but they merit this misfortune which they have made for themselves. They have been the victims of the popes who wanted to have in them slaves, soldiers without families and without fatherland, living solely for the Church: but I, magistrate, who serve the state all day, I need a wife in the evening; and the Church has not the right to deprive me of a benefit which God accords me. The apostles were married, Joseph was married, and I want to be. If I, Alsacian, am dependent on a priest who dwells at Rome, if this priest has the barbarous power to rob me of a wife, let him make a eunuch of me for the singing of *Misereres* in his chapel.

Note for Women

Equity demands that, having recorded this note in favour of husbands, we should also put before the public the case in favour of wives, presented to the junta of Portugal by a Countess of Arcira. This is the substance of it:

The Gospel has forbidden adultery for my husband just as for me; he will be damned as I shall, nothing is better established. When he committed twenty infidelities, when he gave my necklace to one of my rivals, and my ear-rings to another, I did not ask the judges to have him shaved, to shut him up among monks and to give me his property. And I, for having imitated him once, for having done with the most handsome young man in Lisbon what he did every day with impunity with the most idiotic strumpets of the court and the town, have to answer at the bar before licentiates each of whom would be at my feet if we were alone together in my closet; have to endure at the court the usher cutting off my hair which is the most beautiful in the world; and being shut up among nuns who have no common sense, deprived of my dowry and my marriage covenants, with all my property given to my coxcomb of a husband to help him seduce other women and to commit fresh adulteries.

I ask if it is just, and if it is not evident that the laws were made by cuckolds?

In answer to my plea I am told that I should be happy not to be stoned at the city gate by the canons, the priests of the parish and the whole populace. This was the practice among the first nation of the earth, the chosen nation, the cherished nation, the only one which was right when all the others were wrong.

To these barbarities I reply that when the poor adulteress was presented by her accusers to the Master of the old and new law, He did not have her stoned; that on the contrary He reproached them with their injustice, that he laughed at them by writing on the ground with his finger, that he quoted the old Hebraic proverb—"He that is without sin among you, let him first cast a stone at her"; that then they all retired, the oldest fleeing first, because the older they were the more adulteries had they committed.

The doctors of canon law answer me that this history of the adulteress is related only in the Gospel of St. John, that it was not inserted there until later. Leontius, Maldonat, affirm that it is not to be found in a single ancient Greek copy; that none of the twenty-three early commentators mentions it. Origin, St. Jerome, St. John Chrysostom, Theophilact, Nonnus, do not recognize it at all. It is not to be found in the Syriac Bible, it is not in Ulphilas' version.

That is what my husband's advocates say, they who would have me not only shaved, but also stoned.

But the advocates who pleaded for me say that Ammonius, author of the third century, recognized this story as true, and that if St. Jerome rejects it in some places, he adopts it in others; that, in a word, it is authentic to-day. I leave there, and I say to my husband: "If you are without sin, shave me, imprison me, take my property; but if you have

13

committed more sins than I have, it is for me to shave you, to have you imprisoned, and to seize your fortune. In justice these things should be equal."

My husband answers that he is my superior and my chief, that he is more than an inch taller, that he is shaggy as a bear; that consequently I owe him everything, and that he owes me nothing.

But I ask if Queen Anne of England is not her husband's chief? if her husband the Prince of Denmark, who is her High Admiral, does not owe her entire obedience? and if she would not have him condemned by the court of peers if the little man's infidelity were in question? It is therefore clear that if the women do not have the men punished, it is when they are not the stronger.

ADVOCATE

An advocate is a man who, not having a sufficient fortune to buy one of those resplendent offices on which the universe has its eyes, studies the laws of Theodosius and Justinian for three years, so that he may learn the usages of Paris, and who finally, being registered, has the right to plead causes for money, if he have a strong voice.

ANCIENTS AND MODERNS

The great dispute between the ancients and the moderns is not yet settled; it has been on the table since the silver age succeeded the golden age. Mankind has always maintained that the good old times were much better than the present day. Nestor, in the "Iliad," wishing to insinuate himself as a wise conciliator into the minds of Achilles and Agamemnon, starts by saying to them—"I lived formerly with better men than you; no, I have never seen and I shall never see such great personages as Dryas, Cenæus, Exadius, Polyphemus equal to the gods, etc."

Posterity has well avenged Achilles for Nestor's poor compliment. Nobody knows Dryas any longer; one has hardly heard speak of Exadius, or of Cenæus; and as for Polyphemus equal to the gods, he has not too good a reputation, unless the possession of a big eye in one's forehead, and the eating of men raw, are to have something of the divine.

14

Lucretius does not hesitate to say that nature has degenerated (lib. II. v. 1159). Antiquity is full of eulogies of another more remote antiquity. Horace combats this prejudice with as much finesse as force in his beautiful Epistle to Augustus (Epist. I. liv. ii.). "Must our poems, then," he says, "be like our wines, of which the oldest are always preferred?"

The learned and ingenious Fontenelle expresses himself on this subject as follows:

"The whole question of the pre-eminence between the ancients and the moderns, once it is well understood, is reduced to knowing whether the trees which formerly were in our countryside were bigger than those of to-day. In the event that they were, Homer, Plato, Demosthenes cannot be equalled in these latter centuries.

"Let us throw light on this paradox. If the ancients had more intellect than us, it is that the brains of those times were better ordered, formed of firmer or more delicate fibres, filled with more animal spirits; but in virtue of what were the brains of those times better ordered? The trees also would have been bigger and more beautiful; for if nature was then younger and more vigorous, the trees, as well as men's brains, would have been conscious of this vigour and this youth." ("Digression on the Ancients and the Moderns," vol. 4, 1742 edition.)

With the illustrious academician's permission, that is not at all the state of the question. It is not a matter of knowing whether nature has been able to produce in our day as great geniuses and as good works as those of Greek and Latin antiquity; but to know whether we have them in fact. Without a doubt it is not impossible for there to be as big oaks in the forest of Chantilli as in the forest of Dodona; but supposing that the oaks of Dodona had spoken, it would be quite clear that they had a great advantage over ours, which in all probability will never speak.

Nature is not bizarre; but it is possible that she gave the Athenians a country and a sky more suitable than Westphalia and the Limousin for forming certain geniuses. Further, it is possible that the government of Athens, by seconding the climate, put into Demosthenes' head something that the air of Climart and La Grenouillère and the government of Cardinal de Richelieu did not put into the heads of Omer Talon and Jérome Bignon.

This dispute is therefore a question of fact. Was antiquity more fecund in great monuments of all kinds, up to the time of Plutarch, than modern centuries have been from the century of the Medicis up to Louis XIV. inclusive?

The Chinese, more than two hundred years before our era, constructed that great wall which was not able to save them from the invasion of the Tartars. The Egyptians, three thousand years before, had overloaded the earth with their astonishing pyramids, which had a base of about ninety thousand square feet. Nobody doubts that, if one wished to undertake to-day these useless works, one could easily succeed by a lavish expenditure of money. The great wall of China is a monument to fear; the pyramids are monuments to vanity and superstition. Both bear witness to a great patience in the peoples, but to no superior genius. Neither the Chinese nor the Egyptians would have been able to make even a statue such as those which our sculptors form to-day.

The chevalier Temple, who has made it his business to disparage all the moderns, claims that in architecture they have nothing comparable to the temples of Greece and Rome: but, for all that he is English, he must agree that the Church of St. Peter is incomparably more beautiful than the Capitol was.

It is curious with what assurance he maintains that there is nothing new in our astronomy, nothing in the knowledge of the human body, unless perhaps, he says, the circulation of the blood. Love of his own opinion, founded on his vast self-esteem, makes him forget the discovery of the satellites of Jupiter, of the five moons and the ring of Saturn, of the rotation of the sun on its axis, of the calculated position of three thousand stars, of the laws given by Kepler and Newton for the heavenly orbs, of the causes of the precession of the equinoxes, and of a hundred other pieces of knowledge of which the ancients did not suspect even the possibility.

The discoveries in anatomy are as great in number. A new universe in little, discovered by the microscope, was counted for nothing by the chevalier Temple; he closed his eyes to the marvels of his contemporaries, and opened them only to admire ancient ignorance.

He goes so far as to pity us for having nothing left of the magic of the Indians, the Chaldeans, the Egyptians; and by this magic he understands a profound knowledge of nature, whereby they produced miracles: but he does not cite one miracle, because in fact there never were any. "What has become," he asks, "of the charms of that music which so often enchanted man and beast, the fishes, the birds, the snakes, and changed their nature?"

This enemy of his century really believes the fable of Orpheus, and has not apparently heard either the beautiful music of Italy, or even that of France, which in truth does not charm snakes, but does charm the ears of connoisseurs.

What is still more strange is that, having all his life cultivated belles-lettres, he does not reason better about our good authors than about our philosophers. He looks on Rabelais as a great man. He cites the "Amours des Gaules" as one of our best works. He was, however, a scholar, a courtier, a man of much wit, an ambassador, a man who had reflected profoundly on all he had seen. He possessed great knowledge: a prejudice sufficed to spoil all this merit.

16

There are beauties in Euripides, and in Sophocles still more; but they have many more defects. One dares say that the beautiful scenes of Corneille and the touching tragedies of Racine surpass the tragedies of Sophocles and Euripides as much as these two Greeks surpass Thespis. Racine was quite conscious of his great superiority over Euripides; but he praised the Greek poet in order to humiliate Perrault.

Molière, in his good pieces, is as superior to the pure but cold Terence, and to the droll Aristophanes, as to Dancourt the buffoon.

There are therefore spheres in which the moderns are far superior to the ancients, and others, very few in number, in which we are their inferiors. It is to this that the whole dispute is reduced.

ANIMALS

What a pitiful, what a sorry thing to have said that animals are machines bereft of understanding and feeling, which perform their operations always in the same way, which learn nothing, perfect nothing, etc.!

What! that bird which makes its nest in a semi-circle when it is attaching it to a wall, which builds it in a quarter circle when it is in an angle, and in a circle upon a tree; that bird acts always in the same way? That hunting-dog which you have disciplined for three months, does it not know more at the end of this time than it knew before your lessons? Does the canary to which you teach a tune repeat it at once? do you not spend a considerable time in teaching it? have you not seen that it has made a mistake and that it corrects itself?

Is it because I speak to you, that you judge that I have feeling, memory, ideas? Well, I do not speak to you; you see me going home looking disconsolate, seeking a paper anxiously, opening the desk where I remember having shut it, finding it, reading it joyfully. You judge that I have experienced the feeling of distress and that of pleasure, that I have memory and understanding.

Bring the same judgment to bear on this dog which has lost its master, which has sought him on every road with sorrowful cries, which enters the house agitated, uneasy, which goes down the stairs, up the stairs, from room to room, which at last finds in his study the master it loves, and which shows him its joy by its cries of delight, by its leaps, by its caresses.

Barbarians seize this dog, which in friendship surpasses man so prodigiously; they nail it on a table, and they dissect it alive in order to show the mesenteric veins. You discover in it all the same organs of feeling that are in yourself. Answer me, machinist, has nature arranged all the means of feeling in this animal, so that it may not feel? has it nerves in order to be impassible? Do not suppose this impertinent contradiction in nature.

But the schoolmasters ask what the soul of animals is? I do not understand this question. A tree has the faculty of receiving in its fibres its sap which circulates, of unfolding the buds of its leaves and its fruit; will you ask what the soul of this tree is? it has received these gifts; the animal has received those of feeling, of memory, of a certain number of ideas. Who has bestowed these gifts? who has given these faculties? He who has made the grass of the fields to grow, and who makes the earth gravitate toward the sun.

"Animals' souls are substantial forms," said Aristotle, and after Aristotle, the Arab school, and after the Arab school, the angelical school, and after the angelical school, the Sorbonne, and after the Sorbonne, nobody at all.

"Animals' souls are material," cry other philosophers. These have not been in any better fortune than the others. In vain have they been asked what a material soul is; they have to admit that it is matter which has sensation: but what has given it this sensation? It is a material soul, that is to say that it is matter which gives sensation to matter; they cannot issue from this circle.

Listen to other brutes reasoning about the brutes; their soul is a spiritual soul which dies with the body; but what proof have you of it? what idea have you of this spiritual soul, which, in truth, has feeling, memory, and its measure of ideas and ingenuity; but which will never be able to know what a child of six knows? On what ground do you imagine that this being, which is not body, dies with the body? The greatest fools are those who have advanced that this soul is neither body nor spirit. There is a fine system. By spirit we can understand only some unknown thing which is not body. Thus these gentlemen's system comes back to this, that the animals' soul is a substance which is neither body nor something which is not body.

Whence can come so many contradictory errors? From the habit men have always had of examining what a thing is, before knowing if it exists. The clapper, the valve of a bellows, is called in French the "soul" of a bellows. What is this soul? It is a name that I have given to this valve which falls, lets air enter, rises again, and thrusts it through a pipe, when I make the bellows move.

There is not there a distinct soul in the machine: but what makes animals' bellows move? I have already told you, what makes the stars

18

move. The philosopher who said, *"Deus est anima brutorum,"* was right; but he should go further.

ANTIQUITY

Have you sometimes seen in a village Pierre Aoudri and his wife Peronelle wishing to go before their neighbours in the procession? "Our grandfathers," they say, "were tolling the bells before those who jostle us to-day owned even a pig-sty."

The vanity of Pierre Aoudri, his wife and his neighbours, knows nothing more about it. Their minds kindle. The quarrel is important; honour is in question. Proofs are necessary. A scholar who sings in the choir, discovers an old rusty iron pot, marked with an "A," first letter of the name of the potter who made the pot. Pierre Aoudri persuades himself that it was his ancestors' helmet. In this way was Cæsar descended from a hero and from the goddess Venus. Such is the history of nations; such is, within very small margins, the knowledge of early antiquity.

The scholars of Armenia *demonstrate* that the terrestrial paradise was in their land. Some profound Swedes *demonstrate* that it was near Lake Vener which is visibly a remnant of it. Some Spaniards *demonstrate* also that it was in Castille; while the Japanese, the Chinese, the Indians, the Africans, the Americans are not sufficiently unfortunate to know even that there was formerly a terrestrial paradise at the source of the Phison, the Gehon, the Tigris and the Euphrates, or, if you prefer it, at the source of the Guadalquivir, the Guadiana, the Douro and the Ebro; for from Phison one easily makes Phaetis; and from Phaetis one makes the Baetis which is the Guadalquivir. The Gehon is obviously the Guadiana, which begins with a "G." The Ebro, which is in Catalonia, is incontestably the Euphrates, of which the initial letter is "E."

But a Scotsman appears who *demonstrates* in his turn that the garden of Eden was at Edinburgh, which has retained its name; and it is to be believed that in a few centuries this opinion will make its fortune.

The whole globe was burned once upon a time, says a man versed in ancient and modern history; for I read in a newspaper that some absolutely black charcoal has been found in Germany at a depth of a hundred feet, between mountains covered with wood. And it is suspected even that there were charcoal burners in this place.

Phaeton's adventure makes it clear that everything has boiled right to the bottom of the sea. The sulphur of Mount Vesuvius proves invincibly that the banks of the Rhine, Danube, Ganges, Nile and the great Yellow River are merely sulphur, nitre and Guiac oil, which only await the moment of the explosion to reduce the earth to ashes, as it has already been. The sand on which we walk is evident proof that the earth has been vitrified, and that our globe is really only a glass ball, just as are our ideas.

But if fire has changed our globe, water has produced still finer revolutions. For you see clearly that the sea, the tides of which mount as high as eight feet in our climate, has produced mountains of a height of sixteen to seventeen thousand feet. This is so true that some learned men who have never been in Switzerland have found a big ship with all its rigging petrified on Mount St. Gothard, or at the bottom of a precipice, one knows not where; but it is quite certain that it was there. Therefore men were originally fish, *quod erat demonstrandum*.

To descend to a less antique antiquity, let us speak of the times when the greater part of the barbarous nations left their countries, to go to seek others which were hardly any better. It is true, if there be anything true in ancient history, that there were some Gaulish brigands who went to pillage Rome in the time of Camillus. Other Gaulish brigands had passed, it is said, through Illyria on the way to hire their services as murderers to other murderers, in the direction of Thrace; they exchanged their blood for bread, and later established themselves in Galatia. But who were these Gauls? were they Berichons and Angevins? They were without a doubt Gauls whom the Romans called Cisalpines, and whom we call Transalpines, famished mountain-dwellers, neighbours of the Alps and the Apennines. The Gauls of the Seine and the Marne did not know at that time that Rome existed, and could not take it into their heads to pass Mount Cenis, as Hannibal did later, to go to steal the wardrobes of Roman senators who at that time for all furniture had a robe of poor grey stuff, ornamented with a band the colour of ox blood; two little pummels of ivory, or rather dog's bone, on the arms of a wooden chair; and in their kitchens a piece of rancid bacon.

The Gauls, who were dying of hunger, not finding anything to eat in Rome, went off therefore to seek their fortune farther away, as was the practice of the Romans later, when they ravaged so many countries one after the other; as did the peoples of the North when they destroyed the Roman Empire.

And, further, what is it which instructs very feebly about these emigrations? It is a few lines that the Romans wrote at hazard; because for the Celts, the Velches or the Gauls, these men who it is desired to make pass for eloquent, at that time did not know, they and their bards, how either to read or write.

But to infer from that that the Gauls or Celts, conquered after by a few of Cæsar's legions, and by a horde of Bourguignons, and lastly by a horde of Sicamores, under one Clodovic, had previously subjugated the whole world, and given their names and laws to Asia, seems to me to be very strange: the thing is not mathematically impossible, and if it be *demonstrated*, I give way; it would be very uncivil to refuse to the Velches what one accords to the Tartars.

ARTS

That the Newness of the Arts in no wise proves the Newness of the Globe

All the philosophers thought matter eternal but the arts appear new. There is not one, even to the art of making bread, which is not recent. The first Romans ate pap; and these conquerors of so many nations never thought of either windmills or watermills. This truth seems at first to contradict the antiquity of the globe such as it is, or supposes terrible revolutions in this globe. The inundations of barbarians can hardly annihilate arts which have become necessary. I suppose that an army of negroes come among us like locusts, from the mountains of Cobonas, through the Monomotapa, the Monoemugi, the Nosseguais, the Maracates; that they have traversed Abyssinia, Nubia, Egypt, Syria, Asia Minor, the whole of our Europe; that they have overthrown everything, ransacked everything; there will still remain a few bakers, a few cobblers, a few tailors, a few carpenters: the necessary arts will survive; only luxury will be annihilated. It is what was seen at the fall of the Roman Empire; the art of writing even became very rare; almost all those which contributed to the comfort of life were reborn only long after. We invent new ones every day.

From all this one can at bottom conclude nothing against the antiquity of the globe. For, supposing even that an influx of barbarians had made us lose entirely all the arts even to the arts of writing and making bread; supposing, further, that for ten years past we had no bread, pens, ink and paper; the land which has been able to subsist for ten years without eating bread and without writing its thoughts, would be able to pass a century, and a hundred thousand centuries without these aids.

It is quite clear that man and the other animals can exist very well without bakers, without novelists, and without theologians, witness the whole of America, witness three quarters of our continent.

The newness of the arts among us does not therefore prove the newness of the globe, as was claimed by Epicurus, one of our predecessors in reverie, who supposed that by chance the eternal atoms in declining, had one day formed our earth. Pomponace said: *"Se il mondo non è eterno, per tutti santi è molto vecchio."*

ASTROLOGY

Astrology may rest on better foundations than Magic. For if no one has seen either Goblins, or Lemures, or Dives, or Peris, or Demons, or Cacodemons, the predictions of astrologers have often been seen to succeed. If of two astrologers consulted on the life of a child and on the weather, one says that the child will live to manhood, the other not; if one announces rain, and the other fine weather, it is clear that one of them will be a prophet.

The great misfortune of the astrologers is that the sky has changed since the rules of the art were established. The sun, which at the equinox was in Aries in the time of the Argonauts, is to-day in Taurus; and the astrologers, to the great ill-fortune of their art, to-day attribute to one house of the sun what belongs visibly to another. However, that is not a demonstrative reason against astrology. The masters of the art deceive themselves; but it is not demonstrated that the art cannot exist.

There is no absurdity in saying: Such and such a child is born in the waxing of the moon, during stormy weather, at the rising of such and such star; his constitution has been feeble, and his life unhappy and short; which is the ordinary lot of poor constitutions: this child, on the contrary, was born when the moon was full, the sun strong, the weather calm, at the rising of such and such star; his constitution has been good, his life long and happy. If these observations had been repeated, if they had been found accurate, experience would have been able after some thousands of years to form an art which it would have been difficult to doubt: one would have thought, with some likelihood, that men are like trees and vegetables which must be planted and sown only in certain seasons. It would have been of no avail against the astrologers to say: My son was born at a fortunate time, and nevertheless died in his cradle; the astrologer would have answered: It often happens that trees planted in the proper season perish; I answered to you for the stars, but I did not answer for the flaw of conformation you communicated to your child. Astrology operates only when no cause opposes itself to the good the stars can do.

One would not have succeeded better in discrediting the astrologer by saying: Of two children who were born in the same minute, one has been king, the other has been only churchwarden of his parish; for the astrologer could very well have defended himself by pointing out that the peasant made his fortune when he became churchwarden, as the prince when he became king.

And if one alleged that a bandit whom Sixtus V. had hanged was born at the same time as Sixtus V., who from a pig-herd became Pope, the astrologers would say one had made a mistake of a few seconds, and that it is impossible, according to the rules, for the same star to give the triple crown and the gibbet. It is then only because a host of experiences belied the predictions, that men perceived at last that the art was illusory; but before being undeceived, they were long credulous.

One of the most famous mathematicians in Europe, named Stoffler, who flourished in the fifteenth and sixteenth centuries, and who long worked at the reform of the calendar, proposed at the Council of Constance, foretold a universal flood for the year 1524. This flood was to arrive in the month of February, and nothing is more plausible; for Saturn, Jupiter and Mars were then in conjunction in the sign of Pisces. All the peoples of Europe, Asia and Africa, who heard speak of the prediction, were dismayed. Everyone expected the flood, despite the rainbow. Several contemporary authors record that the inhabitants of the maritime provinces of Germany hastened to sell their lands dirt cheap to those who had most money, and who were not so credulous as they. Everyone armed himself with a boat as with an ark. A Toulouse doctor, named Auriol, had a great ark made for himself, his family and his friends; the same precautions were taken over a large part of Italy. At last the month of February arrived, and not a drop of water fell: never was month more dry, and never were the astrologers more embarrassed. Nevertheless they were not discouraged, nor neglected among us; almost all princes continued to consult them.

I have not the honour of being a prince; but the celebrated Count of Boulainvilliers and an Italian, named Colonne, who had much prestige in Paris, both foretold that I should die infallibly at the age of thirty-two. I have been so malicious as to deceive them already by nearly thirty years, wherefore I humbly beg their pardon.

ATHEISM

SECTION I

Of the Comparison so often made between Atheism and Idolatry

It seems to me that in the "Encyclopedic Dictionary" the opinion of the Jesuit Richeome, on atheists and idolaters, has not been refuted as strongly as it might have been; opinion held formerly by St. Thomas, St. Gregory of Nazianze, St. Cyprian and Tertullian, opinion that Arnobius set forth with much force when he said to the pagans: "Do you not blush to reproach us with despising your gods, and is it not much more proper to believe in no God at all, than to impute to them infamous actions?"[1] opinion established long before by Plutarch, who says "that he much prefers people to say there is no Plutarch, than to say—'There is an inconstant, choleric, vindictive Plutarch'";[2] opinion strengthened finally by all the effort of Bayle's dialectic.

Here is the ground of dispute, brought to fairly dazzling light by the Jesuit Richeome, and rendered still more plausible by the way Bayle has turned it to account.[3]

"There are two porters at the door of a house; they are asked: 'Can one speak to your master?' 'He is not there,' answers one. 'He is there,' answers the other, 'but he is busy making counterfeit money, forged contracts, daggers and poisons, to undo those who have but accomplished his purposes.' The atheist resembles the first of these porters, the pagan the other. It is clear, therefore, that the pagan offends the Deity more gravely than does the atheist."

With Father Richeome's and even Bayle's permission, that is not at all the position of the matter. For the first porter to resemble the atheists, he must not say—"My master is not here": he should say—"I have no master; him whom you claim to be my master does not exist; my comrade is a fool to tell you that he is busy compounding poisons and sharpening daggers to assassinate those who have executed his caprices. No such being exists in the world."

Richeome has reasoned, therefore, very badly. And Bayle, in his somewhat diffuse discourses, has forgotten himself so far as to do Richeome the honour of annotating him very malapropos.

Plutarch seems to express himself much better in preferring people who affirm there is no Plutarch, to those who claim Plutarch to be an unsociable man. In truth, what does it matter to him that people say he is not in the world? But it matters much to him that his reputation be not tarnished. It is not thus with the Supreme Being.

---

[1] Arnobius, *Adversus Gentes.*, lib. v.

[2] *Of Superstition*, by Plutarch.

[3] See Bayle, *Continuation of Divers Thoughts*, par. 77, art. XIII.

24

Plutarch even does not broach the real object under discussion. It is not a question of knowing who offends more the Supreme Being, whether it be he who denies Him, or he who distorts Him. It is impossible to know otherwise than by revelation, if God is offended by the empty things men say of Him.

Without a thought, philosophers fall almost always into the ideas of the common herd, in supposing God to be jealous of His glory, to be choleric, to love vengeance, and in taking rhetorical figures for real ideas. The interesting subject for the whole universe, is to know if it be not better, for the good of all mankind, to admit a rewarding and revengeful God, who recompenses good actions hidden, and who punishes secret crimes, than to admit none at all.

Bayle exhausts himself in recounting all the infamies imputed by fable to the gods of antiquity. His adversaries answer him with commonplaces that signify nothing. The partisans of Bayle and his enemies have almost always fought without making contact. They all agree that Jupiter was an adulterer, Venus a wanton, Mercury a rogue. But, as I see it, that is not what needs consideration. One must distinguish between Ovid's Metamorphoses and the religion of the ancient Romans. It is quite certain that never among the Romans or even among the Greeks, was there a temple dedicated to Mercury the rogue, Venus the wanton, Jupiter the adulterer.

The god whom the Romans called *Deus optimus*, very good, very great, was not reputed to encourage Clodius to sleep with Cæsar's wife, or Cæsar to be King Nicomedes' Sodomite.

Cicero does not say that Mercury incited Verres to steal Sicily, although Mercury, in the fable, had stolen Apollo's cows. The real religion of the ancients was that Jupiter, *very good and very just*, and the secondary gods, punished the perjurer in the infernal regions. Likewise the Romans were long the most religious observers of oaths. Religion was very useful, therefore, to the Romans. There was no command to believe in Leda's two eggs, in the changing of Inachus' daughter into a cow, in the love of Apollo for Hyacinthus.

One must not say therefore that the religion of Numa dishonoured the Deity. For a long time, therefore, people have been disputing over a chimera; which happens only too often.

The question is then asked whether a nation of atheists can exist; it seems to me that one must distinguish between the nation properly so called, and a society of philosophers above the nation. It is very true that in every country the populace has need of the greatest curb, and that if Bayle had had only five or six hundred peasants to govern, he would not have failed to announce to them the existence of a God, rewarder and revenger. But Bayle would not have spoken of Him to the Epicureans who were rich people, fond of rest, cultivating all the social virtues, and above all friendship, fleeing the embarrassment and danger of public affairs, in fine, leading a comfortable and innocent life. It seems to me that in this way the dispute is finished as regards society and politics.

For entirely savage races, it has been said already that one cannot count them among either the atheists or the theists. Asking them their belief would be like asking them if they are for Aristotle or Democritus: they know nothing; they are not atheists any more than they are Peripatetics.

In this case, I shall answer that the wolves live like this, and that an assembly of cannibal barbarians such as you suppose them is not a society; and I shall always ask you if, when you have lent your money to someone in your society, you want neither your debtor, nor your attorney, nor your judge, to believe in God.

Of Modern Atheists. Reasons of the Worshippers of God

We are intelligent beings: intelligent beings cannot have been formed by a crude, blind, insensible being: there is certainly some difference between the ideas of Newton and the dung of a mule. Newton's intelligence, therefore, came from another intelligence.

When we see a beautiful machine, we say that there is a good engineer, and that this engineer has excellent judgment. The world is assuredly an admirable machine; therefore there is in the world an admirable intelligence, wherever it may be. This argument is old, and none the worse for that.

All living bodies are composed of levers, of pulleys, which function according to the laws of mechanics; of liquids which the laws of hydrostatics cause to circulate perpetually; and when one thinks that all these beings have a perception quite unrelated to their organization, one is overwhelmed with surprise.

The movement of the heavenly bodies, that of our little earth round the sun, all operate by virtue of the most profound mathematical law. How Plato who was not aware of one of these laws, eloquent but visionary Plato, who said that the earth was erected on an equilateral triangle, and the water on a right-angled triangle; strange Plato, who says there can be only five worlds, because there are only five regular bodies: how, I say, did Plato, who did not know even spherical trigonometry, have nevertheless a genius sufficiently fine, an instinct sufficiently happy, to call God the "Eternal Geometer," to feel the existence of a creative intelligence? Spinoza himself admits it. It is impossible to strive against this truth which surrounds us and which presses on us from all sides.

Reasons of the Atheists

Notwithstanding, I have known refractory persons who say that there is no creative intelligence at all, and that movement alone has by itself formed all that we see and all that we are. They tell you brazenly:

"The combination of this universe was possible, seeing that the combination exists: therefore it was possible that movement alone arranged it. Take four of the heavenly bodies only, Mars, Venus, Mercury and the Earth: let us think first only of the place where they are, setting aside all the rest, and let us see how many probabilities we have that movement alone put them in their respective places. We have only twenty-four chances in this combination, that is, there are only twenty-four chances against one to bet that these bodies will not be where they are with reference to each other. Let us add to these four globes that of Jupiter; there will be only a hundred and twenty against one to bet that Jupiter, Mars, Venus, Mercury and our globe, will not be placed where we see them.

"Add finally Saturn: there will be only seven hundred and twenty chances against one, for putting these six big planets in the arrangement they preserve among themselves, according to their given distances. It is therefore demonstrated that in seven hundred and twenty throws, movement alone has been able to put these six principal planets in their order.

"Take then all the secondary bodies, all their combinations, all their movements, all the beings that vegetate, that live, that feel, that think, that function in all the globes, you will have but to increase the number of chances; multiply this number in all eternity, up to the number which our feebleness calls 'infinity,' there will always be a unity in favour of the formation of the world, such as it is, by movement alone: therefore it is possible that in all eternity the movement of matter alone has produced the entire universe such as it exists. It is even inevitable that in eternity this combination should occur. Thus," they say, "not only is it possible for the world to be what it is by movement alone, but it was impossible for it not to be likewise after an infinity of combinations."

Answer

All this supposition seems to me prodigiously fantastic, for two reasons; first, that in this universe there are intelligent beings, and that you would not know how to prove it possible for movement alone to produce understanding; second, that, from your own avowal, there is infinity against one to bet, that an intelligent creative cause animates the universe. When one is alone face to face with the infinite, one feels very small.

Again, Spinoza himself admits this intelligence; it is the basis of his system. You have not read it, and it must be read. Why do you want to go further than him, and in foolish arrogance plunge your feeble reason in an abyss into which Spinoza dared not descend? Do you realize thoroughly the extreme folly of saying that it is a blind cause that arranges that the square of a planet's revolution is always to the square of the revolutions of other planets, as the cube of its distance is to the cube of the distances of the others to the common centre? Either the heavenly bodies are great geometers, or the Eternal Geometer has arranged the heavenly bodies.

But where is the Eternal Geometer? is He in one place or in all places, without occupying space? I have no idea. Is it of His own substance that He has arranged all things? I have no idea. Is He immense without quantity and without quality? I have no idea. All that I know is that one must worship Him and be just.

New Objection of a Modern Atheist[4]

Can one say that the parts of animals conform to their needs: what are these needs? preservation and propagation. Is it astonishing then that, of the infinite combinations which chance has produced, there has been able to subsist only those that have organs adapted to the nourishment and continuation of their species? have not all the others perished of necessity?

Answer

This objection, oft-repeated since Lucretius, is sufficiently refuted by the gift of sensation in animals, and by the gift of intelligence in man. How should combinations "which chance has produced," produce this sensation and this intelligence (as has just been said in the preceding paragraph)? Without any doubt the limbs of animals are made for their needs with incomprehensible art, and you are not so bold as to deny it. You say no more about it. You feel that you have nothing to answer to this great argument which nature brings against you. The disposition of a fly's wing, a snail's organs suffices to bring you to the ground.

Maupertuis' Objection

Modern natural philosophers have but expanded these so-called arguments, often they have pushed them to trifling and indecency. They have found God in the folds of the skin of the rhinoceros: one could, with equal reason, deny His existence because of the tortoise's shell.

---

[4] See, for this objection, Maupertuis' Essay on Cosmology, first part.

Answer

What reasoning! The tortoise and the rhinoceros, and all the different species, are proof equally in their infinite variety of the same cause, the same design, the same aim, which are preservation, generation and death.

There is unity in this infinite variety; the shell and the skin bear witness equally. What! deny God because shell does not resemble leather! And journalists have been prodigal of eulogies about these ineptitudes, eulogies they have not given to Newton and Locke, both worshippers of the Deity who spoke with full knowledge.

Maupertuis' Objection

Of what use are beauty and proportion in the construction of the snake? They may have uses, some say, of which we are ignorant. At least let us be silent then; let us not admire an animal which we know only by the harm it does.

Answer

And be you silent too, seeing that you cannot conceive its utility any more than I can; or avow that in reptiles everything is admirably proportioned.

Some are venomous, you have been so yourself. Here there is question only of the prodigious art which has formed snakes, quadrupeds, birds, fish and bipeds. This art is sufficiently evident. You ask why the snake does harm? And you, why have you done harm so many times? Why have you been a persecutor? which is the greatest of all crimes for a philosopher. That is another question, a question of moral and physical ill. For long has one asked why there are so many snakes and so many wicked men worse than snakes. If flies could reason, they would complain to God of the existence of spiders; but they would admit what Minerva admitted about Arachne, in the fable, that she arranges her web marvellously.

One is bound therefore to recognize an ineffable intelligence which even Spinoza admitted. One must agree that this intelligence shines in the vilest insect as in the stars. And as regards moral and physical ill, what can one say, what do? console oneself by enjoying physical and moral good, in worshipping the Eternal Being who has made one and permitted the other.

One more word on this subject. Atheism is the vice of a few intelligent persons, and superstition is the vice of fools. But rogues! what are they? rogues.

Let us say a word on the moral question set in action by Bayle, to know "if a society of atheists could exist?" Let us mark first of all in this matter what is the enormous contradiction of men in this dispute; those who have risen against Bayle's opinion with the greatest ardour; those who have denied with the greatest insults the possibility of a society of atheists, have since maintained with the same intrepidity that atheism is the religion of the government of China.

Assuredly they are quite mistaken about the Chinese government; they had but to read the edicts of the emperors of this vast country to have seen that these edicts are sermons, and that everywhere there is mention of the Supreme Being, ruler, revenger, rewarder.

But at the same time they are not less mistaken on the impossibility of a society of atheists; and I do not know how Mr. Bayle can have forgotten one striking example which was capable of making his cause victorious.

In what does a society of atheists appear impossible? It is that one judges that men who had no check could never live together; that laws can do nothing against secret crimes; that a revengeful God who punishes in this world or the other the wicked who have escaped human justice is necessary.

The laws of Moses, it is true, did not teach a life to come, did not threaten punishments after death, did not teach the first Jews the immortality of the soul; but the Jews, far from being atheists, far from believing in avoiding divine vengeance, were the most religious of all men. Not only did they believe in the existence of an eternal God, but they believed Him always present among them; they trembled lest they be punished in themselves, in their wives, in their children, in their posterity, even unto the fourth generation; this curb was very potent.

But, among the Gentiles, many sects had no curb; the sceptics doubted everything: the academicians suspended judgment on everything; the Epicureans were persuaded that the Deity could not mix Himself in the affairs of men; and at bottom, they admitted no Deity. They were convinced that the soul is not a substance, but a faculty which is born and which perishes with the body; consequently they had no yoke other than morality and honour. The Roman senators and knights were veritable atheists, for the gods did not exist for men who neither feared nor hoped anything from them. The Roman senate in the time of Cæsar and Cicero, was therefore really an assembly of atheists.

That great orator, in his harangue for Cluentius, says to the whole senate in assembly: "What ill does death do him? we reject all the inept fables of the nether regions: of what then has death deprived him? of nothing but the consciousness of suffering."

Does not Cæsar, the friend of Cataline, wishing to save his friend's life against this same Cicero, object to him that to make a criminal die is not to punish him at all, that death *is nothing*, that it is merely the end of our ills, that it is a moment more happy than calamitous? And do not Cicero and the whole senate surrender to these reasons? The conquerors and the legislators of the known universe formed visibly therefore a society of men who feared nothing from the gods, who were real atheists.

Further on Bayle examines whether idolatry is more dangerous than atheism, if it is a greater crime not to believe in the Deity than to have unworthy opinions thereof: in that he is of Plutarch's opinion; he believes it is better to have no opinion than to have a bad opinion; but with all deference to Plutarch, it was clearly infinitely better for the Greeks to fear Ceres, Neptune and Jupiter, than to fear nothing at all. The sanctity of oaths is clearly necessary, and one should have more confidence in those who believe that a false oath will be punished, than in those who think they can make a false oath with impunity. It is indubitable that in a civilized town, it is infinitely more useful to have a religion, even a bad one, than to have none at all.

It looks, therefore, that Bayle should have examined rather which is the more dangerous, fanaticism or atheism. Fanaticism is certainly a thousand times more deadly; for atheism inspires no bloody passion, whereas fanaticism does: atheism is not opposed to crime, but fanaticism causes crimes to be committed. Fanatics committed the massacres of St. Bartholomew. Hobbes passed for an atheist; he led a tranquil and innocent life. The fanatics of his time deluged England, Scotland and Ireland with blood. Spinoza was not only atheist, but he taught atheism; it was not he assuredly who took part in the judicial assassination of Barneveldt; it was not he who tore the brothers De Witt in pieces, and who ate them grilled.

The atheists are for the most part impudent and misguided scholars who reason badly, and who not being able to understand the creation, the origin of evil, and other difficulties, have recourse to the hypothesis of the eternity of things and of inevitability.

The ambitious, the sensual, have hardly time for reasoning, and for embracing a bad system; they have other things to do than comparing Lucretius with Socrates. That is how things go among us.

That was not how things went with the Roman senate which was almost entirely composed of atheists in theory and in practice, that is to say, who believed in neither a Providence nor a future life; this senate was an assembly of philosophers, of sensualists and ambitious men, all very dangerous, who ruined the republic. Epicureanism existed under

31

the emperors: the atheists of the senate had been rebels in the time of Sylla and Cæsar: under Augustus and Tiberius they were atheist slaves.

I would not wish to have to deal with an atheist prince, who would find it to his interest to have me ground to powder in a mortar: I should be quite sure of being ground to powder. If I were a sovereign, I would not wish to have to deal with atheist courtiers, whose interest it would be to poison me: I should have to be taking antidotes every day. It is therefore absolutely necessary for princes and for peoples, that the idea of a Supreme Being, creator, ruler, rewarder, revenger, shall be deeply engraved in people's minds.

Bayle says, in his "Thoughts on the Comets," that there are atheist peoples. The Caffres, the Hottentots, the Topinambous, and many other small nations, have no God: they neither deny nor affirm; they have never heard speak of Him; tell them that there is a God: they will believe it easily; tell them that everything happens through the nature of things; they will believe you equally. To claim that they are atheists is to make the same imputation as if one said they are anti-Cartesian; they are neither for nor against Descartes. They are real children; a child is neither atheist nor deist, he is nothing.

What conclusion shall we draw from all this? That atheism is a very pernicious monster in those who govern; that it is also pernicious in the persons around statesmen, although their lives may be innocent, because from their cabinets it may pierce right to the statesmen themselves; that if it is not so deadly as fanaticism, it is nearly always fatal to virtue. Let us add especially that there are less atheists to-day than ever, since philosophers have recognized that there is no being vegetating without germ, no germ without a plan, etc., and that wheat comes in no wise from putrefaction.

Some geometers who are not philosophers have rejected final causes, but real philosophers admit them; a catechist proclaims God to the children, and Newton demonstrates Him to the learned.

If there are atheists, whom must one blame, if not the mercenary tyrants of souls, who, making us revolt against their knaveries, force a few weak minds to deny the God whom these monsters dishonour. How many times have the people's leeches brought oppressed citizens to the point of revolting against their king!

Men fattened on our substance cry to us: "Be persuaded that a she-ass has spoken; believe that a fish has swallowed a man and has given him up at the end of three days safe and sound on the shore; have no doubt that the God of the universe ordered one Jewish prophet to eat excrement (Ezekiel), and another prophet to buy two whores and to make with them sons of whoredom (Hosea). These are the very words that the God of truth and purity has been made to utter; believe a hundred things either visibly abominable or mathematically impossible;

unless you do, the God of pity will burn you, not only during millions of thousands of millions of centuries in the fire of hell, but through all eternity, whether you have a body, whether you have not."

These inconceivable absurdities revolt weak and rash minds, as well as wise and resolute minds. They say: "Our masters paint God to us as the most insensate and the most barbarous of all beings; therefore there is no God;" but they should say: therefore our masters attribute to God their absurdities and their furies, therefore God is the contrary of what they proclaim, therefore God is as wise and as good as they make him out mad and wicked. It is thus that wise men account for things. But if a bigot hears them, he denounces them to a magistrate who is a watchdog of the priests; and this watchdog has them burned over a slow fire, in the belief that he is avenging and imitating the divine majesty he outrages.

AUTHORITY

Wretched human beings, whether you wear green robes, turbans, black robes or surplices, cloaks and neckbands, never seek to use authority where there is question only of reason, or consent to be scoffed at throughout the centuries as the most impertinent of all men, and to suffer public hatred as the most unjust.

A hundred times has one spoken to you of the insolent absurdity with which you condemned Galileo, and I speak to you for the hundred and first, and I hope you will keep the anniversary of it for ever; I desire that there be graved on the door of your Holy Office:

"Here seven cardinals, assisted by minor brethren, had the master of thought in Italy thrown into prison at the age of seventy; made him fast on bread and water because he instructed the human race, and because they were ignorant."

There was pronounced a sentence in favour of Aristotle's categories, and there was decreed learnedly and equitably the penalty of the galleys for whoever should be sufficiently daring as to have an opinion different from that of the Stagyrite, whose books were formerly burned by two councils.

Further on a faculty, which had not great faculties, issued a decree against innate ideas, and later a decree for innate ideas, without the said faculty being informed by its beadles what an idea is.

In the neighbouring schools judicial proceedings were instituted against the circulation of the blood.

33

An action was started against inoculation, and parties have been subpœnaed.

At the Customs of thought twenty-one folio volumes were seized, in which it was stated treacherously and wickedly that triangles always have three angles; that a father is older than his son; that Rhea Silvia lost her virginity before giving birth to her child, and that flour is not an oak leaf.

In another year was judged the action: *Utrum chimera bombinans in vacuo possit comedere secundas intentiones*, and was decided in the affirmative.

In consequence, everyone thought themselves far superior to Archimedes, Euclid, Cicero, Pliny, and strutted proudly about the University quarter.

AUTHORS

Author is a generic name which can, like the name of all other professions, signify good or bad, worthy of respect or ridicule, useful and agreeable, or trash for the wastepaper-basket.

We think that the author of a good work should refrain from three things—from putting his name, save very modestly, from the epistle dedicatory, and from the preface. Others should refrain from a fourth— that is, from writing.

Prefaces are another stumbling-block. "The 'I,'" said Pascal, "is hateful." Speak as little of yourself as possible; for you must know that the reader's self-esteem is as great as yours. He will never forgive you for wanting to condemn him to have a good opinion of you. It is for your book to speak for you, if it comes to be read by the crowd.

If you want to be an author, if you want to write a book; reflect that it must be useful and new, or at least infinitely agreeable.

If an ignoramus, a pamphleteer, presumes to criticize without discrimination, you can confound him; but make rare mention of him, for fear of sullying your writings.

If you are attacked as regards your style, never reply; it is for your work alone to make answer.

Someone says you are ill, be content that you are well, without wanting to prove to the public that you are in perfect health. And above all remember that the public cares precious little whether you are well or ill.

A hundred authors make compilations in order to have bread, and twenty pamphleteers make excerpts from these compilations, or apology for them, or criticism and satire of them, also with the idea of having bread, because they have no other trade. All these persons go on Friday to the police lieutenant of Paris to ask permission to sell their rubbish. They have audience immediately after the strumpets who do not look at them because they know that these are underhand dealings.[5]

Real authors are those who have succeeded in one of the real arts, in epic poetry, in tragedy or comedy, in history or philosophy, who have taught men or charmed them. The others of whom we have spoken are, among men of letters, what wasps are among birds.

BANISHMENT

Banishment for a period or for life, punishment to which one condemns delinquents, or those one wishes to appear as such.

Not long ago one banished outside the sphere of jurisdiction a petty thief, a petty forger, a man guilty of an act of violence. The result was that he became a big robber, a forger on a big scale, and murderer within the sphere of another jurisdiction. It is as if we threw into our neighbours' fields the stones which incommode us in our own.

Those who have written on the rights of men, have been much tormented to know for certain if a man who has been banished from his fatherland still belongs to his fatherland. It is nearly the same thing as asking if a gambler who has been driven away from the gaming-table is still one of the gamblers.

If to every man it is permitted by natural right to choose his fatherland, he who has lost the right of citizen can, with all the more

---

[5] When Voltaire was writing, it was the police lieutenant of Paris who had, under the chancellor, the inspection of books: since then, a part of his department has been taken from him. He has kept only the inspection of theatrical plays and works below those on printed sheets. The detail of this part is immense. In Paris one is not permitted to print that one has lost one's dog, unless the police are assured that in the poor beast's description there is no proposition contrary to morality and religion (1819).

reason, choose for himself a new fatherland; but can he bear arms against his former fellow-citizens? There are a thousand examples of it. How many French protestants naturalized in Holland, England and Germany have served against France, and against armies containing their own kindred and their own brothers! The Greeks who were in the King of Persia's armies made war on the Greeks, their former compatriots. One has seen the Swiss in the Dutch service fire on the Swiss in the French service. It is still worse than to fight against those who have banished you; for, after all, it seems less dishonest to draw the sword for vengeance than to draw it for money.

BANKRUPTCY

Few bankruptcies were known in France before the sixteenth century. The great reason is that there were no bankers. Lombards, Jews lent on security at ten per cent: trade was conducted in cash. Exchange, remittances to foreign countries were a secret unknown to all judges.

It is not that many people were not ruined; but that was not called *bankruptcy*; one said *discomfiture*; this word is sweeter to the ear. One used the word *rupture* as did the Boulonnais; but rupture does not sound so well.

The bankruptcies came to us from Italy, *bancorotto, bancarotta, gambarotta e la giustizia non impicar*. Every merchant had his bench (*banco*) in the place of exchange; and when he had conducted his business badly, declared himself *fallito*, and abandoned his property to his creditors with the proviso that he retain a good part of it for himself, be free and reputed a very upright man. There was nothing to be said to him, his bench was broken, *banco rotto, banca rotta*; he could even, in certain towns, keep all his property and baulk his creditors, provided he seated himself bare-bottomed on a stone in the presence of all the merchants. This was a mild derivation of the old Roman proverb—*solvere aut in aere aut in cute*, to pay either with one's money or one's skin. But this custom no longer exists; creditors have preferred their money to a bankrupt's hinder parts.

In England and in some other countries, one declares oneself bankrupt in the gazettes. The partners and creditors gather together by virtue of this announcement which is read in the coffee-houses, and they come to an arrangement as best they can.

As among the bankruptcies there are frequently fraudulent cases, it has been necessary to punish them. If they are taken to court they are everywhere regarded as theft, and the guilty are condemned to ignominious penalties.

It is not true that in France the death penalty was decreed against bankrupts without distinction. Simple failures involved no penalty; fraudulent bankrupts suffered the penalty of death in the states of Orleans, under Charles IX., and in the states of Blois in 1576, but these edicts, renewed by Henry IV., were merely comminatory.

It is too difficult to prove that a man has dishonoured himself on purpose, and has voluntarily ceded all his goods to his creditors in order to cheat them. When there has been a doubt, one has been content with putting the unfortunate man in the pillory, or with sending him to the galleys, although ordinarily a banker makes a poor convict.

Bankrupts were very favourably treated in the last year of Louis XIV.'s reign, and during the Regency. The sad state to which the interior of the kingdom was reduced, the multitude of merchants who could not or would not pay, the quantity of unsold or unsellable effects, the fear of interrupting all commerce, obliged the government in 1715, 1716, 1718, 1721, 1722, and 1726 to suspend all proceedings against all those who were in a state of insolvency. The discussions of these actions were referred to the judge-consuls; this is a jurisdiction of merchants very expert in these cases, and better constituted for going into these commercial details than the parliaments which have always been more occupied with the laws of the kingdom than with finance. As the state was at that time going bankrupt, it would have been too hard to punish the poor middle-class bankrupts.

Since then we have had eminent men, fraudulent bankrupts, but they have not been punished.

BEAUTY

Ask a toad what beauty is, the *to kalon*? He will answer you that it is his toad wife with two great round eyes issuing from her little head, a wide, flat mouth, a yellow belly, a brown back. Interrogate a Guinea negro, for him beauty is a black oily skin, deep-set eyes, a flat nose. Interrogate the devil; he will tell you that beauty is a pair of horns, four claws and a tail. Consult, lastly, the philosophers, they will answer you with gibberish: they have to have something conforming to the arch-type of beauty in essence, to the *to kalon*.

One day I was at a tragedy near by a philosopher. "How beautiful that is!" he said.

"What do you find beautiful there?" I asked.

"It is beautiful," he answered, "because the author has reached his goal."

The following day he took some medicine which did him good. "The medicine has reached its goal," I said to him. "What a beautiful medicine!" He grasped that one cannot say a medicine is beautiful, and that to give the name of "beauty" to something, the thing must cause you to admire it and give you pleasure. He agreed that the tragedy had inspired these sentiments in him, and that there was the *to kalon*, beauty.

We journeyed to England: the same piece, perfectly translated, was played there; it made everybody in the audience yawn. "Ho, ho!" he said, "the *to kalon* is not the same for the English and the French." After much reflection he came to the conclusion that beauty is often very relative, just as what is decent in Japan is indecent in Rome, and what is fashionable in Paris, is not fashionable in Pekin; and he saved himself the trouble of composing a long treatise on beauty.

There are actions which the whole world finds beautiful. Two of Cæsar's officers, mortal enemies, send each other a challenge, not as to who shall shed the other's blood with tierce and quarte behind a thicket as with us, but as to who shall best defend the Roman camp, which the Barbarians are about to attack. One of them, having repulsed the enemy, is near succumbing; the other rushes to his aid, saves his life, and completes the victory.

A friend sacrifices his life for his friend; a son for his father.... The Algonquin, the Frenchman, the Chinaman, will all say that that is very *beautiful*, that these actions give them pleasure, that they admire them.

They will say as much of the great moral maxims, of Zarathustra's—"In doubt if an action be just, abstain..."; of Confucius'—"Forget injuries, never forget kindnesses."

The negro with the round eyes and flat nose, who will not give the name of "beauties" to the ladies of our courts, will without hesitation give it to these actions and these maxims. The wicked man even will recognize the beauty of these virtues which he dare not imitate. The beauty which strikes the senses merely, the imagination, and that which is called "intelligence," is often uncertain therefore. The beauty which speaks to the heart is not that. You will find a host of people who will tell you that they have found nothing beautiful in three-quarters of the Iliad; but nobody will deny that Codrus' devotion to his people was very beautiful, supposing it to be true.

There are many other reasons which determine me not to write a treatise on beauty.

BISHOP

Samuel Ornik, native of Basle, was, as you know, a very amiable young man who, besides, knew his New Testament by heart in Greek and German. When he was twenty his parents sent him on a journey. He was charged to carry some books to the coadjutor of Paris, at the time of the Fronde. He arrived at the door of the archbishop's residence; the Swiss told him that Monseigneur saw nobody. "Comrade," said Ornik to him, "you are very rude to your compatriots. The apostles let everyone approach, and Jesus Christ desired that people should suffer all the little children to come to him. I have nothing to ask of your master; on the contrary, I have brought him something."

"Come inside, then," said the Swiss.

He waits an hour in a first antechamber. As he was very naïve, he began a conversation with a servant, who was very fond of telling all he knew of his master. "He must be mightily rich," said Ornik, "to have this crowd of pages and flunkeys whom I see running about the house."

"I don't know what his income is," answered the other, "but I heard it said to Joly and the Abbé Charier that he already had two millions of debts."

"But who is that lady coming out of the room?"

"That is Madame de Pomereu, one of his mistresses."

"She is really very pretty; but I have not read that the apostles had such company in their bedrooms in the mornings. Ah! I think the archbishop is going to give audience."

"Say—'His Highness, Monseigneur.'"

"Willingly." Ornik salutes His Highness, presents his books, and is received with a very gracious smile. The archbishop says four words to him, then climbs into his coach, escorted by fifty horsemen. In climbing, Monseigneur lets a sheath fall. Ornik is quite astonished that Monseigneur carries so large an ink-horn in his pocket. "Don't you see that's his dagger?" says the chatterbox. "Everyone carries a dagger when he goes to parliament."

"That's a pleasant way of officiating," says Ornik; and he goes away very astonished.

He traverses France, and enlightens himself from town to town; thence he passes into Italy. When he is in the Pope's territory, he meets one of those bishops with a thousand crowns income, walking on foot.

Ornik was very polite; he offers him a place in his cambiature. "You are doubtless on your way to comfort some sick man, Monseigneur?"

"Sir, I am on my way to my master's."

"Your master? that is Jesus Christ, doubtless?"

"Sir, it is Cardinal Azolin; I am his almoner. He pays me very poorly; but he has promised to place me in the service of Donna Olimpia, the favourite sister-in-law *di nostro signore*."

"What! you are in the pay of a cardinal? But do you not know that there were no cardinals in the time of Jesus Christ and St. John?"

"Is it possible?" cried the Italian prelate.

"Nothing is more true; you have read it in the Gospel."

"I have never read it," answered the bishop; "all I know is Our Lady's office."

"I tell you there were neither cardinals nor bishops, and when there were bishops, the priests were their equals almost, according to Jerome's assertions in several places."

"Holy Virgin," said the Italian. "I knew nothing about it: and the popes?"

"There were not any popes any more than cardinals."

The good bishop crossed himself; he thought he was with an evil spirit, and jumped out of the cambiature.

BOOKS

You despise them, books, you whose whole life is plunged in the vanities of ambition and in the search for pleasure or in idleness; but think that the whole of the known universe, with the exception of the savage races is governed by books alone. The whole of Africa right to Ethiopia and Nigritia obeys the book of the Alcoran, after having staggered under the book of the Gospel. China is ruled by the moral book of Confucius; a greater part of India by the book of the Veidam. Persia was governed for centuries by the books of one of the Zarathustras.

If you have a law-suit, your goods, your honour, your life even depends on the interpretation of a book which you never read.

Robert the Devil, the *Four Sons of Aymon*, the *Imaginings of Mr. Oufle*, are books also; but it is with books as with men; the very small number play a great part, the rest are mingled in the crowd.

Who leads the human race in civilized countries? those who know how to read and write. You do not know either Hippocrates, Boerhaave or Sydenham; but you put your body in the hands of those who have read them. You abandon your soul to those who are paid to read the Bible, although there are not fifty among them who have read it in its entirety with care.

To such an extent do books govern the world, that those who command to-day in the city of the Scipios and the Catos have desired that the books of their law should be only for them; it is their sceptre; they have made it a crime of *lèse-majesté* for their subjects to look there without express permission. In other countries it has been forbidden to think in writing without letters patent.

There are nations among whom thought is regarded purely as an object of commerce. The operations of the human mind are valued there only at two sous the sheet.

In another country, the liberty of explaining oneself by books is one of the most inviolable prerogatives. Print all that you like under pain of boring or of being punished if you abuse too considerably your natural right.

Before the admirable invention of printing, books were rarer and more expensive than precious stones. Almost no books among the barbarian nations until Charlemagne, and from him to the French king Charles V., surnamed "the wise"; and from this Charles right to François Ier, there is an extreme dearth.

The Arabs alone had books from the eighth century of our era to the thirteenth.

China was filled with them when we did not know how to read or write.

Copyists were much employed in the Roman Empire from the time of the Scipios up to the inundation of the barbarians.

The Greeks occupied themselves much in transcribing towards the time of Amyntas, Philip and Alexander; they continued this craft especially in Alexandria.

This craft is somewhat ungrateful. The merchants always paid the authors and the copyists very badly. It took two years of assiduous labour for a copyist to transcribe the Bible well on vellum. What time and what trouble for copying correctly in Greek and Latin the works of Origin, of Clement of Alexandria, and of all those other authors called "fathers."

The poems of Homer were long so little known that Pisistratus was the first who put them in order, and who had them transcribed in Athens, about five hundred years before the era of which we are making use.

To-day there are not perhaps a dozen copies of the Veidam and the Zend-Avesta in the whole of the East.

You would not have found a single book in the whole of Russia in 1700, with the exception of Missals and a few Bibles in the homes of aged men drunk on brandy.

To-day people complain of a surfeit: but it is not for readers to complain; the remedy is easy; nothing forces them to read. It is not any the more for authors to complain. Those who make the crowd must not cry that they are being crushed. Despite the enormous quantity of books, how few people read! and if one read profitably, one would see the deplorable follies to which the common people offer themselves as prey every day.

What multiplies books, despite the law of not multiplying beings unnecessarily, is that with books one makes others; it is with several volumes already printed that a new history of France or Spain is fabricated, without adding anything new. All dictionaries are made with dictionaries; almost all new geography books are repetitions of geography books. The Summation of St. Thomas has produced two thousand fat volumes of theology; and the same family of little worms that have gnawed the mother, gnaw likewise the children.

BOULEVERD OR BOULEVART

Boulevart, fortification, rampart. Belgrade is the boulevart of the Ottoman Empire on the Hungarian side. Who would believe that this word originally signified only a game of bowls? The people of Paris played bowls on the grass of the rampart; this grass was called the *verd*, like the grass market. *On boulait sur le verd.* From there it comes that the English, whose language is a copy of ours in almost all the words which are not Saxon, have called the game of bowls "bowling-green," the *verd* (green) of the game of bowls. We have taken back from them what we had lent them. Following their example, we gave the name of *boulingrins*, without knowing the strength of the word, to the grass-plots we introduced into our gardens.

I once heard two good dames who were going for a walk on the *Bouleverd*, and not on the *Boulevart*. People laughed at them, and wrongly. But in all matters custom carries the day; and everyone who is right against custom is hissed or condemned.

BOURGES

Our questions barely turn on geography; but let us be permitted to mark in two words our astonishment about the town of Bourges. The "Dictionnaire de Trévoux" claims that "it is one of the most ancient towns of Europe, that it was the seat of the empire of the Gauls, and gave kings to the Celts."

I do not wish to combat the ancientness of any town or any family. But was there ever an empire of the Gauls? Did the Celts have kings? This mania for antiquity is a malady from which one will not be healed so soon. The Gauls, Germany, Scandinavia have nothing that is antique save the land, the trees and the animals. If you want antiquities, go toward Asia, and even then it is very small beer. Man is ancient and monuments new, that is what we have in view in more than one article.

If it were a real benefit to be born in a stone or wooden enclosure more ancient than another, it would be very reasonable to make the foundation of one's town date back to the time of the war of the giants; but since there is not the least advantage in this vanity, one must break away from it. That is all I had to say about Bourges.

BRAHMINS

Is it not probable that the Brahmins were the first legislators of the earth, the first philosophers, the first theologians?

Do not the few monuments of ancient history which remain to us form a great presumption in their favour, since the first Greek philosophers went to them to learn mathematics, and since the most ancient curiosities collected by the emperors of China are all Indian?

We will speak elsewhere of the "Shasta"; it is the first book of theology of the Brahmins, written about fifteen hundred years before their "Veidam," and anterior to all the other books.

Their annals make no mention of any war undertaken by them at any time. The words for *arms*, to *kill*, to *maim*, are not to be found either in the fragments of the "Shasta" which we have, or in the "Ezourveidam," or in the "Cormoveidam." I can at least give the assurance that I did not see them in these last two collections: and what is still more singular is that the "Shasta" which speaks of a conspiracy in heaven, makes no mention of any war in the great peninsula enclosed between the Indus and the Ganges.

The Hebrews, who were known so late, never name the Brahmins; they had no knowledge of India until after the conquests of Alexander, and their settling in Egypt, of which they had said so much evil. The name of India is to be found only in the Book of Esther, and in that of Job which was not Hebrew. One remarks a singular contrast between the sacred books of the Hebrews, and those of the Indians. The Indian books announce only peace and gentleness; they forbid the killing of animals: the Hebrew books speak only of killing, of the massacre of men and beasts; everything is slaughtered in the name of the Lord; it is quite another order of things.

It is incontestably from the Brahmins that we hold the idea of the fall of the celestial beings in revolt against the Sovereign of nature; and it is from there probably that the Greeks drew the fable of the Titans. It is there also that the Jews at last took the idea of the revolt of Lucifer, in the first century of our era.

How could these Indians suppose a revolt in heaven without having seen one on earth? Such a jump from human nature to divine nature is barely conceivable. Usually one goes from known to unknown.

One does not imagine a war of giants until one has seen some men more robust than the others tyrannize over their fellows. The first Brahmins must either have experienced violent discords, or at least have seen them in heaven.

It is a very astonishing phenomenon for a society of men who have never made war to have invented a species of war made in the imaginary spaces, or in a globe distant from ours, or in what is called the "firmament," the "empyrean." But it must be carefully observed that in this revolt of celestial beings against their Sovereign no blows were struck, no celestial blood flowed, no mountains hurled at the head, no angels cut in two, as in Milton's sublime and grotesque poem.

According to the "Shasta," it is only a formal disobedience to the orders of the Most High, a cabal which God punishes by relegating the rebellious angels to a vast place of shadows called "Ondera" during the period of an entire mononthour. A mononthour is four hundred and twenty-six millions of our years. But God deigned to pardon the guilty after five thousand years, and their ondera was only a purgatory.

He made "Mhurd" of them, men, and placed them in our globe on condition that they should not eat animals, and that they should not copulate with the males of their new species, under pain of returning to ondera.

Those are the principal articles of the Brahmins' faith, which have lasted without interruption from immemorial times right to our day: it seems strange to us that among them it should be as grave a sin to eat a chicken as to commit sodomy.

This is only a small part of the ancient cosmogony of the Brahmins. Their rites, their pagodas, prove that among them everything was allegorical; they still represent virtue beneath the emblem of a woman who has ten arms, and who combats ten mortal sins represented by monsters. Our missionaries have not failed to take this image of virtue for that of the devil, and to assure us that the devil is worshipped in India. We have never been among these people but to enrich ourselves and to calumniate them.

Really we have forgotten a very essential thing in this little article on the Brahmins; it is that their sacred books are filled with contradictions. But the people do not know of them, and the doctors have solutions ready, figurative meanings, allegories, symbols, express declarations of Birma, Brahma and Vitsnou, which should close the mouths of all who reason.

CHARACTER

From the Greek word *impression, engraving*.

It is what nature has graved in us.

Can one change one's character? Yes, if one changes one's body. It is possible for a man born blunderer, unbending and violent, being stricken with apoplexy in his old age, to become a foolish, tearful child, timid and peaceable. His body is no longer the same. But as long as his nerves, his blood and his marrow are in the same state, his nature will not change any more than a wolf's and a marten's instinct.

The character is composed of our ideas and our feelings: well, it is substantiated that we give ourselves neither feelings nor ideas; therefore our character does not depend on us.

If it depended on us, there is nobody who would not be perfect.

We cannot give ourselves tastes, talents; why should we give ourselves qualities?

If one does not reflect, one thinks oneself master of everything; when one reflects thereon, one sees that one is master of nothing.

Should you wish to change a man's character completely, purge him with diluents every day until you have killed him. Charles XII., in his suppurative fever on the road to Bender, was no longer the same man. One prevailed upon him as upon a child.

If I have a crooked nose and two cat's eyes, I can hide them with a mask. Can I do more with the character which nature has given me?

A man born violent, hasty, presented himself before François I., King of France, to complain of an injustice; the prince's countenance, the respectful bearing of the courtiers, the very place where he is, make a powerful impression on this man; mechanically he lowers his eyes, his rough voice softens, he presents his petition humbly, one would believe him born as gentle as are (at that moment at least) the courtiers, amongst whom he is even disconcerted; but François I. understands physiognomy, he easily discovers in the lowered eyes, burning nevertheless with sombre fire, in the strained facial muscles, in the compressed lips, that this man is not so gentle as he is forced to appear. This man follows him to Pavia, is taken with him, led to the same prison in Madrid: François I.'s majesty no longer makes the same impression on him; he grows familiar with the object of his respect. One day when pulling off the king's boots, and pulling them off badly, the king, embittered by his misfortune, gets angry; my man sends the king about his business, and throws his boots out of the window.

Sixtus V. was born petulant, stubborn, haughty, impetuous, vindictive, arrogant; this character seemed softened during the trials of his novitiate. He begins to enjoy a certain credit in his order; he flies into a passion with a guard, and batters him with his fist: he is inquisitor at Venice; he performs his duties with insolence: behold him cardinal, he is possessed *dalla rabbia papale*: this fury triumphs over his nature; he buries his person and his character in obscurity; he apes the humble and the dying man; he is elected Pope; this moment gives back to the spring, which politics have bent, all its long curbed elasticity; he is the haughtiest and most despotic of sovereigns.

Naturam expella furca, tamen usque recurret.
(Hor. L. I., ep. x).

Drive away nature, it returns at the gallop.

(Destouches, *Glorieux*, Act 3, Sc. 5.)

Religion, morality put a brake on a nature's strength; they cannot destroy it. The drunkard in a cloister, reduced to a half-sétier of cider at each meal, will no longer get drunk, but he will always like wine.

Age enfeebles character; it is a tree that produces only degenerate fruit, but the fruit is always of the same nature; it is knotted and covered with moss, it becomes worm-eaten, but it is always oak or pear tree. If one could change one's character, one would give oneself one, one would be master of nature. Can one give oneself anything? do we not receive everything? Try to animate an indolent man with a continued activity; to freeze with apathy the boiling soul of an impetuous fellow, to inspire someone who has neither ear nor taste with a taste for music and poetry, you will no more succeed than if you undertook to give sight to a man born blind. We perfect, we soften, we conceal what nature has put in us, but we do not put in ourselves anything at all.

One says to a farmer: "You have too many fish in this pond, they will not prosper; there are too many cattle in your meadows, grass lacks, they will grow thin." It happens after this exhortation that the pikes eat half my man's carp, and the wolves the half of his sheep; the rest grow fat. Will he congratulate himself on his economy? This countryman, it is you; one of your passions has devoured the others, and you think you have triumphed over yourself. Do not nearly all of us resemble that old general of ninety who, having met some young officers who were debauching themselves with some girls, says to them angrily: "Gentlemen, is that the example I give you?"

CHARLATAN

The article entitled "Charlatan" in the "Encyclopedic Dictionary" is filled with useful truths agreeably presented. The Chevalier de Jaucourt has there presented the charlatanry of medicine.

We will take the liberty of adding here a few reflections. The abode of the doctors is in the large towns; there are barely any doctors in the country. It is in the great towns that the rich invalids are; debauchery, the excesses of the table, the passions, are the cause of their maladies. Dumoulin, not the lawyer, the doctor, who was as good a practician as the other, said as he was dying, that he left two great doctors behind him, diet and river water.

In 1728, in the time of Law, the most famous charlatan of the first species, another, Villars by name, confided to some friends that his uncle who had lived nearly a hundred years, and who died only by accident, had left him the secret of a water which could easily prolong life to a hundred and fifty years, provided a man was temperate. When he saw a funeral pass, he shrugged his shoulders in pity; if the defunct, he observed, had drunk my water, he would not be where he is. His friends to whom he gave generously of the water, and who observed the prescribed regime in some degree, thrived on it and praised it. He then sold the bottle for six francs; the sale was prodigious. It was water from the Seine with a little nitre. Those who took it and who subjected themselves to a certain amount of regime, above all those who were born with a good constitution, recovered perfect health in a few days. He said to the others: "It is your fault if you are not entirely cured: correct these two vices and you will live at least a hundred and fifty years." Some of them reformed; this good charlatan's fortune increased like his reputation. The Abbé de Pons, the enthusiast, put him far above the Maréchal de Villars: "The Maréchal kills men," he said to him, "but you make them live."

People learned at last that Villars Water was only river water; they would have no more of it; and went to other charlatans.

It is certain that he had done good, and that the only reproach one could make against him was that he had sold Seine water a little too dear. He led men to temperance by which fact he was superior to the apothecary Arnoult, who stuffed Europe with his sachets against apoplexy, without recommending any virtue.

I knew in London a doctor named Brown, who practised in Barbados. He had a sugar refinery and negroes; he was robbed of a considerable sum; he assembled his negroes: "My lads," he said to them, "the great serpent appeared to me during the night, he told me that the thief would at this moment have a parrot's feather on the end of his nose." The guilty man promptly put his hand to his nose. "It is you who robbed me," said the master; "the great serpent has just told me so." And he regained his money. One can hardly condemn such a charlatanry; but one must be dealing with negroes.

Scipio Africanus, this great Scipio very different otherwise from Dr. Brown, willingly made his soldiers believe that he was inspired by the gods. This great charlatanry was long the custom. Can one blame Scipio to have availed himself of it? he was the man who perhaps did most honour to the Roman Republic; but why did the gods inspire him not to render his accounts?

Numa did better; it was necessary to police some brigands and a senate which was the most difficult section of these brigands to govern. If he had proposed his laws to the assembled tribes, the assassins of his predecessor would have made a thousand difficulties. He addressed himself to the goddess Egeria, who gave him some pandects from Jupiter; he was obeyed without contradiction, and he reigned happily. His instructions were good, his charlatanry did good; but if some secret enemy had discovered the imposture, if he had said: "Exterminate an impostor who prostitutes the name of the gods in order to deceive men," Numa ran the risk of being sent to heaven with Romulus.

It is probable that Numa took his measures very carefully, and that he deceived the Romans for their benefit, with a dexterity suitable to the time, the place, the intelligence of the early Romans.

Mahomet was twenty times on the point of failing, but he succeeded at last with the Arabs of Medina; and people believed that he was the intimate friend of the Archangel Gabriel. If to-day someone came to Constantinople to announce that he was the favourite of the Archangel Raphael, far superior to Gabriel in dignity, and that it was in him alone people should believe, he would be impaled in the public place. It is for charlatans to choose their time well.

Was there not a little charlatanry in Socrates with his familiar demon, and Apollo's precise declaration which proclaimed him the wisest of all men? How can Rollin, in his history, reason from this oracle? How is it that he does not let the young idea know that it was pure charlatanry? Socrates chose his time badly. A hundred years earlier, maybe, he would have governed Athens.

All leaders of sects in philosophy have been somewhat charlatans: but the greatest of all have been those who have aspired to domination. Cromwell was the most terrible of all our charlatans. He appeared at precisely the only time he could succeed: under Elizabeth he would have been hanged; under Charles II. he would have been merely ridiculous. He came happily at a time when people were disgusted with kings; and his son, at a time when people were weary of a protector.

Of Charlatanry in Science and Literature

The sciences can barely be without charlatanry. People wish to have their opinions accepted; the quibbling doctor wishes to eclipse the angelic doctor; the recondite doctor wishes to reign alone. Each builds his system of physics, metaphysics, scholastic theology; it is a competition in turning one's merchandise to account. You have agents who extol it, fools who believe you, protectors who support you.

Is there a greater charlatanry than that of substituting words for things, and of wanting others to believe what you do not believe yourself?

One establishes whirlwinds of subtle matter, ramous, globulous, striated, channelled; the other elements of matter which are not matter at all, and a pre-established harmony which makes the clock of the body sound the hour, when the clock of the soul shows it with its hand. These chimeras find partisans for a few years. When this rubbish has passed out of fashion, new fanatics appear on the itinerant theatre; they banish germs from the world, they say that the sea produced the mountains, and that men were once fish.

How much charlatanry has been put into history, either by astonishing the reader with prodigies, by titillating human malignity with satire, or by flattering the families of tyrants with infamous eulogy?

The wretched species that writes for a living is charlatan in another way. A poor man who has no trade, who has had the misfortune to go to college, and who thinks he knows how to write, goes to pay his court to a bookseller, and asks him for work. The bookseller knows that the majority of most people who live in houses want to have little libraries, that they need abridgments and new titles; he orders from the writer an abridgment of the "History by Rapin-Thoyras," an abridgment of the "History of the Church," a "Collection of Witty Sayings" drawn from the "Menagiana," a "Dictionary of Great Men," where an unknown pedant is placed beside Cicero, and a *sonettiero* of Italy near Virgil.

Another bookseller orders novels, or translations of novels. "If you have no imagination," he says to the workman, "you will take a few of the adventures in 'Cyrus,' in 'Gusman d'Alfarache,' in the 'Secret Memoirs of a Gentleman of Quality,' or 'Of a Lady of Quality'; and from the total you will prepare a volume of four hundred pages at twenty sous the sheet."

Another bookseller gives the gazettes and almanacs for ten years past to a man of genius. "You will make me an extract of all that, and you will bring it me back in three months under the name of 'Faithful History of the Times,' by the Chevalier de Trois Etoiles, Lieutenant of the Navy, employed in the Ministry of Foreign Affairs."

Of this kind of book there are about fifty thousand in Europe; and it all passes just like the secret of whitening the skin, of darkening the hair, and the universal panacea.

CIVIL LAWS

Extract from Some Notes found among a Lawyer's Papers, which maybe merit Examination.

Let the punishments of criminals be useful. A hanged man is good for nothing, and a man condemned to public works still serves the country, and is a living lesson.

Let all laws be clear, uniform and precise: to interpret laws is almost always to corrupt them.

Let nothing be infamous save vice.

Let taxes be always proportional.

Let the law never be contradictory to custom: for if the custom be good, the law is worthless.

CLIMATE

Climate influences religion as regards customs and ceremonies. A legislator will not have had difficulty in making the Indians bathe in the Ganges at certain seasons of the moon; it is a great pleasure for them. He would have been stoned if he had proposed the same bath to the peoples who dwell on the banks of the Dwina near Archangel. Forbid pig to an Arab who would have leprosy if he ate of this flesh which is very bad and disgusting in his country, he will obey you joyfully. Issue the same veto to a Westphalian and he will be tempted to fight you.

Abstinence from wine is a good religious precept in Arabia where orange water, lemon water, lime water are necessary to health. Mohammed would not have forbidden wine in Switzerland perhaps, especially before going to battle.

There are customs of pure fantasy. Why did the priests of Egypt imagine circumcision? it is not for health. Cambyses who treated them as they deserved, they and their bull Apis, Cambyses' courtiers, Cambyses' soldiers, had not had their prepuces lopped, and were very well. Climate does nothing to a priest's genitals. One offered one's prepuce to Isis, probably as one presented everywhere the first fruits of the earth. It was offering the first fruits of life.

51

Religions have always rolled on two pivots; observance and creed: observance depends largely on climate; creed not at all. One could as easily make a dogma accepted on the equator as the polar circle. It would later be rejected equally at Batavia and in the Orkneys, while it would be maintained *unguibus et rostro* at Salamanca. That depends in no way on the soil and the atmosphere, but solely on opinion, that fickle queen of the world.

Certain libations of wine will be precept in a vine-growing country, and it will not occur to a legislator's mind to institute in Norway sacred mysteries which cannot be performed without wine.

It will be expressly ordered to burn incense in the parvis of a temple where beasts are slaughtered in the Deity's honour, and for the priests' supper. This butcher's shop called "temple" would be a place of abominable infection if it were not continually purified: and without the assistance of aromatics, the religion of the ancients would have caused the plague. Even the interior of the temple was decked with festoons of flowers in order to make the air sweeter.

No cow will be sacrificed in the burning land of the Indian peninsula; because this animal which furnishes necessary milk is very rare in an arid country, its flesh is dry, tough, contains very little nourishment, and the Brahmins would live very badly. On the contrary, the cow will become sacred, in view of its rarity and utility.

One will only enter barefoot the temple of Jupiter Ammon where the heat is excessive: one must be well shod to perform one's devotions in Copenhagen.

It is not so with dogma. People have believed in polytheism in all climates; and it is as easy for a Crimean Tartar as for an inhabitant of Mecca to recognize a single God, incommunicable, non-begetting, non-begotten. It is through its dogma still more than through its rites that a religion is spread from one climate to another. The dogma of the unity of God soon passed from Medina to the Caucasus; then the climate cedes to opinion.

The Arabs said to the Turks: "We had ourselves circumcised in Arabia without really knowing why; it was an old fashion of the priests of Egypt to offer to Oshireth or Osiris a little part of what they held most precious. We had adopted this custom three thousand years before we became Mohammedans. You will be circumcised like us; like us you will be obliged to sleep with one of your wives every Friday, and to give each year two and a half per cent of your income to the poor. We drink only water and sherbet; all intoxicating liquor is forbidden us; in Arabia it is pernicious. You will embrace this regime although you love wine passionately, and although it may even be often necessary for you to go on the banks of the Phasis and Araxes. Lastly, if you want to go to Heaven, and be well placed there, you will take the road to Mecca."

The inhabitants of the north of the Caucasus submit to these laws, and embrace throughout the country a religion which was not made for them.

In Egypt the symbolic worship of animals succeeded the dogmas of Thaut. The gods of the Romans later shared Egypt with the dogs, the cats and the crocodiles. To the Roman religion succeeded Christianity; it was entirely driven out by Mohammedanism, which perhaps will cede its place to a new religion.

In all these vicissitudes climate has counted for nothing: government has done everything. We are considering here second causes only, without raising profane eyes to the Providence which directs them. The Christian religion, born in Syria, having received its principal development in Alexandria, inhabits to-day the lands where Teutate, Irminsul, Frida, Odin were worshipped.

There are peoples whose religion has been made by neither climate nor government. What cause detached the north of Germany, Denmark, three-quarters of Switzerland, Holland, England, Scotland, Ireland, from the Roman communion? Poverty. Indulgences and deliverance from purgatory were sold too dear to souls whose bodies had at that time very little money. The prelates, the monks devoured a province's whole revenue. People took a cheaper religion. At last, after twenty civil wars, people believed that the Pope's religion was very good for great lords, and the reformed religion for citizens. Time will show whether the Greek religion or the Turkish religion will prevail by the Ægean Sea and the Pont-Euxine.

COMMON SENSE

There are sometimes in common expressions an image of what passes in the depths of all men's hearts. Among the Romans *sensus communis* signified not only common sense, but humanity, sensibility. As we are not as good as the Romans, this word signifies among us only half of what it signified among them. It means only good sense, plain reason, reason set in operation, a first notion of ordinary things, a state midway between stupidity and intelligence. "This man has no common sense" is a great insult. "A common-sense man" is an insult likewise; it means that he is not entirely stupid, and that he lacks what is called wit and understanding. But whence comes this expression *common sense*, unless it be from the senses? Men, when they invented this word, avowed that nothing entered the soul save through the senses;

otherwise, would they have used the word *sense* to signify common reasoning?

People say sometimes—"Common sense is very rare." What does this phrase signify? that in many men reason set in operation is stopped in its progress by prejudices, that such and such man who judges very sanely in one matter, will always be vastly deceived in another. This Arab, who will be a good calculator, a learned chemist, an exact astronomer, will believe nevertheless that Mohammed put half the moon in his sleeve.

Why will he go beyond common sense in the three sciences of which I speak, and why will he be beneath common sense when there is question of this half moon? Because in the first cases he has seen with his eyes, he has perfected his intelligence; and in the second, he has seen with other people's eyes, he has closed his own, he has perverted the common sense which is in him.

How has this strange mental alienation been able to operate? How can the ideas which move with so regular and so firm a step in the brain on a great number of subjects limp so wretchedly on another a thousand times more palpable and easy to comprehend? This man always has inside him the same principles of intelligence; he must have some organ vitiated then, just as it happens sometimes that the finest *gourmet* may have a depraved taste as regards a particular kind of food.

How is the organ of this Arab, who sees half the moon in Mohammed's sleeve, vitiated? It is through fear. He has been told that if he did not believe in this sleeve, his soul, immediately after his death, when passing over the pointed bridge, would fall for ever into the abyss. He has been told even worse things: If ever you have doubts about this sleeve, one dervish will treat you as impious; another will prove to you that you are an insensate fool who, having all possible motives for believing, have not wished to subordinate your superb reason to the evidence; a third will report you to the little divan of a little province, and you will be legally impaled.

All this terrifies the good Arab, his wife, his sister, all his little family into a state of panic. They have good sense about everything else, but on this article their imagination is wounded, as was the imagination of Pascal, who continually saw a precipice beside his armchair. But does our Arab believe in fact in Mohammed's sleeve? No. He makes efforts to believe; he says it is impossible, but that it is true; he believes what he does not believe. On the subject of this sleeve he forms in his head a chaos of ideas which he is afraid to disentangle; and this veritably is not to have common sense.

CONCATENATION OF EVENTS

The present is delivered, it is said, of the future. Events are linked to each other by an invincible fatality: it is Destiny which, in Homer, is above even Jupiter. This master of gods and men declares roundly that he cannot stop his son Sarpedon dying in his appointed time. Sarpedon was born at the moment when he had to be born, and could not be born at another moment; he could not die otherwise than before Troy; he could not be buried elsewhere than in Lycia; had at the appointed time to produce vegetables which had to be changed into the substance of a few Lycians; his heirs had to establish a new order in his states; this new order had to exert an influence over the neighbouring kingdoms; from it resulted a new arrangement of war and peace with the neighbours of the neighbours of Lycia: thus, step by step, the destiny of the whole world has been dependent on Sarpedon's death, which depended on Helen being carried off; and this carrying off was necessarily linked to Hecuba's marriage, which by tracing back to other events was linked to the origin of things.

If only one of these facts had been arranged differently, another universe would have resulted: but it was not possible for the present universe not to exist; therefore it was not possible for Jupiter to save his son's life, for all that he was Jupiter.

This system of necessity and fatality has been invented in our time by Leibnitz, according to what people say, under the name of *self-sufficient reason*; it is, however, very ancient: that there is no effect without a cause and that often the smallest cause produces the greatest effects, does not date from to-day.

Lord Bolingbroke avows that the little quarrels of Madame Marlborough and Madame Masham gave birth to his chance of making Queen Anne's private treaty with Louis XIV.; this treaty led to the Peace of Utrecht; this Peace of Utrecht established Philip V. on the throne of Spain. Philip V. took Naples and Sicily from the house of Austria; the Spanish prince who is to-day King of Naples clearly owes his kingdom to my lady Masham: and he would not have had it, he would not perhaps even have been born, if the Duchess of Marlborough had been more complaisant towards the Queen of England. His existence at Naples depended on one foolishness more or less at the court of London.

Examine the position of all the peoples of the universe; they are established like this on a sequence of facts which appear to be connected with nothing and which are connected with everything. Everything is cog, pulley, cord, spring, in this vast machine.

It is likewise in the physical sphere. A wind which blows from the depths of Africa and the austral seas, brings a portion of the African atmosphere, which falls in rain in the valleys of the Alps; these rains fertilize our lands; our north wind in its turn sends our vapours among the negroes; we do good to Guinea, and Guinea does good to us. The chain stretches from one end of the universe to the other.

But it seems to me that a strange abuse is made of the truth of this principle. From it some people conclude that there is not a sole minute atom whose movement has not exerted its influence in the present arrangement of the world; that there is not a single minute accident, among either men or animals, which is not an essential link in the great chain of fate.

Let us understand each other: every effect clearly has its cause, going back from cause to cause in the abyss of eternity; but every cause has not its effect going forward to the end of the centuries. All events are produced by each other, I admit; if the past is delivered of the present, the present is delivered of the future; everything has father, but everything has not always children. Here it is precisely as with a genealogical tree; each house goes back, as we say, to Adam; but in the family there are many persons who have died without leaving issue.

There is a genealogical tree of the events of this world. It is incontestable that the inhabitants of Gaul and Spain are descended from Gomer, and the Russians from Magog, his younger brother: one finds this genealogy in so many fat books! On this basis one cannot deny that the Great Turk, who is also descended from Magog, was not bound to be well beaten in 1769 by Catherine II., Empress of Russia. This adventure is clearly connected with other great adventures. But that Magog spat to right or left, near Mount Caucasus, and that he made two circles in a well or three, that he slept on the left side or on the right; I do not see that that has had much influence on present affairs.

One must think that everything is not complete in nature, as Newton has demonstrated, and that every movement is not communicated step by step until it makes a circuit of the world, as he has demonstrated still further. Throw into water a body of like density, you calculate easily that after a short time the movement of this body, and the movement it has communicated to the water, are destroyed; the movement disappears and is effaced; therefore the movement that Magog might produce by spitting in a well cannot influence what is passing to-day in Moldavia and Wallachia; therefore present events are not the children of all past events: they have their direct lines; but a thousand little collateral lines do not serve them at all. Once more, every being has a father, but every being has not children.

CONTRADICTIONS

If some literary society wishes to undertake the dictionary of contradictions, I subscribe for twenty folio volumes.

The world can exist only by contradictions: what is needed to abolish them? to assemble the states of the human race. But from the manner in which men are made, it would be a fresh contradiction if they were to agree. Assemble all the rabbits of the universe, there will not be two different opinions among them.

I know only two kinds of immutable beings on the earth, mathematicians and animals; they are led by two invariable rules, demonstration and instinct: and even the mathematicians have had some disputes, but the animals have never varied.

The contrasts, the light and shade in which public men are represented in history, are not contradictions, they are faithful portraits of human nature.

Every day people condemn and admire Alexander the murderer of Clitus, but the avenger of Greece, the conqueror of the Persians, and the founder of Alexandria;

Cæsar the debauchee, who robs the public treasury of Rome to reduce his country to dependence; but whose clemency equals his valour, and whose intelligence equals his courage;

Mohammed, impostor, brigand; but the sole religious legislator who had courage, and who founded a great empire;

Cromwell the enthusiast, a rogue in his fanaticism even, judicial assassin of his king, but as profound politician as brave warrior.

A thousand contrasts frequently crowd together, and these contrasts are in nature; they are no more astonishing than a fine day followed by storm.

Men are equally mad everywhere; they have made the laws little by little, as gaps are repaired in a wall. Here eldest sons have taken all they could from younger sons, there younger sons share equally. Sometimes the Church has commanded the duel, sometimes she has anathematized it. The partisans and the enemies of Aristotle have each been excommunicated in their turn, as have those who wore long hair and those who wore short. In this world we have perfect law only to rule a species of madness called gaming. The rules of gaming are the only ones which admit neither exception, relaxation, variety nor tyranny. A man who has been a lackey, if he play at lansquenet with kings, is paid without difficulty if he win; everywhere else the law is a sword with which the stronger cut the weaker in pieces.

Nevertheless, this world exists as if everything were well ordered; the irregularity is of our nature; our political world is like our globe, a misshapen thing which always preserves itself. It would be mad to wish that the mountains, the seas, the rivers, were traced in beautiful regular forms; it would be still more mad to ask perfect wisdom of men; it would be wishing to give wings to dogs or horns to eagles.

CORN

The Gauls had corn in Cæsar's time: one is curious to know where they and the Teutons found it to sow. People answer you that the Tyrians had brought it into Spain, the Spaniards into Gaul, the Gauls into Germany. And where did the Tyrians get this corn? Among the Greeks probably, from whom they received it in exchange for their alphabet.

Who had made this present to the Greeks? It was formerly Ceres without a doubt; and when one has gone back to Ceres one can hardly go farther. Ceres must have come down on purpose from the sky to give us wheat, rye, barley, etc.

But as the credit of Ceres who gave the corn to the Greeks, and that of Isheth or Isis who bestowed it on the Egyptians, is very much fallen in these days, we remain in uncertainty as to the origin of corn.

Sanchoniathon affirms that Dagon or Dagan, one of the grandsons of Thaut, had the control of corn in Phœnicia. Well, his Thaut is of about the same time as our Jared. From this it results that corn is very old, and that it is of the same antiquity as grass. Perhaps this Dagon was the first man to make bread, but that is not demonstrated.

Strange thing! we know positively that it is to Noah that we are under an obligation for wine, and we do not know to whom we owe bread. And, still more strange thing, we are so ungrateful to Noah, that we have more than two thousand songs in honour of Bacchus, and we chant barely one in honour of Noah our benefactor.

A Jew has assured me that corn came by itself in Mesopotamia, like the apples, wild pears, chestnuts, medlars in the West. I want to believe it until I am sure of the contrary; for corn must certainly grow somewhere. It has become the ordinary and indispensable food in the good climates, and throughout the North.

Some great philosophers whose talents we esteem and whose systems we do not follow (Buffon) have claimed on page 195 of the "Natural History of the Dog," that mankind has made corn; that our fathers by virtue of sowing lolium and gramina changed them into wheat. As these philosophers are not of our opinion about shells, they will permit us not to be of theirs about corn. We do not believe that one has ever made tulips grow from jasmin. We find that the germ of corn is quite different from that of lolium, and we do not believe in any transmutation. When somebody shows it to us we will retract.

Corn assuredly is not the food of the greater part of the world. Maize, tapioca, feed the whole of America. We have entire provinces where the peasants eat nothing but chestnut bread, more nourishing and of better flavour than that of rye and barley which so many people eat, and which is much better than the ration bread which is given to the soldier. The whole of southern Africa does not know of bread. The immense archipelago of the Indies, Siam, Laos, Pegu, Cochin China, Tonkin, a part of China, Japan, the coast of Malabar and Coromandel, the banks of the Ganges furnish a rice, the cultivation of which is much easier than that of wheat, and which causes it to be neglected. Corn is absolutely unknown for the space of fifteen hundred leagues on the coasts of the Glacial Sea. This food, to which we are accustomed, is among us so precious that the fear of seeing a dearth of it alone causes riots among the most subjugated peoples. The corn trade is everywhere one of the great objects of government; it is a part of our being, and yet this essential commodity is sometimes squandered ridiculously. The powder merchants use the best flour for covering the heads of our young men and women. But over three-quarters of the earth bread is not eaten at all. People maintain that the Ethiopians mocked at the Egyptians who lived on bread. But since it is our chief food, corn has become one of the great objects of trade and politics. So much has been written on this subject, that if a husbandman sowed as much corn as the weight of the volumes we have about this commodity, he might hope for the amplest harvest, and become richer than those who in their gilded and lacquered drawing-rooms ignore his exceeding labour and wretchedness.

CROMWELL

SECTION I

Cromwell is painted as a man who was an impostor all his life. I have difficulty in believing it. I think that first of all he was an enthusiast, and that later he made even his fanaticism serve his greatness. A novice who is fervent at the age of twenty often becomes a skilful rogue at forty. In the great game of human life one begins by being a dupe, and one finishes by being a rogue. A statesman takes as almoner a monk steeped in the pettinesses of his monastery, devout, credulous, clumsy, quite new to the world: the monk learns, forms himself, intrigues, and supplants his master.

Cromwell did not know at first whether he would be an ecclesiastic or a soldier. He was both. In 1622 he served a campaign in the army of Frederick Henry, Prince of Orange, a great man, brother of two great men; and when he returned to England, he went into the service of Bishop Williams, and was his grace's theologian, while his grace passed as his wife's lover. His principles were those of the Puritans; thus he had to hate a bishop with all his heart, and not have a liking for kings. He was driven from Bishop Williams' house because he was a Puritan; and there is the origin of his fortune. The English Parliament declared itself against the throne and against the episcopacy; some of his friends in this parliament procured the nomination of a village for him. Only at this time did he begin to exist, and he was more than forty before he had ever made himself talked of. In vain was he conversant with Holy Writ, in vain did he argue about the rights of priests and deacons, and preach a few poor sermons and libels, he was ignored. I have seen one of his sermons which is very insipid, and which bears sufficient resemblance to the predications of the quakers; assuredly there is to be found there no trace of that persuasive eloquence with which later he carried the parliaments away. The reason is that in fact he was much more suited to public affairs than to the Church. It was above all in his tone and in his air that his eloquence consisted; a gesture of that hand that had won so many battles and killed so many royalists, was more persuasive than the periods of Cicero. It must be avowed that it was his incomparable bravery which made him known, and which led him by degrees to the pinnacle of greatness.

He began by launching out as a volunteer who wished to make his fortune, in the town of Hull, besieged by the king. There he did many fine and happy actions, for which he received a gratification of about six thousand francs from the parliament. This present made by the parliament to an adventurer made it clear that the rebel party must prevail. The king was not in a position to give to his general officers what the parliament gave to volunteers. With money and fanaticism one is bound in the long run to be master of everything. Cromwell was made colonel. Then his great talents for war developed to the point that when the parliament created the Count of Manchester general of its armies, it made Cromwell lieutenant-general, without his having passed through the other ranks. Never did man appear more worthy of commanding; never were more activity and prudence, more boldness and more resource seen than in Cromwell. He is wounded at the battle of York; and while the first dressing is being put on his wound, he learns that his general, Manchester, is retiring, and that the battle is lost. He hastens to Manchester's side; he finds him fleeing with some officers; he takes him by the arm, and says to him with an air of confidence and grandeur: "You are mistaken, my lord; it is not on this side that the enemy is." He leads him back near the battlefield, rallies during the night more than twelve thousand men, speaks to them in the name of God, quotes Moses, Gideon and Joshua, at daybreak recommences the battle against the victorious royal army, and defeats it completely. Such a man had to perish or be master. Nearly all the officers of his army were enthusiasts who carried the New Testament at their saddle-bow: in the army as in the parliament men spoke only of making Babylon fall, of establishing the religion in Jerusalem, of shattering the colossus. Among so many madmen Cromwell ceased to be mad, and thought that it was better to govern them than to be governed by them. The habit of preaching as though he were inspired remained to him. Picture a fakir who has put an iron belt round his waist as a penitence, and who then takes off his belt to beat the other fakirs' ears: there you have Cromwell. He becomes as intriguing as he was intrepid; he associates himself with all the colonels of the army, and thus forms among the troops a republic which forces the commander-in-chief to resign. Another commander-in-chief is nominated, he disgusts him. He governs the army, and by it he governs the parliament; he puts this parliament in the necessity of making him commander-in-chief at last. All this was a great deal; but what is essential is that he wins all the battles he engages in in England, Scotland and Ireland; and he wins them, not in watching the fighting and in taking care of himself, but always by charging the enemy, rallying his troops, rushing everywhere, often wounded, killing many royalist officers with his own hand, like a desperate and infuriated grenadier.

Amid this frightful war Cromwell made love; he went, his Bible under his arm, to sleep with the wife of his major-general, Lambert. She loved the Count of Holland, who was serving in the king's army. Cromwell took him prisoner in a battle, and enjoyed the pleasure of having his rival's head cut off. His maxim was to shed the blood of every important enemy, either on the field of battle, or by the executioner's hand. He always increased his power, by always daring to abuse it; the profundity of his plans took away nothing from his ferocious impetuosity. He goes into the House of Parliament and, taking his watch, which he threw on the ground and which he shattered to atoms: "I will break you," he said, "like this watch." He returns there some time after, drives all the members out one after the other, making them defile before him. Each is obliged, as he passes, to make him a deep bow: one of them passes with his hat on his head; Cromwell takes his hat from him and throws it on the ground: "Learn to respect me," he says.

When he had outraged all kings by having his own legitimate king's head cut off, and when he started to reign himself, he sent his portrait to a crowned head; it was to Christine, Queen of Sweden. Marvell, a famous English poet, who wrote very good Latin verse, accompanied this portrait with six verses where he made Cromwell himself speak. Cromwell corrected the last two as follows:

At tibi submittit frontem reverentior umbra,
Non sunt hi vultus regibus usque truces.

This queen was the first to recognize him as soon as he was protector of the three kingdoms. Almost all the sovereigns of Europe sent their ambassadors *to their brother* Cromwell, to this bishop's servant, who had just caused a sovereign, their own kin, to perish at the hand of the executioner. They vied with each in soliciting his alliance. Cardinal Mazarin, to please him, drove out of France the two sons of Charles I., the two grandsons of Henry IV., the two first cousins of Louis XIV. France conquered Dunkirk for him, and sent him the keys. After his death, Louis XIV. and all his court wore mourning, excepting Mademoiselle, who had the courage to come to the company in a coloured habit, and alone maintained the honour of her race.

Never was a king more absolute than he was. He said that he had preferred governing under the name of *protector* rather than under that of *king*, because the English knew the point to which a King of England's prerogative extended, and did not know to what point a protector's might go. That was to understand men, who are governed by opinion, and whose opinion depends on a name. He had conceived a profound scorn for the religion which had served to his fortune. There is a certain anecdote preserved in the house of St. John, which proves sufficiently the little account which Cromwell made of the instrument which had produced such great effects in his hands. He was drinking one day with Ireton, Fleetwood and St. John, great-grandfather of the celebrated Lord Bolingbroke; they wished to uncork a bottle, and the corkscrew fell under the table; they all looked for it and did not find it. Meanwhile a deputation from the Presbyterian churches was waiting in the antechamber, and an usher came to announce them. "Tell them," said Cromwell, "that I have retired, *and that I am seeking the Lord*." It was the expression which the fanatics used when they were saying their prayers. When he had thus dismissed the band of ministers, he said these very words to his confidants: "Those puppies think that we are seeking the Lord, and we are only seeking the corkscrew."

There is barely an example in Europe of any man who, come from so low, raised himself so high. But what was absolutely essential to him with all his talents? Fortune. He had this fortune; but was he happy? He lived poorly and anxiously until he was forty-three; from that time he bathed himself in blood, passed his life in turmoil, and died before his time at the age of fifty-seven. Let us compare this life with that of Newton, who lived eighty-four years, always tranquil, always honoured, always the light of all thinking beings, seeing increase each day his renown, his reputation, his fortune, without ever having either care or remorse; and let us judge which of the two had the better part.

SECTION II

Oliver Cromwell was regarded with admiration by the Puritans and independents of England; he is still their hero; but Richard Cromwell, his son, is my man.

The first is a fanatic who would be hissed to-day in the House of Commons, if he uttered there one single one of the unintelligible absurdities which he gave out with so much confidence before other fanatics who listened to him open-mouthed and wide-eyed, in the name of the Lord. If he said that one must seek the Lord, and fight the Lord's battles; if he introduced the Jewish jargon into the parliament of England, to the eternal shame of the human intelligence, he would be nearer to being led to Bedlam than to being chosen to command armies.

He was brave without a doubt; so are wolves; there are even monkeys as fierce as tigers. From being a fanatic he became an adroit politician, that is to say that from a wolf he became fox, climbed by imposture from the first steps where the infuriated enthusiasm of the times had placed him, right to the pinnacle of greatness; and the impostor walked on the heads of the prostrated fanatics. He reigned, but he lived in the horrors of anxiety. He knew neither serene days nor tranquil nights. The consolations of friendship and society never approached him; he died before his time, more worthy, without a doubt, of execution than the king whom he had conducted from a window of his own palace to the scaffold.

Richard Cromwell, on the contrary, born with a gentle, wise spirit, refused to keep his father's crown at the price of the blood of two or three rebels whom he could sacrifice to his ambition. He preferred to be reduced to private life rather than be an omnipotent assassin. He left the protectorate without regret to live as a citizen. Free and tranquil in the country, he enjoyed health there, and there did he possess his soul in peace for eighty-six years, loved by his neighbours, to whom he was arbiter and father.

Readers, give your verdict. If you had to choose between the destiny of the father and that of the son, which would you take?

CUSTOMS

Contemptible Customs do not always Suppose a Contemptible Nation

63

There are cases where one must not judge a nation by its customs and popular superstitions. I suppose that Cæsar, having conquered Egypt, wanting to make trade flourish in the Roman Empire, has sent an embassy to China, by the port of Arsinoë, the Red Sea, and the Indian Ocean. The Emperor Yventi, first of his name, was then reigning; the annals of China represent him as a very wise and learned prince. After receiving Cæsar's ambassadors with all the Chinese politeness, he informs himself secretly through his interpreters of the customs, science and religion of this Roman people, as celebrated in the West as the Chinese people is in the East. He learns first of all that this people's pontiffs have arranged their year in so absurd a fashion that the sun has already the heavenly signs of spring when the Romans are celebrating the first festivals of winter.

He learns that this nation supports at great cost a college of priests who know exactly the time when one should set sail and when one should give battle, by inspecting an ox's liver, or by the way in which the chickens eat barley. This sacred science was brought formerly to the Romans by a little god named Tages, who emerged from the earth in Tuscany. These peoples worship one supreme God whom they always call the very great and very good God. Nevertheless, they have built a temple to a courtesan named Flora; and almost all the good women of Rome have in their homes little household gods four or five inches high. One of these little divinities is the goddess of the breasts; the other the goddess of the buttocks. There is a household god who is called the god Pet. The emperor Yventi starts laughing: the tribunals of Nankin think first of all with him that the Roman ambassadors are madmen or impostors who have taken the title of envoys of the Roman Republic; but as the emperor is as just as he is polite, he has private talks with the ambassadors. He learns that the Roman pontiffs have been very ignorant, but that Cæsar is now reforming the calendar; they admit to him that the college of augurs was established in early barbarous times; that this ridiculous institution, become dear to a people long uncivilized, has been allowed to subsist; that all honest people laugh at the augurs; that Cæsar has never consulted them; that according to a very great man named Cato, never has an augur been able to speak to his comrade without laughter; and that finally Cicero, the greatest orator and the best philosopher in Rome, has just written against the augurs a little work entitled "Of Divination," in which he commits to eternal ridicule all the soothsayers, all the predictions, and all the sorcery of which the world is infatuated. The emperor of China is curious to read Cicero's book, the interpreters translate it; he admires the book and the Roman Republic.

DEMOCRACY

Ordinarily there is no comparison between the crimes of the great who are always ambitious, and the crimes of the people who always want, and can want only liberty and equality. These two sentiments, Liberty and Equality, do not lead direct to calumny, rapine, assassination, poisoning, the devastation of one's neighbours' lands, etc.; but ambitious might and the mania for power plunge into all these crimes whatever be the time, whatever be the place.

Popular government is in itself, therefore, less iniquitous, less abominable than despotic power.

The great vice of democracy is certainly not tyranny and cruelty: there have been mountain-dwelling republicans, savage, ferocious; but it is not the republican spirit that made them so, it is nature.

The real vice of a civilized republic is in the Turkish fable of the dragon with many heads and the dragon with many tails. The many heads hurt each other, and the many tails obey a single head which wants to devour everything.

Democracy seems suitable only to a very little country, and further it must be happily situated. Small though it be, it will make many mistakes, because it will be composed of men. Discord will reign there as in a monastery; but there will be no St. Bartholomew, no Irish massacres, no Sicilian vespers, no inquisition, no condemnation to the galleys for having taken some water from the sea without paying for it, unless one supposes this republic composed of devils in a corner of hell.

One questions every day whether a republican government is preferable to a king's government? The dispute ends always by agreeing that to govern men is very difficult. The Jews had God Himself for master; see what has happened to them on that account: nearly always have they been beaten and slaves, and to-day do you not find that they cut a pretty figure?

DESTINY

Of all the books of the Occident which have come down to us, the most ancient is Homer; it is there that one finds the customs of profane antiquity, of the gross heroes, of the gross gods, made in the image of men; but it is there that among the reveries and inconsequences, one finds too the seeds of philosophy, and above all the idea of the destiny which is master of the gods, as the gods are masters of the world.

When the magnanimous Hector wishes absolutely to fight the magnanimous Achilles, and with this object starts fleeing with all his might, and three times makes the circuit of the city before fighting, in order to have more vigour; when Homer compares fleet-of-foot Achilles, who pursues him, to a man who sleeps; when Madame Dacier goes into ecstasies of admiration over the art and mighty sense of this passage, then Jupiter wants to save great Hector who has made so many sacrifices to him, and he consults the fates; he weighs the destinies of Hector and Achilles in the balance (Iliad, liv. xxii.): he finds that the Trojan must absolutely be killed by the Greek; he cannot oppose it; and from this moment, Apollo, Hector's guardian genius, is forced to abandon him. It is not that Homer is not often prodigal, and particularly in this place, of quite contrary ideas, following the privilege of antiquity; but he is the first in whom one finds the notion of destiny. This notion, therefore, was very much in vogue in his time.

The Pharisees, among the little Jewish people, did not adopt destiny until several centuries later; for these Pharisees themselves, who were the first literates among the Jews, were very new fangled. In Alexandria they mixed a part of the dogmas of the Stoics with the old Jewish ideas. St. Jerome claims even that their sect is not much anterior to the Christian era.

The philosophers never had need either of Homer or the Pharisees to persuade themselves that everything happens through immutable laws, that everything is arranged, that everything is a necessary effect. This is how they argued.

Either the world exists by its own nature, by its physical laws, or a supreme being has formed it according to his supreme laws: in both cases, these laws are immutable; in both cases everything is necessary; heavy bodies tend towards the centre of the earth, without being able to tend to pause in the air. Pear-trees can never bear pineapples. A spaniel's instinct cannot be an ostrich's instinct; everything is arranged, in gear, limited.

Man can have only a certain number of teeth, hair and ideas; there comes a time when he necessarily loses his teeth, hair and ideas.

It would be a contradiction that what was yesterday was not, that what is to-day is not; it is also a contradiction that what must be cannot be.

If you could disturb the destiny of a fly, there would be no reason that could stop your making the destiny of all the other flies, of all the other animals, of all men, of all nature; you would find yourself in the end more powerful than God.

Imbeciles say: "My doctor has extricated my aunt from a mortal malady; he has made my aunt live ten years longer than she ought to have lived." Others who affect knowledge, say: "The prudent man makes his own destiny."

But often the prudent, far from making their destinies, succumb to them; it is destiny which makes them prudent.

Profound students of politics affirm that, if Cromwell, Ludlow, Ireton and a dozen other parliamentarians had been assassinated a week before Charles I.'s head was cut off, this king might have lived longer and died in his bed; they are right; they can add further that if the whole of England had been swallowed up in the sea, this monarch would not have perished on a scaffold near Whitehall; but things were arranged so that Charles had to have his neck severed.

Cardinal d'Ossat was doubtless more prudent than a madman in Bedlam; but is it not clear that the organs of d'Ossat the sage were made otherwise than those of the scatter-brain? just as a fox's organs are different from a stork's and a lark's.

Your doctor saved your aunt; but assuredly he did not in that contradict nature's order; he followed it. It is clear that your aunt could not stop herself being born in such and such town, that she could not stop herself having a certain malady at a particular time, that the doctor could not be elsewhere than in the town where he was, that your aunt had to call him, that he had to prescribe for her the drugs which cured her, or which one thinks cured her, when nature was the only doctor.

A peasant thinks that it has hailed on his field by chance; but the philosopher knows that there is no chance, and that it was impossible, in the constitution of this world, for it not to hail on that day in that place.

There are persons who, frightened by this truth, admit half of it as debtors who offer half to their creditors, and ask respite for the rest. "There are," they say, "some events which are necessary, and others which are not." It would be very comic that one part of the world was arranged, and that the other were not; that a part of what happens had to happen, and that another part of what happens did not have to happen. If one looks closely at it, one sees that the doctrine contrary to that of destiny is absurd; but there are many people destined to reason badly, others not to reason at all, others to persecute those who reason.

Some say to you: "Do not believe in fatalism; for then everything appearing inevitable, you will work at nothing, you will wallow in indifference, you will love neither riches, nor honours, nor glory; you will not want to acquire anything, you will believe yourself without merit as

67

without power; no talent will be cultivated, everything will perish through apathy."

Be not afraid, gentlemen, we shall ever have passions and prejudices, since it is our destiny to be subjected to prejudices and passions: we shall know that it no more depends on us to have much merit and great talent, than to have a good head of hair and beautiful hands: we shall be convinced that we must not be vain about anything, and yet we shall always have vanity.

I necessarily have the passion for writing this, and you have the passion for condemning me; both of us are equally fools, equally the toys of destiny. Your nature is to do harm, mine is to love truth, and to make it public in spite of you.

The owl, which feeds on mice in its ruins, said to the nightingale: "Finish singing under your beautiful shady trees, come into my hole, that I may eat you"; and the nightingale answered: "I was born to sing here, and to laugh at you."

You ask me what will become of liberty? I do not understand you. I do not know what this liberty is of which you speak; so long have you been disputing about its nature, that assuredly you are not acquainted with it. If you wish, or rather, if you are able to examine peaceably with me what it is, pass to the letter L.

DEVOUT

The word "devout" signifies "devoted"; and in the strict sense of the term this qualification should belong only to monks and nuns who make vows. But as in the Gospel there is no more mention of vows than of devout persons, this title does not in fact belong to anyone. Everyone should be equally righteous. A man who styles himself devout resembles a commoner who styles himself a marquis; he arrogates to himself a quality he does not possess. He thinks himself more worthy than his neighbour. One can forgive such foolishness in women; their frailty and their frivolity render them excusable; the poor creatures pass from a lover to a director in good faith: but one cannot pardon the rogues who direct them, who abuse their ignorance, who establish the throne of their pride on the credulity of the sex. They resolve themselves into a little mystic seraglio composed of seven or eight aged beauties, subdued by the weight of their lack of occupation, and almost always do these persons pay tribute to their new masters. No young woman without a lover, no aged devout woman without a director. Oh! the Orientals are wiser than we are! Never does a pasha say: "We supped yesterday with the Aga of the Janissaries who is my sister's lover, and the vicar of the mosque who is my wife's director."

THE ECCLESIASTICAL MINISTRY

The institution of religion exists only to keep mankind in order, and to make men merit the goodness of God by their virtue. Everything in a religion which does not tend towards this goal must be considered foreign or dangerous.

Instruction, exhortation, menaces of pains to come, promises of immortal beatitude, prayers, counsels, spiritual help are the only means ecclesiastics may use to try to make men virtuous here below, and happy for eternity.

All other means are repugnant to the liberty of the reason, to the nature of the soul, to the inalterable rights of the conscience, to the essence of religion and of the ecclesiastical ministry, to all the rights of the sovereign.

Virtue supposes liberty, as the carrying of a burden supposes active force. Under coercion no virtue, and without virtue no religion. Make a slave of me, I shall be no better for it.

The sovereign even has no right to use coercion to lead men to religion, which supposes essentially choice and liberty. My thought is subordinate to authority no more than is sickness or health.

In order to disentangle all the contradictions with which books on canon law have been filled, and to fix our ideas on the ecclesiastical ministry, let us investigate amid a thousand equivocations what the Church is.

The Church is the assembly of all the faithful summoned on certain days to pray in common, and at all times to do good actions.

The priests are persons established under the authority of the sovereign to direct these prayers and all religious worship.

A numerous Church could not exist without ecclesiastics; but these ecclesiastics are not the Church.

It is no less evident that if the ecclesiastics, who are part of civil society, had acquired rights which might trouble or destroy society, these rights ought to be suppressed.

It is still more evident that, if God has attached to the Church prerogatives or rights, neither these rights nor these prerogatives should belong exclusively either to the chief of the Church or to the ecclesiastics, because they are not the Church, just as the magistrates are not the sovereign in either a democratic state or in a monarchy.

Finally, it is quite evident that it is our souls which are under the clergy's care, solely for spiritual things.

Our soul acts internally; internal acts are thought, volition, inclinations, acquiescence in certain truths. All these acts are above all coercion, and are within the ecclesiastical minister's sphere only in so far as he must instruct and never command.

This soul acts also externally. External actions are under the civil law. Here coercion may have a place; temporal or corporal pains maintain the law by punishing those who infringe it.

Obedience to ecclesiastical order must consequently always be free and voluntary: no other should be possible. Submission, on the other hand, to civil order may be coerced and compulsory.

For the same reason, ecclesiastical punishments, always spiritual, do not reach here below any but those who are convinced inwardly of their fault. Civil pains, on the contrary, accompanied by a physical ill, have their physical effects, whether or no the guilty recognize their justice.

From this it results obviously that the authority of the clergy is and can be spiritual only; that it should not have any temporal power; that no coercive force is proper to its ministry, which would be destroyed by it.

It follows from this further that the sovereign, careful not to suffer any partition of his authority, must permit no enterprise which puts the members of society in external and civil dependence on an ecclesiastical body.

Such are the incontestable principles of real canon law, of which the rules and decisions should be judged at all times by the eternal and immutable truths which are founded on natural law and the necessary order of society.

EMBLEM

In antiquity everything is symbol or emblem. In Chaldea it starts by putting a ram, two kids, a bull in the sky, to mark the productions of the earth in the spring. Fire is the symbol of the Deity in Persia; the celestial dog warns the Egyptians of the Nile floods; the serpent which hides its tail in its head, becomes the image of eternity. The whole of nature is represented and disguised.

In India again you find many of those old statues, uncouth and frightful, of which we have already spoken, representing virtue provided with ten great arms with which to combat vice, and which our poor missionaries have taken for the picture of the devil.

Put all these symbols of antiquity before the eyes of a man of the soundest sense, who has never heard speak of them, he will not understand anything: it is a language to be learned.

The old theological poets were in the necessity of giving God eyes, hands, feet; of announcing Him in the form of a man. St. Clement of Alexandria records some verses of Xenophanes the Colophonian (Stromates liv. v.), from which one sees that it is not merely from to-day that men have made God in their own image. Orpheus of Thrace, the first theologian of the Greeks, long before Homer, expresses himself similarly, according to the same Clement of Alexandria.

Everything being symbol and emblem, the philosophers, and especially those who had travelled in India, employed this method; their precepts were emblems and enigmas.

Do not stir the fire with a sword, that is, do not irritate angry men.

Do not hide the light under the bushel.—Do not hide the truth from men.

Abstain from beans.—Flee frequently public assemblies in which one gave one's suffrage with black or white beans.

Do not have swallows in your house.—That it may not be filled with chatterers.

In the tempest worship the echo.—In times of public trouble retire to the country.

Do not write on the snow.—Do not teach feeble and sluggish minds.

Do not eat either your heart or your brain.—Do not give yourself up to either grief or to too difficult enterprises, etc.

Such are the maxims of Pythagoras, the sense of which is not hard to understand.

The most beautiful of all the emblems is that of God, whom Timæus of Locres represents by this idea: *A circle the centre of which is everywhere and the circumference nowhere.* Plato adopted this emblem; Pascal had inserted it among the material which he intended using, and which has been called his "Thoughts."

In metaphysics, in moral philosophy, the ancients have said everything. We coincide with them, or we repeat them. All modern books of this kind are only repetitions.

It is above all among the Indians, the Egyptians, the Syrians, that these emblems, which to us appear most strange, were consecrated. It is there that the two organs of generation, the two symbols of life, were carried in procession with the greatest respect. We laugh at it, we dare treat these peoples as barbarous idiots, because they innocently thanked God for having given them existence. What would they have said if they had seen us enter our temples with the instrument of destruction at our side?

At Thebes the sins of the people were represented by a goat. On the coast of Phœnicia a naked woman, with a fish's tail, was the emblem of nature.

One must not be astonished, therefore, if this use of symbols reached the Hebrews when they had formed a body of people near the Syrian desert.

One of the most beautiful emblems of the Judaic books is this passage of Ecclesiastes: "... when the grinders cease because they are few, and those that look out of the windows be darkened, when the almond-tree shall flourish and the grasshopper shall be a burden: or ever the silver cord be loosed, or the golden bowl be broken, or the pitcher be broken at the fountain...."

That signifies that the old men lose their teeth, that their sight is dim, that their hair whitens like the flower of the almond-tree, that their feet swell like the grasshopper, that they are no more fit for engendering children, and that then they must prepare for the great journey.

The "Song of Songs" is (as one knows) a continual emblem of the marriage of Jesus Christ with the Church. It is an emblem from beginning to end. Especially does the ingenious Dom Calmet demonstrate that the palm-tree to which the well-beloved goes is the cross to which our Lord Jesus Christ was condemned. But it must be avowed that a pure and healthy moral philosophy is still preferable to these allegories.

One sees in this people's books a crowd of typical emblems which revolt us to-day and which exercise our incredulity and our mockery, but which appeared ordinary and simple to the Asiatic peoples.

In Ezekiel are images which appear to us as licentious and revolting: in those times they were merely natural. There are thirty examples in the "Song of Songs," model of the most chaste union. Remark carefully that these expressions, these images are always quite serious, and that in no book of this distant antiquity will you find the least mockery on the great subject of generation. When lust is condemned it is in definite terms; but never to excite to passion, nor to make the smallest pleasantry. This far-distant antiquity did not have its Martial, its Catullus, or its Petronius.

It results from all the Jewish prophets and from all the Jewish books, as from all the books which instruct us in the usages of the Chaldeans, the Persians, the Phœnicians, the Syrians, the Indians, the Egyptians; it results, I say, that their customs were not ours, that this ancient world in no way resembled our world. Go from Gibraltar to Mequinez merely, the manners are no longer the same; no longer does one find the same ideas; two leagues of sea have changed everything.

ON THE ENGLISH THEATRE

I have cast my eyes on an edition of Shakespeare issued by Master Samuel Johnson. I saw there that foreigners who are astonished that in the plays of the great Shakespeare a Roman senator plays the buffoon, and that a king appears on the stage drunk, are treated as little-minded. I do not desire to suspect Master Johnson of being a sorry jester, and of being too fond of wine; but I find it somewhat extraordinary that he counts buffoonery and drunkenness among the beauties of the tragic stage: and no less singular is the reason he gives, that the poet disdains accidental distinctions of circumstance and country, like a painter who, content with having painted the figure, neglects the drapery. The comparison would be more just if he were speaking of a painter who in a noble subject should introduce ridiculous grotesques, should paint Alexander the Great mounted on an ass in the battle of Arbela, and Darius' wife drinking at an inn with rapscallions.

But there is one thing more extraordinary than all, that is that Shakespeare is a genius. The Italians, the French, the men of letters of all other countries, who have not spent some time in England, take him only for a clown, for a joker far inferior to Harlequin, for the most contemptible buffoon who has ever amused the populace. Nevertheless, it is in this same man that one finds pieces which exalt the imagination and which stir the heart to its depths. It is Truth, it is Nature herself who speaks her own language with no admixture of artifice. It is of the sublime, and the author has in no wise sought it.

73

What can one conclude from this contrast of grandeur and sordidness, of sublime reason and uncouth folly, in short from all the contrasts that we see in Shakespeare? That he would have been a perfect poet had he lived in the time of Addison.

The famous Addison, who flourished under Queen Anne, is perhaps of all English writers the one who best knew how to guide genius with taste. He had a correct style, an imagination discreet in expression, elegance, strength and simplicity in his verse and in his prose. A friend of propriety and orderliness, he wanted tragedy to be written with dignity, and it is thus that his "Cato" is composed.

From the very first act the verses are worthy of Virgil, and the sentiments worthy of Cato. There is no theatre in Europe where the scene of Juba and Syphax was not applauded as a masterpiece of skill, of well-developed characters, of fine contrasts, and of pure and noble diction. Literary Europe, which knows the translations of this piece, applauded even to the philosophic traits with which the rôle of Cato is filled.

The piece had the great success which its beauty of detail merited, and which was assured to it by the troubles in England to which this tragedy was in more than one place a striking allusion. But the appositeness of these allusions having passed, the verse being only beautiful, the maxims being only noble and just, and the piece being cold, people no longer felt anything more than the coldness. Nothing is more beautiful than Virgil's second canto; recite it on the stage, it will bore: on the stage one must have passion, live dialogue, action. People soon returned to Shakespeare's uncouth but captivating aberrations.

ENVY

One knows well enough what antiquity has said of this shameful passion, and what the moderns have repeated. Hesiod is the first classic author who speaks of it.

"The potter is envious of the potter, the artisan of the artisan, the poor man even of the poor man, the musician of the musician (or if one would give another sense to the word *Aoidos*) the poet of the poet."

Long before Hesiod, Job had said: "Envy slayeth the silly one" (Job. chap. v. verse 2).

I think that Mandeville, author of the "Fable of the Bees," was the first to try to prove that envy is a very good thing, a very useful passion. His first reason is that envy is as natural to man as hunger and thirst; that it can be found in children, as well as in horses and dogs. Do you want your children to hate each other, kiss one more than the other; the secret is infallible.

He maintains that the first thing that two young women meeting each other do is to cast about for what is ridiculous in each other, and the second to flatter each other.

He believes that without envy the arts would be indifferently cultivated, and that Raphael would not have been a great painter if he had not been jealous of Michael Angelo.

Mandeville has taken emulation for envy, maybe; maybe, also, emulation is only envy kept within the bounds of decency.

Michael Angelo might say to Raphael: "Your envy has only led you to work still better than me; you have not decried me, you have not intrigued against me with the Pope, you have not tried to have me excommunicated for having put cripples and one-eyed men in paradise, and succulent cardinals with beautiful women naked as your hand in hell, in my picture of the last judgment. Your envy is very praiseworthy; you are a fine envious fellow; let us be good friends."

But if the envious man is a wretch without talent, jealous of merit as beggars are of the rich; if, pressed by the indigence as by the turpitude of his character he writes you some "News from Parnassus," some "Letters of Madame la Comtesse," some "Années Littéraires," this animal displays an envy that is good for nothing, and for which Mandeville could never make an apology.

One asks why the ancients thought that the eye of the envious man bewitched those who looked at it. It is the envious, rather, who are bewitched.

Descartes says: "That envy impels the yellow bile which comes from the lower part of the liver, and the black bile which comes from the spleen, which is diffused from the heart through the arteries, etc." But as no kind of bile is formed in the spleen, Descartes, by speaking thus, does not seem to merit too much that his natural philosophy should be envied.

A certain Voët or Voëtius, a theological scamp, who accused Descartes of atheism, was very ill with the black bile; but he knew still less than Descartes how his detestable bile was diffused in his blood.

Madame Pernelle is right: "The envious will die, but envy never." (Tartufe, Act v, Scene iii.)

But it is good proverb which says that "it is better to be envious than to have pity." Let us be envious, therefore, as hard as we can.

EQUALITY

SECTION I

It is clear that men, enjoying the faculties connected with their nature, are equal; they are equal when they perform animal functions, and when they exercise their understanding. The King of China, the Great Mogul, the Padisha of Turkey, cannot say to the least of men: "I forbid you to digest, to go to the privy and to think." All the animals of each species are equal among themselves. Animals by nature have over us the advantage of independence. If a bull which is wooing a heifer is driven away with the blows of the horns by a stronger bull, it goes in search of another mistress in another field, and lives free. A cock, beaten by a cock, consoles itself in another poultry-house. It is not so with us. A little vizier exiles a bostangi to Lemnos: the vizier Azem exiles the little vizier to Tenedos: the padisha exiles the little vizier Azem to Rhodes: the Janissaries put the padisha in prison, and elect another who will exile good Mussulmans as he chooses; people will still be very obliged to him if he limits his sacred authority to this little exercise.

If this world were what it seems it should be, if man could find everywhere in it an easy subsistence, and a climate suitable to his nature, it is clear that it would be impossible for one man to enslave another. If this globe were covered with wholesome fruits; if the air, which should contribute to our life, gave us no diseases and a premature death; if man had no need of lodging and bed other than those of the buck and the deer; then the Gengis-kans and the Tamerlans would have no servants other than their children, who would be folk honourable enough to help them in their old age.

In the natural state enjoyed by all untamed quadrupeds, birds and reptiles, man would be as happy as they; domination would then be a chimera, an absurdity of which no one would think; for why seek servants when you have no need of their service?

If it came into the head of some individual of tyrannous mind and brawny arm to enslave a neighbour less strong than he, the thing would be impossible; the oppressed would be on the Danube before the oppressor had taken his measures on the Volga.

All men would then be necessarily equal, if they were without needs; the poverty connected with our species subordinates one man to another; it is not the inequality which is the real misfortune, it is the dependence. It matters very little that So-and-so calls himself "His Highness," and So-and-so "His Holiness"; but to serve the one or the other is hard.

A big family has cultivated fruitful soil; two little families near by have thankless and rebellious fields; the two poor families have to serve the opulent family, or slaughter it: there is no difficulty in that. One of the two indigent families offers its arms to the rich family in order to have bread; the other goes to attack it and is beaten. The serving family is the origin of the servants and the workmen; the beaten family is the origin of the slaves.

In our unhappy world it is impossible for men living in society not to be divided into two classes, the one the rich that commands, the other the poor that serves; and these two are subdivided into a thousand, and these thousand still have different gradations.

When the prizes are drawn you come to us: "I am a man like you," you say. "I have two hands and two feet, as much pride as you, nay more, a mind as disordered, at least, as inconsequent, as contradictory as yours. I am a citizen of San Marino, or of Ragusa, or Vaugirard: give me my share of the land. In our known hemisphere there are about fifty thousand million arpents to cultivate, some passable, some sterile. We are only about a thousand million featherless bipeds in this continent; that makes fifty arpents apiece: be just; give me my fifty arpents."

"Go and take them in the land of the Cafres," we answer, "or the Hottentots, or the Samoyedes; come to an amicable arrangement with them; here all the shares are taken. If among us you want to eat, be clothed, lodged, warmed, work for us as your father did; serve us or amuse us, and you will be paid; otherwise you will be obliged to ask charity, which would be too degrading to your sublime nature, and would stop your being really the equal of kings, and even of country parsons, according to the pretensions of your noble pride."

SECTION II

All the poor are not unhappy. The majority were born in that state, and continual work stops their feeling their position too keenly; but when they feel it, then one sees wars, like that of the popular party against the senate party in Rome, like those of the peasants in Germany, England and France. All these wars finish sooner or later with the subjection of the people, because the powerful have money, and money is master of everything in a state: I say in a state; for it is not the same between nations. The nation which makes the best use of the sword will always subjugate the nation which has more gold and less courage.

All men are born with a sufficiently violent liking for domination, wealth and pleasure, and with much taste for idleness; consequently, all men want their money and the wives or daughters of others, to be their master, to subject them to all their caprices, and to do nothing, or at least to do only very agreeable things. You see clearly that with these fine inclinations it is as impossible for men to be equal as it is impossible for two predicants or two professors of theology not to be jealous of each other.

The human race, such as it is, cannot subsist unless there is an infinity of useful men who possess nothing at all; for it is certain that a man who is well off will not leave his own land to come to till yours; and if you have need of a pair of shoes, it is not the Secretary to the Privy Council who will make them for you. Equality, therefore, is at once the most natural thing and the most fantastic.

As men go to excess in everything when they can, this inequality has been exaggerated. It has been maintained in many countries that it was not permissible for a citizen to leave the country where chance has caused him to be born; the sense of this law is visibly: "This land is so bad and so badly governed, that we forbid any individual to leave it, for fear that everyone will leave it." Do better: make all your subjects want to live in your country, and foreigners to come to it.

All men have the right in the bottom of their hearts to think themselves entirely equal to other men: it does not follow from that that the cardinal's cook should order his master to prepare him his dinner; but the cook can say: "I am a man like my master; like him I was born crying; like me he will die with the same pangs and the same ceremonies. Both of us perform the same animal functions. If the Turks take possession of Rome, and if then I am cardinal and my master cook, I shall take him into my service." This discourse is reasonable and just; but while waiting for the Great Turk to take possession of Rome, the cook must do his duty, or else all human society is perverted.

As regards a man who is neither a cardinal's cook, nor endowed with any other employment in the state; as regards a private person who is connected with nothing, but who is vexed at being received everywhere with an air of being patronized or scorned, who sees quite clearly that many *monsignors* have no more knowledge, wit or virtue than he, and who at times is bored at waiting in their antechambers, what should he decide to do? Why, to take himself off.

EXPIATION

Maybe the most beautiful institution of antiquity is that solemn ceremony which repressed crimes by warning that they must be punished, and which calmed the despair of the guilty by making them atone for their transgressions by penitences. Remorse must necessarily have preceded the expiations; for the maladies are older than the medicine, and all needs have existed before relief.

It was, therefore, before all the creeds, a natural religion, which troubled man's heart when in his ignorance or in his hastiness he had committed an inhuman action. A friend killed his friend in a quarrel, a brother killed his brother, a jealous and frantic lover even killed her without whom he could not live. The head of a nation condemned a virtuous man, a useful citizen. These are men in despair, if they have sensibility. Their conscience harries them; nothing is more true; and it is the height of unhappiness. Only two choices remain, either reparation, or a settling in crime. All sensitive souls choose the first, monsters choose the second.

As soon as religions were established, there were expiations; the ceremonies accompanying them were ridiculous: for what connection between the water of the Ganges and a murder? how could a man repair a homicide by bathing himself? We have already remarked this excess of aberration and absurdity, of imagining that he who washes his body washes his soul, and wipes away the stains of bad actions.

The water of the Nile had later the same virtue as the water of the Ganges: to these purifications other ceremonies were added: I avow that they were still more impertinent. The Egyptians took two goats, and drew lots for which of the two should be thrown below, charged with the sins of the guilty. The name of "Hazazel," the expiator, was given to this goat. What connection, I ask you, between a goat and a man's crime?

It is true that since, God permitted this ceremony to be sanctified among the Jews our fathers, who took so many Egyptian rites; but doubtless it was the repentance, and not the goat, which purified the Jewish souls.

Jason, having killed Absyrthe his step-brother, comes, it is said, with Medea, more guilty than he, to have himself absolved by Circe, queen and priestess of Aea, who ever after passed for a great magician. Circe absolves them with a sucking-pig and salt cakes. That may make a fairly good dish, but can barely either pay for Absyrthe's blood or render Jason and Medea more honourable people, unless they avow a sincere repentance while eating their sucking-pig.

Orestes' expiation (he had avenged his father by murdering his mother) was to go to steal a statue from the Tartars of Crimea. The statue must have been very badly made, and there was nothing to gain on such an effect. Since then we have done better, we have invented the mysteries; the guilty might there receive their absolution by undergoing painful ordeals, and by swearing that they would lead a new life. It is from this oath that the new members were called among all nations by a name which corresponds to initiates, *qui ineunt vitam novam*, who began a new career, who entered into the path of virtue.

The Christian catechumens were called *initiates* only when they were baptised.

It is undoubted that in these mysteries one was washed of one's faults only by the oath to be virtuous; that is so true that the hierophant in all the Greek mysteries, in sending away the assembly, pronounced these two Egyptian words—"*Koth, ompheth*, watch, be pure"; which is a proof at once that the mysteries came originally from Egypt, and that they were invented only to make men better.

The sages in all times did what they could, therefore, to inspire virtue, and not to reduce human frailty to despair; but also there are crimes so horrible that no mystery accorded expiation for them. Nero, for all that he was emperor, could not get himself initiated into the mysteries of Ceres. Constantine, on the Report of Zosimus, could not obtain pardon for his crimes: he was stained with the blood of his wife, his son and all his kindred. It was in the interest of the human race that such great transgressions should remain without expiation, in order that absolution should not invite their committal, and that universal horror might sometimes stop the villains.

The Roman Catholics have expiations which are called "penitences."

By the laws of the barbarians who destroyed the Roman Empire, crimes were expiated with money. That was called *compounding*, *componat cum decem, viginti, triginta solidis*. It cost two hundred sous of that time to kill a priest, and four hundred for killing a bishop; so that a bishop was worth precisely two priests.

Having thus compounded with men, one compounded with God, when confession was generally established. Finally, Pope John XXII., who made money out of everything, prepared a tariff of sins.

The absolution of an incest, four turonenses for a layman; *ab incestu pro laico in foro conscientiæ turonenses quatuor*. For the man and the woman who have committed incest, eighteen turonenses four ducats and nine carlins. That is not just; if one person pays only four turonenses, the two owed only eight turonenses.

Sodomy and bestiality are put at the same rate, with the inhibitory clause to title XLIII: that amounts to ninety turonenses twelve ducats and six carlins: *cum inhibitione turonenses 90, ducatos 12, carlinos 6, etc.*

It is very difficult to believe that Leo X. was so imprudent as to have this impost printed in 1514, as is asserted; but it must be considered that no spark appeared at that time of the conflagration which reformers kindled later, that the court of Rome slumbered on the people's credulity, and neglected to cover its exactions with the lightest veil. The public sale of indulgences, which followed soon after, makes it clear that this court took no precaution to hide the turpitudes to which so many nations were accustomed. As soon as complaints against the Church's abuses burst forth, the court did what it could to suppress the book; but it could not succeed.

If I dare give my opinion of this impost, I think that the various editions are not reliable; the prices are not at all proportionate: these prices do not agree with those which are alleged by d'Aubigné, grandfather of Madame de Maintenon, in the "Confession de Sanci"; he rates virginity at six *gros*, and incest with his mother and sister at five *gros*; this account is ridiculous. I think that there was in fact a tariff established in the datary's office, for those who came to Rome to be absolved, or to bargain for dispensations; but that the enemies of Rome added much to it in order to render it more odious.

What is quite certain is that these imposts were never authorized by any council; that it was an enormous abuse invented by avarice, and respected by those whose interest it was not to abolish it. The buyers and the sellers were equally satisfied: thus, barely anybody protested, until the troubles of the reformation. It must be admitted that an exact note of all these imposts would be of great service to the history of the human mind.

EXTREME

We shall try to extract from this word *extreme* a notion which may be useful.

One disputes every day if, in war, luck or leadership produces successes.

If, in disease, nature acts more than medicine for curing or killing.

If, in jurisprudence, it is not very advantageous to come to terms when one is in the right, and to plead when one is in the wrong.

If literature contributes to the glory of a nation or to its decadence.

If one should or should not make the people superstitious.

If there is anything true in metaphysics, history and moral philosophy.

If taste is arbitrary, and if there is in fact good taste and bad taste, etc., etc.

To decide all these questions right away, take an example of what is the most extreme in each; compare the two opposed extremes, and you will at once discover which is true.

You wish to know if leadership can infallibly determine the success of the war; look at the most extreme case, the most opposed situations, in which leadership alone will infallibly triumph. The enemy's army is forced to pass through a deep mountain gorge; your general knows it: he makes a forced march, he takes possession of the heights, he holds the enemy shut in a pass; they must either die or surrender. In this extreme case, luck cannot have any part in the victory. It is therefore demonstrated that skill can determine the success of a campaign; from that alone is it proved that war is an art.

Now imagine an advantageous but less decisive position; success is not so certain, but it is always very probable. You arrive thus, step by step, to a perfect equality between the two armies. What will decide then? luck, that is to say an unforeseen event, a general officer killed when he is on his way to execute an important order, a corps which is shaken by a false rumour, a panic and a thousand other cases which cannot be remedied by prudence; but it still remains certain that there is an art, a generalship.

As much must be said of medicine, of this art of operating on the head and the hand, to restore life to a man who is about to lose it.

The first man who at the right moment bled and purged a sufferer from an apoplectic fit; the first man who thought of plunging a knife into the bladder in order to extract a stone, and of closing the wound again; the first man who knew how to stop gangrene in a part of the body, were without a doubt almost divine persons, and did not resemble Molière's doctors.

Descend from this obvious example to experiments that are less striking and more equivocal; you see fevers, ills of all kinds which are cured, without it being well proved if it be nature or the doctor who has cured them; you see diseases of which the result cannot be guessed; twenty doctors are deceived; the one that has the most intelligence, the surest eye, guesses the character of the malady. There is therefore an art; and the superior man knows the finenesses of it. Thus did La Peyronie guess that a man of the court had swallowed a pointed bone which had caused an ulcer, and put him in danger of death; thus did Boerhaave guess the cause of the malady as unknown as cruel of a count of Vassenaar. There is therefore really an art of medicine; but in all arts there are men like Virgil and Mævius.

In jurisprudence, take a clear case, in which the law speaks clearly; a bill of exchange properly prepared and accepted; the acceptor must be condemned to pay it in every country. There is therefore a useful jurisprudence, although in a thousand cases judgments are arbitrary, to the misfortune of the human race, because the laws are badly made.

Do you desire to know if literature does good to a nation; compare the two extremes, Cicero and an uncouth ignoramus. See if it is Pliny or Attila who caused the fall of Rome.

One asks if one should encourage superstition in the people; see above all what is most extreme in this disastrous matter, St. Bartholomew, the massacres in Ireland, the crusades; the question is soon answered.

Is there any truth in metaphysics? Seize first of all the points that are most astonishing and the most true; something exists for all eternity. An eternal Being exists by Himself; this Being cannot be either wicked or inconsequent. One must surrender to these truths; almost all the rest is given over to dispute, and the justest mind unravels the truth while the others are seeking in the shadows.

It is with all things as with colours; the weakest eyes distinguish black from white; the better, more practised eyes, discern shades that resemble each other.

EZOURVEIDAM

What is this "Ezourveidam" which is in the King of France's library? It is an ancient commentary which an ancient Brahmin composed once upon a time, before the epoch of Alexander, on the ancient "Veidam," which was itself much less ancient than the book of the "Shasta."

Let us respect, I tell you, all these ancient Indians. They invented the game of chess, and the Greeks went among them to learn geometry.

This "Ezourveidam" was lastly translated by a Brahmin, correspondent of the unfortunate French India Company. It was brought to me on Mount Krapack, where I have long been observing the snows; and I sent it to the great Library of Paris, where it is better placed than in my home.

Those who wish to consult it will see that after many revolutions produced by the Eternal, it pleased the Eternal to form a man who was called *Adimo*, and a woman whose name corresponds to that of life.

Is this Indian anecdote taken from the Jewish books? have the Jews copied it from the Indians? or can one say that both wrote it originally, and that fine minds meet?

The Jews were not permitted to think that their writers had drawn anything from the Brahmins, for they had never heard tell of them. We are not permitted to think about Adam otherwise than the Jews. Consequently I hold my tongue, and I do not think at all.

FAITH

We have long pondered whether or no we should print this article, which we found in an old book. Our respect for St. Peter's see restrained us. But some pious men having convinced us that Pope Alexander VI. had nothing in common with St. Peter, we at last decided to bring this little piece into the light, without scruple.

One day Prince Pico della Mirandola met Pope Alexander VI. at the house of the courtesan Emilia, while Lucretia, the holy father's daughter, was in child-bed, and one did not know in Rome if the child was the Pope's, or his son's the Duke of Valentinois, or Lucretia's husband's, Alphonse of Aragon, who passed for impotent. The conversation was at first very sprightly. Cardinal Bembo records a part of it.

"Little Pic," said the Pope, "who do you think is my grandson's father?"

"Your son-in-law, I think," answered Pic.

"Eh! how can you believe such folly?"

"I believe it through faith."

"But do you not know quite well that a man who is impotent does not make children?"

"Faith consists," returned Pic, "in believing things because they are impossible; and, further, the honour of your house demands that Lucretia's son shall not pass as the fruit of an incest. You make me believe more incomprehensible mysteries. Have I not to be convinced that a serpent spoke, that since then all men have been damned, that Balaam's she-ass also spoke very eloquently, and that the walls of Jericho fell at the sound of trumpets?" Pic forthwith ran through a litany of all the admirable things he believed.

Alexander fell on his sofa by dint of laughing.

84

"I believe all that like you," he said, "for I know well that only by faith can I be saved, and that I shall not be saved by my works."

"Ah! Holy Father," said Pic, "you have need of neither works nor faith; that is good for poor profane people like us; but you who are vice-god can believe and do all you want to. You have the keys of heaven; and without a doubt St. Peter will not close the door in your face. But for myself, I avow I should need potent protection if, being only a poor prince, I had slept with my daughter, and if I had used the stiletto and the cantarella as often as your Holiness."

Alexander could take a jest. "Let us talk seriously," he said to Prince della Mirandola. "Tell me what merit one can have in telling God that one is persuaded of things of which in fact one cannot be persuaded? What pleasure can that give God? Between ourselves, saying that one believes what is impossible to believe is lying."

Pico della Mirandola made a great sign of the cross. "Eh! paternal God," he cried, "may your Holiness pardon me, you are not a Christian."

"No, by my faith," said the Pope.

"I thought as much," said Pico della Mirandola.

FALSE MINDS

We have blind men, one-eyed men, squint-eyed men, men with long sight, short sight, clear sight, dim sight, weak sight. All that is a faithful enough image of our understanding; but we are barely acquainted with false sight. There are hardly men who always take a cock for a horse, or a chamber-pot for a house. Why do we often come across minds otherwise just enough, which are absolutely false on important things? Why does this same Siamese who will never let himself be cheated when there is question of counting him three rupees, firmly believe in the metamorphoses of Sammonocodom? By what strange singularity do sensible men resemble Don Quixote who thought he saw giants where other men saw only windmills? Still, Don Quixote was more excusable than the Siamese who believes that Sammonocodom came several times on earth, and than the Turk who is persuaded that Mahomet put half the moon in his sleeve; for Don Quixote, struck with the idea that he must fight giants, can figure to himself that a giant must have a body as big as a mill; but from what supposition can a sensible man set off to persuade himself that the half of the moon has gone into a sleeve, and that a Sammonocodom has come down from heaven to play at shuttlecock, cut down a forest, and perform feats of legerdemain?

85

The greatest geniuses can have false judgment about a principle they have accepted without examination. Newton had very false judgment when he commentated the Apocalypse.

All that certain tyrants of the souls desire is that the men they teach shall have false judgment. A fakir rears a child who gives much promise; he spends five or six years in driving into his head that the god Fo appeared to men as a white elephant, and he persuades the child that he will be whipped after his death for five hundred thousand years if he does not believe these metamorphoses. He adds that at the end of the world the enemy of the god Fo will come to fight against this divinity.

The child studies and becomes a prodigy; he argues on his master's lessons; he finds that Fo has only been able to change himself into a white elephant, because that is the most beautiful of animals. "The kings of Siam and Pegu," he says, "have made war for a white elephant; certainly if Fo had not been hidden in that elephant, these kings would not have been so senseless as to fight simply for the possession of an animal.

"The enemy of Fo will come to defy him at the end of the world; certainly this enemy will be a rhinoceros, for the rhinoceros fights the elephant." It is thus that in mature age the fakir's learned pupil reasons, and he becomes one of the lights of India; the more subtle his mind, the more false is it, and he forms later minds as false as his.

One shows all these fanatics a little geometry, and they learn it easily enough; but strange to relate, their minds are not straightened for that; they perceive the truths of geometry; but they do not learn to weigh probabilities; they have got into a habit; they will reason crookedly all their lives, and I am sorry for them.

There are unfortunately many ways of having a false mind:

1. By not examining if the principle is true, even when one deduces accurate consequences therefrom; and this way is common.

2. By drawing false consequences from a principle recognized as true. For example, a servant is asked if his master is in his room, by persons he suspects of wanting his life: if he were foolish enough to tell them the truth on the pretext that one must not lie, it is clear he would be drawing an absurd consequence from a very true principle.

A judge who would condemn a man who has killed his assassin, because homicide is forbidden, would be as iniquitous as he was poor reasoner.

Similar cases are subdivided in a thousand different gradations. The good mind, the just mind, is that which distinguishes them; whence comes that one has seen so many iniquitous judgments, not because the judges' hearts were bad, but because they were not sufficiently enlightened.

FATHERLAND

A young journeyman pastrycook who had been to college, and who still knew a few of Cicero's phrases, boasted one day of loving his fatherland. "What do you mean by your fatherland?" a neighbour asked him. "Is it your oven? is it the village where you were born and which you have never seen since? is it the street where dwelled your father and mother who have been ruined and have reduced you to baking little pies for a living? is it the town-hall where you will never be police superintendent's clerk? is it the church of Our Lady where you have not been able to become a choir-boy, while an absurd man is archbishop and duke with an income of twenty thousand golden louis?"

The journeyman pastrycook did not know what to answer. A thinker who was listening to this conversation, concluded that in a fatherland of some extent there were often many thousand men who had no fatherland.

You, pleasure loving Parisian, who have never made any great journey save that to Dieppe to eat fresh fish; who know nothing but your varnished town house, your pretty country house, and your box at that Opera where the rest of Europe persists in feeling bored; who speak your own language agreeably enough because you know no other, you love all that, and you love further the girls you keep, the champagne which comes to you from Rheims, the dividends which the Hôtel-de-Ville pays you every six months, and you say you love your fatherland!

In all conscience, does a financier cordially love his fatherland?

The officer and the soldier who will pillage their winter quarters, if one lets them, have they a very warm love for the peasants they ruin?

Where was the fatherland of the scarred Duc de Guise, was it in Nancy, Paris, Madrid, Rome?

What fatherland have you, Cardinals de La Balue, Duprat, Lorraine, Mazarin?

Where was the fatherland of Attila and of a hundred heroes of this type?

I would like someone to tell me which was Abraham's fatherland.

87

The first man to write that the fatherland is wherever one feels comfortable was, I believe, Euripides in his "Phaeton." But the first man who left his birthplace to seek his comfort elsewhere had said it before him.

Where then is the fatherland? Is it not a good field, whose owner, lodged in a well-kept house, can say: "This field that I till, this house that I have built, are mine; I live there protected by laws which no tyrant can infringe. When those who, like me, possess fields and houses, meet in their common interest, I have my voice in the assembly; I am a part of everything, a part of the community, a part of the dominion; there is my fatherland."?

Well now, is it better for your fatherland to be a monarchy or a republic? For four thousand years has this question been debated. Ask the rich for an answer, they all prefer aristocracy; question the people, they want democracy: only kings prefer royalty. How then is it that nearly the whole world is governed by monarchs? Ask the rats who proposed to hang a bell round the cat's neck. But in truth, the real reason is, as has been said, that men are very rarely worthy of governing themselves.

It is sad that often in order to be a good patriot one is the enemy of the rest of mankind. To be a good patriot is to wish that one's city may be enriched by trade, and be powerful by arms. It is clear that one country cannot gain without another loses, and that it cannot conquer without making misery. Such then is the human state that to wish for one's country's greatness is to wish harm to one's neighbours. He who should wish that his fatherland might never be greater, smaller, richer, poorer, would be the citizen of the world.

FINAL CAUSES

If a clock is not made to tell the hour, I will then admit that final causes are chimeras; and I shall consider it quite right for people to call me "*cause-finalier*," that is—an imbecile.

All the pieces of the machine of this world seem, however, made for each other. A few philosophers affect to mock at the final causes rejected by Epicurus and Lucretius. It is, it seems to me, at Epicurus and Lucretius rather that they should mock. They tell you that the eye is not made for seeing, but that man has availed himself of it for this purpose when he perceived that eyes could be so used. According to them, the mouth is not made for speaking, for eating, the stomach for digesting, the heart for receiving the blood from the veins and for dispatching it through the arteries, the feet for walking, the ears for hearing. These persons avow nevertheless that tailors make them coats to clothe them, and masons houses to lodge them, and they dare deny to nature, to the great Being, to the universal Intelligence, what they accord to the least of their workmen.

Of course one must not make an abuse of final causes; we have remarked that in vain Mr. Prieur, in "The Spectacle of Nature," maintains that the tides are given to the ocean so that vessels may enter port more easily, and to stop the water of the sea from putrefying. In vain would he say that legs are made to be booted, and the nose to wear spectacles.

In order that one may be certain of the true end for which a cause functions, it is essential that that effect shall exist at all times and in all places. There were not ships at all times and on all the seas; hence one cannot say that the ocean was made for the ships. One feels how ridiculous it would be to maintain that nature had worked from all time in order to adjust herself to the inventions of our arbitrary arts, which appeared so late; but it is quite evident that if noses were not made for spectacles, they were for smelling, and that there have been noses ever since there have been men. Similarly, hands not having been given on behalf of glove-makers, they are visibly destined for all the purposes which the metacarpal bones and the phalanges and the circular muscle of the wrist may procure for us.

Cicero, who doubted everything, did not, however, doubt final causes.

It seems especially difficult for the organs of generation not to be destined to perpetuate the species. This mechanism is very admirable, but the sensation which nature has joined to this mechanism is still more admirable. Epicurus had to avow that pleasure is divine; and that this pleasure is a final cause, by which are ceaselessly produced sentient beings who have not been able to give themselves sensation.

This Epicurus was a great man for his time; he saw what Descartes denied, what Gassendi affirmed, what Newton demonstrated, that there is no movement without space. He conceived the necessity of atoms to serve as constituent parts of invariable species. Those are exceedingly philosophical ideas. Nothing was especially more worthy of respect than the moral system of the true Epicureans; it consisted in the removal to a distance of public matters incompatible with wisdom, and in friendship, without which life is a burden. But as regards the rest of Epicurus' physics, they do not appear any more admissible than Descartes' channelled matter. It is, it seems to me, to stop one's eyes and understanding to maintain that there is no design in nature; and if there is design, there is an intelligent cause, there exists a God.

People present to us as objections the irregularities of the globe, the volcanoes, the plains of shifting sands, a few small mountains destroyed and others formed by earthquakes, etc. But from the fact that the naves of the wheels of your coach have caught fire, does it ensue that your coach was not made expressly to carry you from one place to another?

The chains of mountains which crown the two hemispheres, and more than six hundred rivers which flow right to the sea from the feet of these rocks; all the streams which come down from these same reservoirs, and which swell the rivers, after fertilizing the country; the thousands of fountains which start from the same source, and which water animal and vegetable kind; all these things seem no more the effect of a fortuitous cause and of a declension of atoms, than the retina which receives the rays of light, the crystalline lens which refracts them, the incus, the malleus, the stapes, the tympanic membrane of the ear, which receives the sounds, the paths of the blood in our veins, the systole and diastole of the heart, this pendulum of the machine which makes life.

FRAUD

Bambabef the fakir one day met one of the disciples of Confutzee, whom we call "Confucius," and this disciple was named "Ouang," and Bambabef maintained that the people had need of being deceived, and Ouang claimed that one should never deceive anybody; and here is the summary of their dispute:

BAMBABEF:

We must imitate the Supreme Being who does not show us things as they are; he makes us see the sun in a diameter of two or three feet, although this star is a million times bigger than the earth; he makes us see the moon and the stars set on the same blue background, whereas they are at different depths. He requires that a square tower shall appear round to us from a distance; he requires that fire shall seem hot to us, although it is neither hot nor cold; in fine, he surrounds us with errors suited to our nature.

OUANG:

What you name error is not one at all. The sun, placed as it is at millions of millions of lis[6] beyond our globe, is not the sun we see. We perceive in reality, and we can perceive, only the sun which is depicted in our retina at a determined angle. Our eyes have not been given us for

---

[6] A li is 124 paces.

appreciating sizes and distances, we need other aids and other operations to appreciate them.

Bambabef seemed very astonished at this proposition. Ouang, who was very patient, explained to him the theory of optics; and Bambabef, who had a quick understanding, surrendered to the demonstrations of Confutzee's disciple, then he resumed the argument.

BAMBABEF:

If God does not deceive us through the medium of our senses, as I believed, avow at least that doctors always deceive children for their good; they tell them that they are giving them sugar, and in fact they are giving them rhubarb. I, a fakir, may then deceive the people who are as ignorant as the children.

OUANG:

I have two sons; I have never deceived them; when they have been ill I have told them that there was a very bitter medicine, and that they must have the courage to take it; "it would harm you if it were sweet." I have never allowed their masters and teachers to make them afraid of spirits, ghosts, goblins, sorcerers; by this means I have made brave, wise young citizens of them.

BAMBABEF:

The people are not born so happily as your family.

OUANG:

All men are alike, or nearly so; they are born with the same dispositions. One must not corrupt men's natures.

BAMBABEF:

We teach them errors, I admit, but it is for their good. We make them believe that if they do not buy the nails we have blessed, if they do not expiate their sins by giving us money, they will become, in another life, post-horses, dogs or lizards. That intimidates them, and they become honest people.

OUANG:

Do you not see that you are perverting these poor people? There are among them many more than you think who reason, who laugh at your miracles, at your superstitions, who see quite well that they will not be changed into either lizards or post-horses. What is the consequence? They have enough sense to see that you are telling them impertinences, and they have not enough to raise themselves toward a religion that is pure and free from superstition, such as ours. Their passions make them believe that there is no religion at all, because the only one that is taught them is ridiculous; you become guilty of all the vices in which they are plunged.

BAMBABEF:

Not at all, for we do not teach them anything but good morality.

OUANG:

You would have yourselves stoned by the people if you taught them impure morality. Men are so made that they want to do evil, but that they do not want it preached to them. All that is necessary is that you should not mix a wise moral system with absurd fables, because you weaken through your impostures, which you can do without, the morality that you are forced to teach.

BAMBABEF:

What! you believe that one can teach the people truth without strengthening it with fables?

OUANG:

I firmly believe it. Our literati are of the same stuff as our tailors, our weavers and our husbandmen. They worship a God creator, rewarder, avenger. They do not sully their worship, either by absurd systems, or by extravagant ceremonies; and there are far less crimes among the literati than among the people. Why not deign to instruct our workmen as we instruct our literati?

BAMBABEF:

You would be very foolish; it is as if you wanted them to have the same courtesy, to be lawyers; that is neither possible nor proper. There must be white bread for the masters, and brown bread for the servants.

OUANG:

I admit that all men should not have the same learning; but there are some things necessary to all. It is necessary that all men should be just; and the surest way of inspiring all men with justice is to inspire in them religion without superstition.

BAMBABEF:

It is a fine project, but it is impracticable. Do you think that men will be satisfied to believe in a God who punishes and rewards? You have told me that it often happens that the most shrewd among the people revolt against my fables; they will revolt in the same way against truth. They will say: "Who will assure me that God punishes and rewards? where is the proof of it? what is your mission? what miracle have you performed that I may believe you?" They will laugh at you much more than at me.

OUANG:

That is where you are mistaken. You imagine that people will shake off the yoke of an honest, probable idea that is useful to everyone, of an idea in accordance with human reason, because people reject things that are dishonest, absurd, useless, dangerous, that make good sense shudder.

The people are very disposed to believe their magistrates: when their magistrates propose to them only a reasonable belief, they embrace it willingly. There is no need of prodigies for believing in a just God, who reads in man's heart; this idea is too natural, too necessary, to be combated. It is not necessary to say precisely how God will punish and reward; it suffices that people believe in His justice. I assure you I have seen entire towns which have had barely any other dogma, and that it is in those towns that I have seen most virtue.

BAMBABEF:

Take care; in those towns you will find philosophers who will deny you both your pains and your recompenses.

OUANG:

You will admit to me that these philosophers will deny your inventions still more strongly; so you gain nothing from that. Though there are philosophers who do not agree with my principles, there are honest people none the less; none the less do they cultivate the virtue of them, which must be embraced by love, and not by fear. But, further, I maintain that no philosopher would ever be assured that Providence did not reserve pains for the wicked and rewards for the good. For if they ask me who told me that God punishes? I shall ask them who has told them that God does not punish. In fine, I maintain that these philosophers, far from contradicting me, will help me. Would you like to be a philosopher?

BAMBABEF:

Willingly; but do not tell the fakirs.

OUANG:

Let us think above all that, if a philosopher wishes to be useful to human society, he must announce a God.

FREE-WILL

Ever since men have reasoned, the philosophers have obscured this matter: but the theologians have rendered it unintelligible by absurd subtleties about grace. Locke is perhaps the first man to find a thread in this labyrinth; for he is the first who, without having the arrogance of trusting in setting out from a general principle, examined human nature by analysis. For three thousand years people have disputed whether or no the will is free. In the "Essay on the Human Understanding," chapter on "Power," Locke shows first of all that the question is absurd, and that liberty can no more belong to the will than can colour and movement.

What is the meaning of this phrase "to be free"? it means "to be able," or assuredly it has no sense. For the will "to be able" is as ridiculous at bottom as to say that the will is yellow or blue, round or square. To will is to wish, and to be free is to be able. Let us note step by step the chain of what passes in us, without obfuscating our minds by any terms of the schools or any antecedent principle.

It is proposed to you that you mount a horse, you must absolutely make a choice, for it is quite clear that you either will go or that you will not go. There is no middle way. It is therefore of absolute necessity that you wish yes or no. Up to there it is demonstrated that the will is not free. You wish to mount the horse; why? The reason, an ignoramus will say, is because I wish it. This answer is idiotic, nothing happens or can happen without a reason, a cause; there is one therefore for your wish. What is it? the agreeable idea of going on horseback which presents itself in your brain, the dominant idea, the determinant idea. But, you will say, can I not resist an idea which dominates me? No, for what would be the cause of your resistance? None. By your will you can obey only an idea which will dominate you more.

Now you receive all your ideas; therefore you receive your wish, you wish therefore necessarily. The word "liberty" does not therefore belong in any way to your will.

You ask me how thought and wish are formed in us. I answer you that I have not the remotest idea. I do not know how ideas are made any more than how the world was made. All that is given to us is to grope for what passes in our incomprehensible machine.

The will, therefore, is not a faculty that one can call free. A free will is an expression absolutely void of sense, and what the scholastics have called will of indifference, that is to say willing without cause, is a chimera unworthy of being combated.

Where will be liberty then? in the power to do what one wills. I wish to leave my study, the door is open, I am free to leave it.

But, say you, if the door is closed, and I wish to stay at home, I stay there freely. Let us be explicit. You exercise then the power that you have of staying; you have this power, but you have not that of going out.

The liberty about which so many volumes have been written is, therefore, reduced to its accurate terms, only the power of acting.

In what sense then must one utter the phrase—"Man is free"? in the same sense that one utters the words, health, strength, happiness. Man is not always strong, always healthy, always happy.

A great passion, a great obstacle, deprive him of his liberty, his power of action.

The word "liberty," "free-will," is therefore an abstract word, a general word, like beauty, goodness, justice. These terms do not state that all men are always beautiful, good and just; similarly, they are not always free.

Let us go further: this liberty being only the power of acting, what is this power? It is the effect of the constitution and present state of our organs. Leibnitz wishes to resolve a geometrical problem, he has an apoplectic fit, he certainly has not liberty to resolve his problem. Is a vigorous young man, madly in love, who holds his willing mistress in his arms, free to tame his passion? undoubtedly not. He has the power of enjoying, and has not the power of refraining. Locke was therefore very right to call liberty "power." When is it that this young man can refrain despite the violence of his passion? when a stronger idea determines in a contrary sense the activity of his body and his soul.

But what! the other animals will have the same liberty, then, the same power? Why not? They have senses, memory, feeling, perceptions, as we have. They act with spontaneity as we act. They must have also, as we have, the power of acting by virtue of their perceptions, by virtue of the play of their organs.

Someone cries: "If it be so, everything is only machine, everything in the universe is subjected to eternal laws." Well! would you have everything at the pleasure of a million blind caprices? Either everything is the sequence of the necessity of the nature of things, or everything is the effect of the eternal order of an absolute master; in both cases we are only wheels in the machine of the world.

It is a vain witticism, a commonplace to say that without the pretended liberty of the will, all pains and rewards are useless. Reason, and you will come to a quite contrary conclusion.

If a brigand is executed, his accomplice who sees him expire has the liberty of not being frightened at the punishment; if his will is determined by itself, he will go from the foot of the scaffold to assassinate on the broad highway; if his organs, stricken with horror, make him experience an unconquerable terror, he will stop robbing. His companion's punishment becomes useful to him and an insurance for society only so long as his will is not free.

Liberty then is only and can be only the power to do what one will. That is what philosophy teaches us. But if one considers liberty in the theological sense, it is a matter so sublime that profane eyes dare not raise themselves to it.[7]

FRENCH

The French language did not begin to have any form until towards the tenth century; it was born from the ruins of Latin and Celtic, mixed with a few Germanic words. This language was first of all the *romanum rusticum*, rustic Roman, and the Germanic language was the court language up to the time of Charles the Bald; Germanic remained the sole language of Germany after the great epoch of the partition of 843. Rustic Roman, the Romance language, prevailed in Western France; the people of the country of Vaud, of the Valais, of the Engadine valley, and of a few other cantons, still retain to-day manifest vestiges of this idiom.

At the end of the tenth century French was formed; people wrote in French at the beginning of the eleventh; but this French still retained more of Rustic Roman than the French of to-day. The romance of Philomena, written in the tenth century in rustic Roman, is not in a tongue very different from that of the Norman laws. One still remarks Celtic, Latin and German derivations. The words signifying the parts of the human body, or things of daily use, and which have nothing in common with Latin or German, are in old Gaulish or Celtic, such as *tête*,

---

[7] See "Liberty."

jambe, sabre, pointe, aller, parler, écouter, regarder, aboyer, crier, coutume, ensemble, and many others of this kind. Most of the terms of war were Frank or German: *Marche, halte, maréchal, bivouac, reitre, lansquenet.* All the rest is Latin; and all the Latin words were abridged, according to the custom and genius of the nations of the north; thus from *palatium,* palais; from *lupus,* loup; from *Auguste,* août; from *Junius,* juin; from *unctus,* oint; from *purpura,* pourpre; from *pretium,* prix, etc. Hardly were there left any vestiges of the Greek tongue, which had been so long spoken at Marseilles.

In the twelfth century there began to be introduced into the language some of the terms of Aristotle's philosophy; and towards the sixteenth century one expressed by Greek terms all the parts of the human body, their diseases, their remedies; whence the words *cardiaque, céphalique, podagre, apoplectique, asthmatique, iliaque, empyème,* and so many others. Although the language then enriched itself from the Greek, and although since Charles VIII. it had drawn much aid from Italian already perfected, the French language had not yet taken regular consistence. François Ier abolished the ancient custom of pleading, judging, contracting in Latin; custom which bore witness to the barbarism of a language which one did not dare use in public documents, a pernicious custom for citizens whose lot was regulated in a language they did not understand. One was obliged then to cultivate French; but the language was neither noble nor regular. The syntax was left to caprice. The genius for conversation being turned to pleasantries, the language became very fertile in burlesque and naïve expressions, and very sterile in noble and harmonious terms: from this it comes that in rhyming dictionaries one finds twenty terms suitable for comic poetry, for one for more exalted use; and it is, further, a reason why Marot never succeeded in a serious style, and why Amyot could render Plutarch's elegance only with naïveté.

French acquired vigour beneath the pen of Montaigne; but it still had neither nobility nor harmony. Ronsard spoiled the language by bringing into French poetry the Greek compounds which the doctors and philosophers used. Malherbe repaired Ronsard's mischief somewhat. The language became more noble and more harmonious with the establishment of the Académie Française, and acquired finally, in the reign of Louis XIV., the perfection whereby it might be carried into all forms of composition.

The genius of this language is order and clarity; for each language has its genius, and this genius consists in the facility which the language gives for expressing oneself more or less happily, for using or rejecting the familiar twists of other languages. French having no declensions, and being always subject to the article, cannot adopt Greek and Latin inversions; it obliges words to arrange themselves in the natural order of ideas. Only in one way can one say *"Plancus a pris soin des affaires de César."* That is the only arrangement one can give to these words. Express this phrase in Latin—*Res Cæsaris Plancus diligenter curavit*: one can arrange these words in a hundred and twenty ways, without injuring the sense and without troubling the language. The auxiliary verbs which eke out and enervate the phrases in modern languages, still render the French tongue little suited to the concise lapidary style. The auxiliary verbs, its pronouns, its articles, its lack of declinable participles, and finally its uniform gait, are injurious to the great enthusiasm of poetry, in which it has less resources than Italian and English; but this constraint and this bondage render it more suitable for tragedy and comedy than any language in Europe. The natural order in which one is obliged to express one's thoughts and construct one's phrases, diffuses in this language a sweetness and easiness that is pleasing to all peoples; and the genius of the nation mingling with the genius of the language has produced more agreeably written books than can be seen among any other people.

The pleasure and liberty of society having been long known only in France, the language has received therefrom a delicacy of expression and a finesse full of simplicity barely to be found elsewhere. This finesse has sometimes been exaggerated, but people of taste have always known how to reduce it within just limits.

Many persons have thought that the French language has become impoverished since the time of Amyot and Montaigne: one does indeed find in many authors expressions which are no longer admissible; but they are for the most part familiar expressions for which equivalents have been substituted. The language has been enriched with a quantity of noble and energetic expressions; and without speaking here of the eloquence of things, it has acquired the eloquence of words. It is in the reign of Louis XIV., as has been said, that this eloquence had its greatest splendour, and that the language was fixed. Whatever changes time and caprice prepare for it, the good authors of the seventeenth and eighteenth centuries will always serve as models.

FRIENDSHIP

Friendship is the marriage of the soul; and this marriage is subject to divorce. It is a tacit contract between two sensitive and virtuous persons. I say "sensitive," because a monk, a recluse can be not wicked and live without knowing what friendship is. I say "virtuous," because the wicked have only accomplices; voluptuaries have companions in debauch, self-seekers have partners, politicians get partisans; the generality of idle men have attachments; princes have courtiers; virtuous men alone have friends. Cethegus was the accomplice of Catilina, and Maecenas the courtier of Octavius; but Cicero was the friend of Atticus.

GOD

During the reign of Arcadius, Logomacos, lecturer in theology of Constantinople, went to Scythia and halted at the foot of the Caucasus, in the fertile plains of Zephirim, on the frontier of Colchis. That good old man Dondindac was in his great lower hall, between his sheepfold and his vast barn; he was kneeling with his wife, his five sons and five daughters, his kindred and his servants, and after a light meal they were all singing God's praises. "What do you there, idolator?" said Logomacos to him.

"I am not an idolator," answered Dondindac.

"You must be an idolator," said Logomacos, "seeing that you are not Greek. Tell me, what was that you were singing in your barbarous Scythian jargon?"

"All tongues are equal in the ears of God," answered the Scythian. "We were singing His praises."

"That's very extraordinary," returned the theologian. "A Scythian family who pray God without having been taught by us!" He soon engaged Dondindac the Scythian in conversation, for he knew a little Scythian, and the other a little Greek. The following conversation was found in a manuscript preserved in the library of Constantinople.

LOGOMACOS:

Let us see if you know your catechism. Why do you pray God?

DONDINDAC:

Because it is right to worship the Supreme Being from whom we hold everything.

LOGOMACOS:

Not bad for a barbarian! And what do you ask of Him?

DONDINDAC:

I thank Him for the benefits I enjoy, and even for the ills with which He tries me; but I take good care not to ask Him for anything; He knows better than us what we need, and besides, I am afraid to ask Him for good weather when my neighbour is asking for rain.

LOGOMACOS:

99

Ah! I thought he was going to say something silly. Let us start again farther back. Barbarian, who has told you there is a God?

DONDINDAC:

The whole of nature.

LOGOMACOS:

That does not suffice. What idea have you of God?

DONDINDAC:

The idea of my creator, of my master, who will reward me if I do good, and who will punish me if I do ill.

LOGOMACOS:

Trash, nonsense all that! Let us come to essentials. Is God infinite *secundum quid*, or in essence?

DONDINDAC:

I don't understand you.

LOGOMACOS:

Brutish fool! Is God in one place, beyond all places, or in all places?

DONDINDAC:

I have no idea ... just as you please.

LOGOMACOS:

Dolt! Is it possible for what has been not to have been, and can a stick not have two ends? Does He see the future as future or as present? how does He draw the being out of non-existence, and how annihilate the being?

DONDINDAC:

I have never examined these things.

LOGOMACOS:

What a blockhead! Come, one must humble oneself, see things in proportion. Tell me, my friend, do you think that matter can be eternal?

DONDINDAC:

What does it matter to me whether it exists from all eternity or not? I do not exist from all eternity. God is always my master; He has given me the notion of justice, I must follow it; I do not want to be a philosopher, I want to be a man.

LOGOMACOS:

These blockheads are troublesome. Let us go step by step. What is God?

DONDINDAC:

My sovereign, my judge, my father.

LOGOMACOS:

That's not what I'm asking you. What is His nature?

DONDINDAC:

To be potent and good.

LOGOMACOS:

But, is He corporeal or spiritual?

DONDINDAC:

How should I know?

LOGOMACOS:

What! you don't know what a spirit is?

DONDINDAC:

Not in the least: of what use would it be to me? should I be more just? should I be a better husband, a better father, a better master, a better citizen?

LOGOMACOS:

It is absolutely essential you should learn what a spirit is. It is, it is, it is ... I will tell you another time.

DONDINDAC:

I'm very much afraid that you may tell me less what it is than what it is not. Allow me to put a question to you in my turn. I once saw one of your temples; why do you depict God with a long beard?

LOGOMACOS:

That's a very difficult question which needs preliminary instruction.

DONDINDAC:

Before receiving your instruction, I must tell you what happened to me one day. I had just built a closet at the end of my garden; I heard a mole arguing with a cockchafer. "That's a very fine building," said the mole. "It must have been a very powerful mole who did that piece of work."

"You're joking," said the cockchafer. "It was a cockchafer bubbling over with genius who is the architect of this building." From that time I resolved never to argue.

HELVETIA

Happy Helvetia! to what charter do you owe your liberty? to your courage, to your resolution, to your mountains.

"But I am your emperor."

"But I do not want you any longer."

"But your fathers were my father's slaves."

"It is for that very reason that their children do not wish to serve you."

"But I had the right belonging to my rank."

"And we have the right of nature."

Why is liberty so rare?

Because it is the chiefest good.

HISTORY

Definition

History is the recital of facts given as true, in contradistinction to the fable, which is the recital of facts given as false.

There is the history of opinions which is hardly anything but a collection of human errors.

The history of the arts can be the most useful of all when it joins to the knowledge of the invention and the progress of the arts the description of their mechanism.

Natural history, improperly called *history*, is an essential part of natural philosophy. The history of events has been divided into sacred history and profane history; sacred history is a series of divine and miraculous operations whereby it pleased God once on a time to lead the Jewish nation, and to-day to exercise our faith.

First Foundations of History

The first foundations of all history are the recitals of the fathers to the children, transmitted afterward from one generation to another; at their origin they are at the very most probable, when they do not shock common sense, and they lose one degree of probability in each generation. With time the fable grows and the truth grows less; from this it comes that all the origins of peoples are absurd. Thus the Egyptians had been governed by the gods for many centuries; then they had been governed by demi-gods; finally they had had kings for eleven thousand three hundred and forty years; and in that space of time the sun had changed four times from east to west.

The Phœnicians of Alexander's time claimed to have been established in their country for thirty thousand years; and these thirty thousand years were filled with as many prodigies as the Egyptian chronology. I avow that physically it is very possible that Phœnicia has existed not merely thirty thousand years, but thirty thousand milliards of centuries, and that it experienced like the rest of the world thirty million revolutions. But we have no knowledge of it.

One knows what a ridiculously marvellous state of affairs ruled in the ancient history of the Greeks.

The Romans, for all that they were serious, did not any the less envelop the history of their early centuries in fables. This nation, so recent compared with the Asiatic peoples, was five hundred years without historians. It is not surprising, therefore, that Romulus was the son of Mars, that a she-wolf was his foster mother, that he marched with a thousand men of his village of Rome against twenty-five thousand combatants of the village of the Sabines: that later he became a god; that Tarquin, the ancient, cut a stone with a razor, and that a vestal drew a ship to land with her girdle, etc.

The early annals of all our modern nations are no less fabulous; the prodigious and improbable things must sometimes be reported, but as proofs of human credulity: they enter the history of opinions and foolishnesses; but the field is too vast.

Of Records

In order to know with a little certainty something of ancient history, there is only one means, it is to see if any incontestable records remain. We have only three in writing: the first is the collection of astronomical observations made for nineteen hundred consecutive years at Babylon, sent by Alexander to Greece. This series of observations, which goes back to two thousand two hundred and thirty-four years before our era, proves invincibly that the Babylonians existed as a body of people several centuries before; for the arts are only the work of time, and men's natural laziness leaves them for some thousands of years without other knowledge and without other talents than those of feeding themselves, of defending themselves against the injuries of the air, and of slaughtering each other. Let us judge by the Germans and by the English in Cæsar's time, by the Tartars to-day, by the two-thirds of Africa, and by all the peoples we have found in America, excepting in some respects the kingdoms of Peru and of Mexico, and the republic of Tlascala. Let us remember that in the whole of this new world nobody knew how to read or write.

The second record is the central eclipse of the sun, calculated in China two thousand one hundred and fifty-five years before our era, and recognized true by our astronomers. Of the Chinese the same thing must be said as of the peoples of Babylon; they already comprised a vast civilized empire without a doubt. But what puts the Chinese above all the peoples of the earth is that neither their laws, nor their customs, nor the language spoken among them by their lettered mandarins has changed for about four thousand years. Nevertheless, this nation and the nation of India, the most ancient of all those that exist to-day, which possess the vastest and the most beautiful country, which invented almost all the arts before we had learned any of them, have always been omitted right to our days in all so-called universal histories. And when a Spaniard and a Frenchman took a census of the nations, neither one nor the other failed to call his country the first monarchy in the world, and his king the greatest king in the world, flattering himself that his king would give him a pension as soon as he had read his book.

The third record, very inferior to the two others, exists in the Arundel marbles: the chronicle of Athens is graved there two hundred and sixty-three years before our era; but it goes back only to Cecrops, thirteen hundred and nineteen years beyond the time when it was engraved. In the history of antiquity those are the sole incontestable epochs that we have.

Let us give serious attention to these marbles brought back from Greece by Lord Arundel. Their chronicle begins fifteen hundred and eighty-two years before our era. That is to-day (1771) an antiquity of 3,353 years, and you do not see there a single fact touching on the miraculous, on the prodigious. It is the same with the Olympiads; it is not there that one should say *Græcia mendax*, lying Greece. The Greeks knew very well how to distinguish between history and fable, between real facts and the tales of Herodotus: just as in their serious affairs their orators borrowed nothing from the speeches of the sophists or from the images of the poets.

The date of the taking of Troy is specified in these marbles; but no mention is made of Apollo's arrows, or of the sacrifice of Iphigenia, or of the ridiculous combats of the gods. The date of the inventions of Triptolemy and Ceres is found there; but Ceres is not called *goddess*. Mention is made of a poem on the abduction of Prosperine; it is not said that she is the daughter of Jupiter and a goddess, and that she is wife of the god of the infernal regions.

Hercules is initiated into the mysteries of Eleusis; but not a word on his twelve labours, nor on his passage into Africa in his cup, nor on his divinity, nor on the big fish by which he was swallowed, and which kept him in its belly three days and three nights, according to Lycophron.

Among us, on the contrary, a standard is brought from heaven by an angel to the monks of Saint-Denis; a pigeon brings a bottle of oil to a church in Rheims; two armies of snakes give themselves over to a pitched battle in Germany; an archbishop of Mayence is besieged and eaten by rats; and, to crown everything, great care has been taken to mark the year of these adventures.

All history is recent. It is not astonishing that we have no ancient profane history beyond about four thousand years. The revolutions of this globe, the long and universal ignorance of that art which transmits facts by writing are the cause of it. This art was common only among a very small number of civilized nations; and was in very few hands even. Nothing rarer among the French and the Germans than to know how to write; up to the fourteenth century of our era nearly all deeds were only attested by witnesses. It was, in France, only under Charles VII., in 1454, that one started to draft in writing some of the customs of France. The art of writing was still rarer among the Spanish, and from that it results that their history is so dry and so uncertain, up to the time of Ferdinand and Isabella. One sees by that to what extent the very small number of men who knew how to write could deceive, and how easy it was to make us believe the most enormous absurdities.

There are nations which have subjugated a part of the world without having the usage of characters. We know that Gengis-khan conquered a part of Asia at the beginning of the thirteenth century, but it is not through either him or the Tartars that we know it. Their history, written by the Chinese and translated by Father Gaubil, states that these Tartars had not at that time the art of writing.

This art cannot have been less unknown to the Scythian Oguskan, named Madies by the Persians and the Greeks, who conquered a part of Europe and Asia so long before the reign of Cyrus. It is almost certain that at that time of a hundred nations there were hardly two or three who used characters. It is possible that in an ancient world destroyed, men knew writing and the other arts; but in ours they are all very recent.

There remain records of another kind, which serve to establish merely the remote antiquity of certain peoples, and which precede all the known epochs, and all the books; these are the prodigies of architecture, like the pyramids and the palaces of Egypt, which have resisted time. Herodotus, who lived two thousand two hundred years ago, and who had seen them, was not able to learn from the Egyptian priests at what time they had been erected.

It is difficult to give to the most ancient of the pyramids less than four thousand years of antiquity; but one must consider that these efforts of the ostentation of the kings could only have been commenced long after the establishment of the towns. But to build towns in a land inundated every year, let us always remark that it was first necessary to raise the land of the towns on piles in this land of mud, and to render them inaccessible to the flood; it was essential, before taking this necessary course, and before being in a state to attempt these great works, for the people to have practised retreating during the rising of the Nile, amid the rocks which form two chains right and left of this river. It was necessary for these mustered peoples to have the instruments for tilling, those of architecture, a knowledge of surveying, with laws and a police. All this necessarily requires a prodigious space of time. We see by the long details which face every day the most necessary and the smallest of our undertakings, how difficult it is to do great things, and it needs not only indefatigable stubbornness, but several generations animated with this stubbornness.

However, whether it be Menes, Thaut or Cheops, or Rameses who erected one or two of these prodigious masses, we shall not be the more instructed of the history of ancient Egypt: the language of this people is lost. We therefore know nothing but that before the most ancient historians there was matter for making an ancient history.

IGNORANCE

I am ignorant of how I was formed, and of how I was born. For a quarter of my life I was absolutely ignorant of the reasons for all that I saw, heard and felt, and I was nothing but a parrot at whom other parrots chattered.

When I looked round me and within me, I conceived that something exists for all eternity; since there are beings who exist to-day, I concluded that there is a being who is necessary and necessarily eternal. Thus, the first step I took to emerge from my ignorance crossed the boundaries of all the centuries.

But when I tried to walk in this infinite quarry open before me, I could neither find a single path, nor discern plainly a single object; and from the leap I made to contemplate eternity, I fell back again into the abyss of my ignorance.

I saw what was called "matter," from the star Sirius and the stars of the Milky Way, as distant from Sirius as Sirius is from us, right to the last atom that can be perceived with the microscope, and I am ignorant as to what matter is.

The light which let me see all these beings is unknown to me; I can, with the help of a prism, dissect this light, and divide it into seven pencils of rays; but I cannot divide these pencils; I am ignorant of what they are composed. Light is of the nature of matter, since it has movement and makes an impression on objects; but it does not tend toward a centre like all bodies: on the contrary, it escapes invincibly from the centre, whereas all matter bears towards its centre. Light seems penetrable, and matter is impenetrable. Is this light matter? is it not matter? with what innumerable properties can it be endowed? I am ignorant thereof.

Is this substance which is so brilliant, so swift and so unknown, are these other substances which roll in the immensity of space, eternal as they seem infinite? I have no idea. Has a necessary being, of sovereign intelligence, created them out of nothing, or has he arranged them? did he produce this order in Time or before Time? What even is this Time of which I speak? I cannot define it. O God! Teach me, for I am enlightened neither by other men's darkness nor by my own.

What is sensation? How have I received it? what connection is there between the air which strikes my ear and the sensation of sound? between this body and the sensation of colour? I am profoundly ignorant thereof, and I shall always be ignorant thereof.

What is thought? where does it dwell? how is it formed? who gives me thought during my sleep? is it by virtue of my will that I think? But always during my sleep, and often while I am awake, I have ideas in spite of myself. These ideas, long forgotten, long relegated to the back shop of my brain, issue from it without my interfering, and present themselves to my memory, which makes vain efforts to recall them.

External objects have not the power to form ideas in me, for one does not give oneself what one has not; I am too sensible that it is not I who give them to me, for they are born without my orders. Who produces them in me? whence do they come? whither do they go? Fugitive phantoms, what invisible hand produces you and causes you to disappear?

Why, alone of all animals, has man the mania for dominating his fellow-men?

Why and how has it been possible that of a hundred thousand million men more than ninety-nine have been immolated to this mania?

How is reason so precious a gift that we would not lose it for anything in the world? and how has this reason served only to make us the most unhappy of all beings?

Whence comes it that loving truth passionately, we are always betrayed to the most gross impostures?

Why is life still loved by this crowd of Indians deceived and enslaved by the bonzes, crushed by a Tartar's descendants, overburdened with work, groaning in want, assailed by disease, exposed to every scourge?

Whence comes evil, and why does evil exist?

O atoms of a day! O my companions in infinite littleness, born like me to suffer everything and to be ignorant of everything, are there enough madmen among you to believe that they know all these things? No, there are not; no, at the bottom of your hearts you feel your nonentity as I render justice to mine. But you are arrogant enough to want people to embrace your vain systems; unable to be tyrants over our bodies, you claim to be tyrants over our souls.

THE IMPIOUS

Who are the impious? those who give a white beard, feet and hands to the Being of beings, to the great Demiourgos, to the eternal intelligence by which nature is governed. But they are only excusably impious, poor impious people against whom one must not grow wroth.

If even they paint the great incomprehensible Being born on a cloud which can bear nothing; if they are foolish enough to put God in a mist, in the rain, or on a mountain, and to surround him with little chubby, flushed faces accompanied by two wings; I laugh and I pardon them with all my heart.

The impious persons who attribute to the Being of beings preposterous predictions and injustices would anger me if this great Being had not given me a reason which quells my wrath. The silly fanatic repeats to me, after others, that it is not for us to judge what is reasonable and just in the great Being, that His reason is not like our reason, that His justice is not like our justice. Eh! how, you mad demoniac, do you want me to judge justice and reason otherwise than by the notions I have of them? do you want me to walk otherwise than with my feet, and to speak otherwise than with my mouth?

The impious man who supposes the great Being jealous, arrogant, malignant, vindictive, is more dangerous. I would not want to sleep under the same roof as this man.

But how would you treat the impious man who says to you: "See only through my eyes, do not think; I announce to you a tyrannical God who has made me to be your tyrant; I am his well-beloved: during all eternity he will torture millions of his creatures whom he detests in order to gladden me; I shall be your master in this world, and I shall laugh at your torments in the other."

Do you not feel an itching to thrash this cruel, impious fellow? If you are born gentle, will you not run with all your might to the west when this barbarian utters his atrocious reveries in the east?

JOAN OF ARC

It is meet that the reader should be acquainted with the true history of Joan of Arc surnamed "the Maid." The details of her adventure are very little known and may give readers pleasure; here they are.

109

Paul Jove says that the courage of the French was stimulated by this girl, and takes good care not to believe her inspired. Neither Robert, Gaguin, Paul Emile, Polydore Vergile, Genebrard, Philip of Bergamo, Papyre Masson, nor even Mariana, say that she was sent by God; and even though Mariana the Jesuit had said it, that would not deceive me.

Mézerai relates "that the prince of the celestial militia appeared to her." I am sorry for Mézerai, and I ask pardon of the prince of the celestial militia.

Most of our historians, who copy each other, suppose that the Maid uttered prophecies, and that her prophecies were accomplished. She is made to say that "she will drive the English out of the kingdom," and they were still there five years after her death. She is said to have written a long letter to the King of England, and assuredly she could neither read nor write; such an education was not given to an inn servant in the Barois; and the information laid against her states that she could not sign her name.

But, it is said, she found a rusted sword, the blade of which was engraved with five golden *fleurs-de-lis*; and this sword was hidden in the church of Sainte Catherine de Fierbois at Tours. There, certainly is a great miracle!

Poor Joan of Arc having been captured by the English, despite her prophecies and her miracles, maintained first of all in her cross-examination that St. Catherine and St. Marguerite had honoured her with many revelations. I am astonished that she never said anything of her talks with the prince of the celestial militia. These two saints apparently liked talking better than St. Michael. Her judges thought her a sorceress, she thought herself inspired.

One great proof that Charles VII.'s captains made use of the marvellous in order to encourage the soldiers, in the deplorable state to which France was reduced, is that Saintrailles had his shepherd, as the Comte de Dunois had his shepherdess. The shepherd made prophecies on one side, while the shepherdess made them on the other.

But unfortunately the Comte de Dunois' prophetess was captured at the siege of Compiègne by a bastard of Vendôme, and Saintrailles' prophet was captured by Talbot. The gallant Talbot was far from having the shepherd burned. This Talbot was one of those true Englishmen who scorn superstition, and who have not the fanaticism for punishing fanatics.

This, it seems to me, is what the historians should have observed, and what they have neglected.

The Maid was taken to Jean de Luxembourg, Comte de Ligny. She was shut up in the fortress of Beaulieu, then in that of Beaurevoir, and from there in that of Crotoy in Picardy.

First of all Pierre Cauchon, Bishop of Beauvais, who was of the King of England's party against his own legitimate king, claims the Maid as a sorceress arrested on the limits of his diocese. He wishes to judge her as a sorceress. He supported the right he claimed by a downright lie. Joan had been captured on the territory of the bishopric of Noyon: and neither the Bishop of Beauvais, nor the Bishop of Noyon assuredly had the right of condemning anybody, and still less of committing to death a subject of the Duke of Lorraine, and a warrior in the pay of the King of France.

There was at that time (who would believe it?) a vicar-general of the Inquisition in France, by name Brother Martin.[8] It was one of the most horrible effects of the total subversion of that unfortunate country. Brother Martin claimed the prisoner as smelling of heresy (*odorantem hæresim*). He called upon the Duke of Burgundy and the Comte de Ligny, "by the right of his office, and of the authority given to him by the Holy See, to deliver Joan to the Holy Inquisition."

The Sorbonne hastened to support Brother Martin, and wrote to the Duke of Burgundy and to Jean de Luxembourg—"You have used your noble power to apprehend this woman who calls herself the Maid, by means of whom the honour of God has been immeasurably offended, the faith exceedingly hurt, and the Church too greatly dishonoured; for by reason of her, idolatry, errors, bad doctrine, and other inestimable evils have ensued in this kingdom ... but what this woman has done would be of small account, if did not ensue what is meet for satisfying the offence perpetrated by her against our gentle Creator and His faith, and the Holy Church with her other innumerable misdeeds ... and it would be intolerable offence against the divine majesty if it happened that this woman were freed."[9]

Finally, the Maid was awarded to Jean Cauchon whom people called the unworthy bishop, the unworthy Frenchman, and the unworthy man. Jean de Luxembourg sold the Maid to Cauchon and the English for ten thousand livres, and the Duke of Bedford paid them. The Sorbonne, the bishop and Brother Martin, then presented a new petition to this Duke of Bedford, regent of France, "in honour of our Lord and Saviour Jesus Christ, for that the said Joan may be briefly put into the hands of the

---

[8] Beuchot says: There was at that time in France an Inquisitor-General, named Brother Jean or Jacques le Graverend. His vice-inquisitor or vicar, who took part in Joan's trial, was not called Brother Martin, but Brother Jean Magistri or the Master.

[9] This is a translation of the Latin of the Sorbonne, made long after.

Church." Joan was led to Rouen. The archbishopric was vacant at that time, and the chapter permitted the Bishop of Beauvais to *work* in the town. (*Besogner* is the term which was used.) He chose as assessors nine doctors of the Sorbonne with thirty-five other assistants, abbots or monks. The vicar of the Inquisition, Martin, presided with Cauchon; and as he was only a vicar, he had but second place.

Joan underwent fourteen examinations; they are singular. She said that she saw St. Catherine and St. Marguerite at Poitiers. Doctor Beaupère asks her how she recognized the saints. She answers that it was by their way of bowing. Beaupère asks her if they are great chatterboxes. "Go look on the register," she says. Beaupère asks her if, when she saw St. Michael, he was naked. She answers: "Do you think our Lord had nothing to clothe him with?"

The curious will carefully observe here that Joan had long been directed with other religious women of the populace by a rogue named Richard,[10] who performed miracles, and who taught these girls to perform them. One day he gave communion three times in succession to Joan, in honour of the Trinity. It was then the custom in matters of importance and in times of great peril. The knights had three masses said, and communicated three times when they went to seek fortune or to fight in a duel. It is what has been observed on the part of the Chevalier Bayard.

The workers of miracles, Joan's companions, who were submissive to Richard, were named Pierrone and Catherine. Pierrone affirmed that she had seen that God appeared to her in human form as a friend to a friend. God was "clad in a long white robe, etc."

Up to the present the ridiculous; here now is the horrible.

One of Joan's judges, doctor of theology and priest, by name Nicholas *the Bird-Catcher*, comes to confess her in prison. He abuses the sacrament to the point of hiding behind a piece of serge two priests who transcribed Joan of Arc's confession. Thus did the judges use sacrilege in order to be murderers. And an unfortunate idiot, who had had enough courage to render very great services to the king and the country, was condemned to be burned by forty-four French priests who immolated her for the English faction.

It is sufficiently well-known how someone had the cunning and meanness to put a man's suit beside her to tempt her to wear this suit again, and with what absurd barbarism this transgression was claimed

---

[10] Beuchot says that Berriat Saint-Prix, in his "Jeanne d'Arc," proves, page 341 *et seq.*, that the imputations against Brother Richard are groundless, and that he could exercise no influence at the trial.

as a pretext for condemning her to the flames, as if in a warrior girl it was a crime worthy of the fire, to put on breeches instead of a skirt. All this wrings the heart, and makes common sense shudder. One cannot conceive how we dare, after the countless horrors of which we have been guilty, call any nation by the name of barbarian.

Most of our historians, lovers of the so-called embellishments of history rather than of truth, say that Joan went fearlessly to the torture; but as the chronicles of the times bear witness, and as the historian Villaret admits, she received her sentence with cries and tears; a weakness pardonable in her sex, and perhaps in ours, and very compatible with the courage which this girl had displayed amid the dangers of war; for one can be fearless in battle, and sensitive on the scaffold.

I must add that many persons have believed without any examination that the Maid of Orleans was not burned at Rouen at all, although we have the official report of her execution. They have been deceived by the account we still have of an adventuress who took the name of the "Maid," deceived Joan of Arc's brothers, and under cover of this imposture, married in Lorraine a nobleman of the house of Armoise. There were two other rogues who also passed themselves off as the "Maid of Orleans." All three claimed that Joan was not burned at all, and that another woman had been substituted for her. Such stories can be admitted only by those who want to be deceived.

KISSING

I ask pardon of the boys and the girls; but maybe they will not find here what they will seek. This article is only for scholars and serious persons for whom it is barely suitable.

There is but too much question of kissing in the comedies of Molière's time. Champagne, in the comedy of "La Mère Coquette" by Quinault, asks kisses of Laurette; she says to him—"You are not content, then; really it is shameful; I have kissed you twice." Champagne answers her—"What! you keep account of your kisses?" (Act I. Sc. 1.).

The valets always used to ask kisses of the soubrettes; people kissed each other on the stage. Usually it was very dull and very intolerable, particularly in the case of ugly actors, who were nauseating.

If the reader wants kisses, let him look for them in the "Pastor Fido"; there is one entire chorus where nothing but kisses is mentioned; and the piece is founded solely on a kiss that Mirtillo gave one day to Amarilli, in a game of blind man's buff, *un bacio molto saporito.*

Everyone knows the chapter on kisses, in which Jean de la Casa, Archbishop of Benevento, says that people can kiss each other from head to foot. He pities the people with big noses who can only approach each other with difficulty; and he counsels ladies with long noses to have flat-nosed lovers.

The kiss was a very ordinary form of salutation throughout ancient times. Plutarch recalls that the conspirators, before killing Cæsar, kissed his face, hand and breast. Tacitus says that when Agricola, his father-in-law, returned from Rome, Domitian received him with a cold kiss, said nothing to him, and left him confounded in the crowd. The inferior who could not succeed in greeting his superior by kissing him, put his mouth to his own hand, and sent him a kiss that the other returned in the same way if he so wished.

This sign was used even for worshipping the gods. Job, in his parable (Chap. xxxi.), which is perhaps the oldest of known books, says that he has not worshipped the sun and the moon like the other Arabs, that he has not carried his hand to his mouth as he looked at the stars.

In our Occident nothing remains of this ancient custom but the puerile and genteel civility that is still taught to children in some small towns, of kissing their right hands when someone has given them some sweets.

It was a horrible thing to betray with a kiss; it was that that made Cæsar's assassination still more hateful. We know all about Judas' kisses; they have become proverbial.

Joab, one of David's captains, being very jealous of Amasa, another captain, says to him (2 Sam. xx. 9): "Art thou in health, my brother? And he took Amasa by the beard with the right hand to kiss him," and with his other hand drew his sword and "smote him therewith in the fifth rib, and shed out his bowels on the ground."

No other kiss is to be found in the other fairly frequent assassinations which were committed among the Jews, unless it be perhaps the kisses which Judith gave to the captain Holophernes, before cutting off his head while he was in bed asleep; but no mention is made of them, and the thing is merely probable.

In one of Shakespeare's tragedies called "Othello," this Othello, who is a black, gives two kisses to his wife before strangling her. That seems abominable to honourable people; but Shakespeare's partisans say it is beautifully natural, particularly in a black.

When Giovanni Galeas Sforza was assassinated in Milan Cathedral, on St. Stephen's day, the two Medici in the Reparata church; Admiral Coligny, the Prince of Orange, the Maréchal d'Ancre, the brothers Witt, and so many others; at least they were not kissed.

There was among the ancients I know not what of symbolic and sacred attached to the kiss, since one kissed the statues of the gods and their beards, when the sculptors had shown them with a beard. Initiates kissed each other at the mysteries of Ceres, as a sign of concord.

The early Christians, men and women, kissed each other on the mouth at their *agapæ*. This word signified "love-feast." They gave each other the holy kiss, the kiss of peace, the kiss of brother and sister, ἅγιον φίλημα. This custom lasted for more than four centuries, and was abolished at last on account of its consequences. It was these kisses of peace, these agapæ of love, these names of "brother" and "sister," that long drew to the little-known Christians, those imputations of debauchery with which the priests of Jupiter and the priestesses of Vesta charged them. You see in Petronius, and in other profane authors, that the libertines called themselves "brother" and "sister." It was thought that among the Christians the same names signified the same infamies. They were innocent accomplices in spreading these accusations over the Roman empire.

There were in the beginning seventeen different Christian societies, just as there were nine among the Jews, including the two kinds of Samaritans. The societies which flattered themselves at being the most orthodox accused the others of the most inconceivable obscenities. The term of "gnostic," which was at first so honourable, signifying "learned," "enlightened," "pure," became a term of horror and scorn, a reproach of heresy. Saint Epiphanius, in the third century, claimed that they used first to tickle each other, the men and the women; that then they gave each other very immodest kisses, and that they judged the degree of their faith by the voluptuousness of these kisses; that the husband said to his wife, in presenting a young initiate to her: "Have an agape with my brother," and that they had an agape.

We do not dare repeat here, in the chaste French tongue,[11] what Saint Epiphanius adds in Greek (Epiphanius, *contra hæres*, lib. I., vol. ii). We will say merely that perhaps this saint was somewhat imposed upon; that he allowed himself to be too carried away by zeal, and that all heretics are not hideous debauchees.

The sect of Pietists, wishing to imitate the early Christians, to-day give each other kisses of peace on leaving the assembly, calling each other "my brother, my sister"; it is what, twenty years ago, a very pretty and very human Pietist lady avowed to me. The ancient custom was to kiss on the mouth; the Pietists have carefully preserved it.

---

[11] Or the English—*Translator.*

There was no other manner of greeting dames in France, Germany, Italy, England; it was the right of cardinals to kiss queens on the mouth, and in Spain even. What is singular is that they had not the same prerogative in France, where ladies always had more liberty than anywhere else, but "every country has its ceremonies," and there is no usage so general that chance and custom have not provided exceptions. It would have been an incivility, an affront, for an honourable woman, when she received a lord's first visit, not to have kissed him, despite his moustaches. "It is a displeasing custom," says Montaigne (Book III., chap. v.), "and offensive to ladies, to have to lend their lips to whoever has three serving-men in his suite, disagreeable though he be." This custom was, nevertheless, the oldest in the world.

If it is disagreeable for a young and pretty mouth to stick itself out of courtesy to an old and ugly mouth, there was a great danger between fresh, red mouths of twenty to twenty-five years old; and that is what finally brought about the abolition of the ceremony of kissing in the mysteries and the agapæ. It is what caused women to be confined among the Orientals, so that they might kiss only their fathers and their brothers; custom long since introduced into Spain by the Arabs.

Behold the danger: there is one nerve of the fifth pair which goes from the mouth to the heart, and thence lower down, with such delicate industry has nature prepared everything! The little glands of the lips, their spongy tissue, their velvety paps, the fine skin, ticklish, gives them an exquisite and voluptuous sensation, which is not without analogy with a still more hidden and still more sensitive part. Modesty may suffer from a lengthily savoured kiss between two Pietists of eighteen.

It is to be remarked that the human species, the turtledoves and the pigeons alone are acquainted with kisses; thence came among the Latins the word *columbatìm*, which our language has not been able to render. There is nothing of which abuse has not been made. The kiss, designed by nature for the mouth, has often been prostituted to membranes which do not seem made for this usage. One knows of what the templars were accused.

We cannot honestly treat this interesting subject at greater length, although Montaigne says: "One should speak thereof shamelessly: brazenly do we utter 'killing,' 'wounding,' 'betraying,' but of that we dare not speak but with bated breath."

LANGUAGES

There is no complete language, no language which can express all our ideas and all our sensations; their shades are too numerous, too imperceptible. Nobody can make known the precise degree of sensation he experiences. One is obliged, for example, to designate by the general names of "love" and "hate" a thousand loves and a thousand hates all different from each other; it is the same with our pleasures and our pains. Thus all languages are, like us, imperfect.

They have all been made successively and by degrees according to our needs. It is the instinct common to all men which made the first grammars without perceiving it. The Lapps, the Negroes, as well as the Greeks, needed to express the past, the present and the future; and they did it: but as there has never been an assembly of logicians who formed a language, no language has been able to attain a perfectly regular plan.

All words, in all possible languages, are necessarily the images of sensations. Men have never been able to express anything but what they felt. Thus everything has become metaphor; everywhere the soul is enlightened, the heart burns, the mind wanders. Among all peoples the infinite has been the negation of the finite; immensity the negation of measure. It is evident that our five senses have produced all languages, as well as all our ideas. The least imperfect are like the laws: those in which there is the least that is arbitrary are the best. The most complete are necessarily those of the peoples who have cultivated the arts and society. Thus the Hebraic language should be one of the poorest languages, like the people who used to speak it. How should the Hebrews have had maritime terms, they who before Solomon had not a boat? how the terms of philosophy, they who were plunged in such profound ignorance up to the time when they started to learn something in their migration to Babylon? The language of the Phœnicians, from which the Hebrews drew their jargon, should be very superior, because it was the idiom of an industrious, commercial, rich people, distributed all over the earth.

The most ancient known language should be that of the nation most anciently gathered together as a body of people. It should be, further, that of the people which has been least subjugated, or which, having been subjugated, has civilized its conquerors. And in this respect, it is constant that Chinese and Arabic are the most ancient of all those that are spoken to-day.

There is no mother-tongue. All neighbouring nations have borrowed from each other: but one has given the name of "mother-tongue" to those from which some known idioms are derived. For example, Latin is the mother-tongue in respect of Italian, Spanish and French: but it was itself derived from Tuscan; and Tuscan was derived from Celtic and Greek.

The most beautiful of all languages must be that which is at once, the most complete, the most sonorous, the most varied in its twists and the most regular in its progress, that which has most compound words, that which by its prosody best expresses the soul's slow or impetuous movements, that which most resembles music.

Greek has all these advantages: it has not the roughness of Latin, in which so many words end in *um*, *ur*, *us*. It has all the pomp of Spanish, and all the sweetness of Italian. It has above all the living languages of the world the expression of music, by long and short syllables, and by the number and variety of its accents. Thus all disfigured as it is to-day in Greece, it can still be regarded as the most beautiful language in the universe.

The most beautiful language cannot be the most widely distributed, when the people which speaks it is oppressed, not numerous, without commerce with other nations, and when these other nations have cultivated their own languages. Thus Greek should be less diffused than Arabic, and even Turkish.

Of all European languages French should be the most general, because it is the most suited to conversation: it has taken its character from that of the people which speaks it.

The French have been, for nearly a hundred and fifty years, the people which has best known society, which the first discarded all embarrassment, and the first among whom women were free and even sovereign, when elsewhere they were only slaves. The always uniform syntax of this language, which admits no inversions, is a further facility barely possessed by other tongues; it is more current coin than others, even though it lacks weight. The prodigious quantity of agreeably frivolous books which this nation has produced is a further reason for the favour which its language has obtained among all nations.

Profound books will not give vogue to a language: they will be translated; people will learn Newton's philosophy; but they will not learn English in order to understand it.

What makes French still more common is the perfection to which the drama has been carried in this tongue. It is to "Cinna," "Phèdre," the "Misanthrope" that it owes its vogue, and not to the conquests of Louis XIV.

It is not so copious and so flexible as Italian, or so majestic as Spanish, or so energetic as English; and yet it has had more success than these three languages from the sole fact that it is more suited to intercourse, and that there are more agreeable books in it than elsewhere. It has succeeded like the cooks of France, because it has more flattered general taste.

The same spirit which has led the nations to imitate the French in their furniture, in the arrangement of rooms, in gardens, in dancing, in all that gives charm, has led them also to speak their language. The great art of good French writers is precisely that of the women of this nation, who dress better than the other women of Europe, and who, without being more beautiful, appear to be so by the art with which they adorn themselves, by the noble and simple charm they give themselves so naturally.

It is by dint of good breeding that this language has managed to make the traces of its former barbarism disappear. Everything would bear witness to this barbarism to whosoever should look closely. One would see that the number *vingt* comes from *viginti*, and that formerly this *g* and this *t* were pronounced with a roughness characteristic of all the northern nations; of the month of *Augustus* has been made the month of *août*. Not so long ago a German prince thinking that in France one never pronounced the term *Auguste* otherwise, called King Auguste of Poland King Août. All the letters which have been suppressed in pronunciation, but retained in writing, are our former barbarous clothes.

It was when manners were softened that the language also was softened: before François Ier summoned women to his court, it was as clownish as we were. It would have been as good to speak old Celtic as the French of the time of Charles VIII. and Louis XII.: German was not more harsh.

It has taken centuries to remove this rust. The imperfections which remain would still be intolerable, were it not for the continual care one takes to avoid them, as a skilful horseman avoids stones in the road. Good writers are careful to combat the faulty expressions which popular ignorance first brings into vogue, and which, adopted by bad authors, then pass into the gazettes and the pamphlets. *Roastbeef* signifies in English *roasted ox*, and our waiters talk to us nowadays of a "roastbeef of mutton." *Riding-coat* means *a coat for going on horseback*; of it people have made *redingote*, and the populace thinks it an ancient word of the language. It has been necessary to adopt this expression with the people because it signifies an article of common use.

In matters of arts and crafts and necessary things, the common people subjugated the court, if one dare say so; just as in matters of religion those who most despise the common run of people are obliged to speak and to appear to think like them.

To call things by the names which the common people has imposed on them is not to speak badly; but one recognizes a people naturally more ingenious than another by the proper names which it gives to each thing.

It is only through lack of imagination that a people adapts the same expression to a hundred different ideas. It is a ridiculous sterility not to have known how to express otherwise *an arm of the sea, a scale arm, an arm of a chair*; there is poverty of thought in saying equally the *head of a nail*, the *head of an army*.

Ignorance has introduced another custom into all modern languages. A thousand terms no longer signify what they should signify. *Idiot* meant *solitary*, to-day it means *foolish*; *epiphany* signified *appearance*, to-day it is the festival of three kings; *baptize* is to dip in water, we say *baptize with the name* of John or James.

To these defects in almost all languages are added barbarous irregularities. Venus is a charming name, *venereal* is abominable. Another result of the irregularity of these languages composed at hazard in uncouth times is the quantity of compound words of which the simple form does not exist any more. They are children who have lost their father. We have *architects* and no *tects*; there are things which are *ineffable* and none which are *effable*. One is *intrepid*, one is not *trepid*. There are *impudent* fellows, *insolent* fellows, but neither *pudent* fellows nor *solent* fellows. All languages more or less retain some of these defects; they are all irregular lands from which the hand of the adroit artist knows how to derive advantage.

Other defects which make a nation's character evident always slip into languages. In France there are fashions in expressions as in ways of doing the hair. A fashionable invalid or doctor will take it into his head to say that he has had a *soupçon* of fever to signify that he has had a slight attack; soon the whole nation has *soupçons* of colics, *soupçons* of hatred, love, ridicule. Preachers in the pulpit tell you that you must have at least a *soupçon* of God's love. After a few months this fashion gives place to another.

What does most harm to the nobility of the language is not this passing fashion with which people are soon disgusted, not the solecisms of fashionable people into which good authors do not fall, but the affectation of mediocre authors in speaking of serious things in a conversational style. Everything conspires to corrupt a language that is rather widely diffused; authors who spoil the style by affectation; those who write to foreign countries, and who almost always mingle foreign expressions with their natural tongue; merchants who introduce into conversation their business terms.

All languages being imperfect, it does not follow that one should change them. One must adhere absolutely to the manner in which the good authors have spoken them; and when one has a sufficient number of approved authors, a language is fixed. Thus one can no longer change anything in Italian, Spanish, English, French, without corrupting them; the reason is clear: it is that one would soon render unintelligible the books which provide the instruction and the pleasure of the nations.

LAWS

Sheep live very placidly in community, they are considered very easy-going, because we do not see the prodigious quantity of animals they devour. It is even to be believed that they eat them innocently and without knowing it, like us when we eat a Sassenage cheese. The republic of the sheep is a faithful representation of the golden age.

A chicken-run is visibly the most perfect monarchic state. There is no king comparable to a cock. If he marches proudly in the midst of his people, it is not out of vanity. If the enemy approaches, he does not give orders to his subjects to go to kill themselves for him by virtue of his certain knowledge and plenary power; he goes to battle himself, ranges his chickens behind him and fights to the death. If he is the victor, he himself sings the *Te Deum*. In civil life there is no one so gallant, so honest, so disinterested. He has all the virtues. Has he in his royal beak a grain of corn, a grub, he gives it to the first lady among his subjects who presents herself. Solomon in his harem did not come near a poultry-yard cock.

If it be true that the bees are governed by a queen to whom all her subjects make love, that is a still more perfect government.

The ants are considered to be an excellent democracy. Democracy is above all the other States, because there everyone is equal, and each individual works for the good of all.

The republic of the beavers is still superior to that of the ants, at least if we judge by their masonry work.

The monkeys resemble strolling players rather than a civilized people; and they do not appear to be gathered together under fixed, fundamental laws, like the preceding species.

We resemble the monkeys more than any other animal by the gift of imitation, the frivolity of our ideas, and by our inconstancy which has never allowed us to have uniform and durable laws.

When nature formed our species and gave us instincts, self-esteem for our preservation, benevolence for the preservation of others, love which is common to all the species, and the inexplicable gift of combining more ideas than all the animals together; when she had thus given us our portion, she said to us: "Do as you can."

There is no good code in any country. The reason for this is evident; the laws have been made according to the times, the place and the need, etc.

When the needs have changed, the laws which have remained, have become ridiculous. Thus the law which forbade the eating of pig and the drinking of wine was very reasonable in Arabia, where pig and wine are injurious; it is absurd at Constantinople.

The law which gives the whole fee to the eldest son is very good in times of anarchy and pillage. Then the eldest son is the captain of the castle which the brigands will attack sooner or later; the younger sons will be his chief officers, the husbandmen his soldiers. All that is to be feared is that the younger son may assassinate or poison the Salian lord his elder brother, in order to become in his turn the master of the hovel; but these cases are rare, because nature has so combined our instincts and our passions that we have more horror of assassinating our elder brother than we have of being envious of his position. But this law, suitable for the owners of dungeons in Chilperic's time is detestable when there is question of sharing stocks in a city.

To the shame of mankind, one knows that the laws of games are the only ones which everywhere are just, clear, inviolable and executed. Why is the Indian who gave us the rules of the game of chess willingly obeyed all over the world, and why are the popes' decretals, for example, to-day an object of horror and scorn? the reason is that the inventor of chess combined everything with precision for the satisfaction of the players, and that the popes, in their decretals, had nothing in view but their own interest. The Indian wished to exercise men's minds equally, and give them pleasure; the popes wished to besot men's minds. Also, the essence of the game of chess has remained the same for five thousand years, it is common to all the inhabitants of the earth; and the decretals are known only at Spoletto, Orvieto, Loretto, where the shallowest lawyer secretly hates and despises them.

But I delight in thinking that there is a natural law independent of all human conventions: the fruit of my work must belong to me; I must honour my father and my mother; I have no right over my fellow's life, and my fellow has none over mine, etc. But when I think that from Chedorlaomer to Mentzel,[12] colonel of hussars, everyone loyally kills and pillages his fellow with a licence in his pocket, I am very afflicted.

I am told that there are laws among thieves, and also laws of war. I ask what are these laws of war. I learn that they mean hanging a brave officer who has held fast in a bad post without cannon against a royal army; that they mean having a prisoner hanged, if the enemy has

---

[12] Chedorlaomer was king of the Elamites, and contemporary with Abraham. See Genesis ch. xiv.

Mentzel was a famous chief of Austrian partisans in the war of 1741. At the head of five thousand men, he made Munich capitulate on February 13th, 1742.

hanged one of yours; that they mean putting to the fire and the sword villages which have not brought their sustenance on the appointed day, according to the orders of the gracious sovereign of the district. "Good," say I, "that is the 'Spirit of the Laws.'"

It seems to me that most men have received from nature enough common sense to make laws, but that everyone is not just enough to make good laws.

LIBERTY

Either I am very much mistaken, or Locke the definer has very well defined liberty as "power." I am mistaken again, or Collins, celebrated London magistrate, is the only philosopher who has really sifted this idea, and Clark's answer to him was merely that of a theologian. But of all that has been written in France on liberty, the following little dialogue seems to me the most clear.

A: There is a battery of guns firing in your ears, have you the liberty to hear them or not to hear them?

B: Without doubt, I cannot stop myself hearing them.

A: Do you want this gun to carry off your head and the heads of your wife and daughter, who are walking with you?

B: What are you talking about? as long as I am of sound mind, I cannot want such a thing; it is impossible.

A: Good; you hear this gun necessarily, and you wish necessarily that neither you nor your family shall die from a cannon shot while you are out for a walk; you have not the power either of not hearing or of wishing to remain here?

B: Clearly.

A: You have consequently taken some thirty steps in order to be sheltered from the gun, you have had the power to walk these few steps with me?

B: Again very clearly.

A: And if you had been a paralytic, you could not have avoided being exposed to this battery, you would necessarily have heard and received a gun shot; and you would be dead necessarily?

B: Nothing is more true.

A: In what then does your liberty consist, unless it be in the power that your self has exercised in performing what your will required of absolute necessity?

B: You embarrass me; liberty then is nothing but the power of doing what I want to do?

A: Think about it, and see if liberty can be understood otherwise.

B: In that case my hunting dog is as free as I am; he has necessarily the will to run when he sees a hare, and the power of running if he has not a pain in his legs. I have then nothing above my dog; you reduce me to the state of the beasts.

A: What poor sophistry from the poor sophists who have taught you. Indeed you are in a bad way to be free like your dog! Do you not eat, sleep, propagate like him, even almost to the attitude? Do you want the sense of smell other than through your nose? Why do you want to have liberty otherwise than your dog has?

B: But I have a soul which reasons much, and my dog reasons hardly at all. He has almost only simple ideas, and I have a thousand metaphysical ideas.

A: Well, you are a thousand times freer than he is; that is, you have a thousand times more power of thinking than he has; but you do not think otherwise than he does.

B: What! I am not free to wish what I wish?

A: What do you mean by that?

B: I mean what everyone means. Doesn't one say every day, wishes are free?

A: A proverb is not a reason; explain yourself more clearly.

B: I mean that I am free to wish as I please.

A: With your permission, that has no sense; do you not see that it is ridiculous to say, I wish to wish? You wish necessarily, as a result of the ideas that have offered themselves to you. Do you wish to be married; yes or no?

B: But if I tell you that I want neither the one nor the other?

A: You will be answering like someone who says: "Some believe Cardinal Mazarin to be dead, others believe him to be alive, and as for me I believe neither the one nor the other."

B: Well, I want to be married.

A: Ah! that is an answer. Why do you want to be married?

B: Because I am in love with a beautiful, sweet, well-bred young girl, who is fairly rich and sings very well, whose parents are very honest people, and because I flatter myself I am loved by her, and very welcome to her family.

A: That is a reason. You see that you cannot wish without reason. I declare to you that you are free to marry; that is, that you have the power to sign the contract, have your nuptials, and sleep with your wife.

B: How now! I cannot wish without reason? And what will become of that other proverb: *Sit pro ratione voluntas*; my will is my reason, I wish because I wish?

A: That is absurd, my dear fellow; there would be in you an effect without a cause.

B: What! When I play at odds and evens, I have a reason for choosing evens rather than odds?

A: Yes, undoubtedly.

B: And what is that reason, if you please?

A: The reason is that the idea of even rather than the opposite idea presents itself to your mind. It would be comic that there were cases where you wished because there was a cause of wishing, and that there were cases where you wished without any cause. When you wish to be married, you evidently feel the dominating reason; you do not feel it when you are playing at odds and evens; and yet there certainly must be one.

B: But, I repeat, I am not free then?

A: Your will is not free, but your actions are. You are free to act, when you have the power to act.

B: But all the books I have read on the liberty of indifference....

A: What do you mean by the liberty of indifference?

B: I mean the liberty of spitting on the right or on the left, of sleeping on my right side or on my left, of taking a walk of four turns or five.

A: Really the liberty you would have there would be a comic liberty! God would have given you a fine gift! It would really be something to boast of! Of what use to you would be a power which was exercised only on such futile occasions? But the fact is that it is ridiculous to suppose the will to wish to spit on the right. Not only is this will to wish absurd, but it is certain that several trifling circumstances determine you in these acts that you call indifferent. You are no more free in these acts than in the others. But, I repeat, you are free at all times, in all places, as soon as you do what you wish to do.

B: I suspect you are right. I will think about it.[13]

LIBRARY

A big library has this in it of good, that it dismays those who look at it. Two hundred thousand volumes discourage a man tempted to print; but unfortunately he at once says to himself: "People do not read all those books, and they may read mine." He compares himself to a drop of water who complains of being lost in the ocean and ignored: a genius had pity on it; he caused it to be swallowed by an oyster; it became the most beautiful pearl in the Orient, and was the chief ornament in the throne of the Great Mogul. Those who are only compilers, imitators, commentators, splitters of phrases, usurious critics, in short, those on whom a genius has no pity, will always remain drops of water.

Our man works in his garret, therefore, in the hope of becoming a pearl.

It is true that in this immense collection of books there are about a hundred and ninety-nine thousand which will never be read, from cover to cover at least; but one may need to consult some of them once in a lifetime. It is a great advantage for whoever wishes to learn to find at his hand in the king's palace the volume and page he seeks, without being kept waiting a moment. It is one of the most noble institutions. No expense is more magnificent and more useful.

The public library of the King of France is the finest in the whole world, less on account of the number and rarity of the volumes than of the ease and courtesy with which the librarians lend them to all scholars. This library is incontestably the most precious monument there is in France.

---

[13] See "Free-Will."

This astounding multitude of books should not scare. We have already remarked that Paris contains about seven hundred thousand men, that one cannot live with them all, and that one chooses three or four friends. Thus must one no more complain of the multitude of books than of the multitude of citizens.

A man who wishes to learn a little about his existence, and who has no time to waste, is quite embarrassed. He wishes to read simultaneously Hobbes, Spinoza, Bayle who wrote against them, Leibnitz who disputed with Bayle, Clarke who disputed with Leibnitz, Malebranche who differed from them all, Locke who passed as having confounded Malebranche, Stillingfleet who thought he had vanquished Locke, Cudworth who thinks himself above them because he is understood by no one. One would die of old age before having thumbed the hundredth part of the metaphysical romances.

One is very content to have the most ancient books, as one inquires into the most ancient medals. It is that which makes the honour of a library. The oldest books in the world are the "Kings" of the Chinese, the "Shastabad" of the Brahmins, of which Mr. Holwell has brought to our knowledge admirable passages, what remains of the ancient Zarathustra, the fragments of Sanchoniathon which Eusebius has preserved for us and which bears the characteristics of the most remote antiquity. I do not speak of the "Pentateuch" which is above all one could say of it.

We still have the prayer of the real Orpheus, which the hierophant recited in the old Greek mysteries. "Walk in the path of justice, worship the sole master of the universe. He is one; He is sole by Himself. All beings owe Him their existence; He acts in them and by them. He sees everything, and never has been seen by mortal eyes."

St. Clement of Alexandria, the most learned of the fathers of the Church, or rather the only scholar in profane antiquity, gives him almost always the name of Orpheus of Thrace, of Orpheus the Theologian, to distinguish him from those who wrote later under his name.

We have no longer anything either of Museus or of Linus. A few passages from these predecessors of Homer would well be an adornment to a library.

Augustus had formed the library called the Palatine. The statue of Apollo presided over it. The emperor embellished it with busts of the best authors. One saw in Rome twenty-nine great public libraries. There are now more than four thousand important libraries in Europe. Choose which suits you, and try not to be bored.

LIMITS OF THE HUMAN MIND

Someone asked Newton one day why he walked when he wanted to, and how his arm and his hand moved at his will. He answered manfully that he had no idea. "But at least," his interlocutor said to him, "you who understand so well the gravitation of the planets will tell me why they turn in one direction rather than in another!" And he again confessed that he had no idea.

Those who taught that the ocean was salt for fear that it might become putrid, and that the tides were made to bring our ships into port (The Abbé Pluche in "The Spectacle of Nature"), were somewhat ashamed when the reply was made to them that the Mediterranean has ports and no ebb. Musschenbroeck himself fell into this inadvertence.

Has anyone ever been able to say precisely how a log is changed on the hearth into burning carbon, and by what mechanism lime is kindled by fresh water?

Is the first principle of the movement of the heart in animals properly understood? does one know clearly how generation is accomplished? has one guessed what gives us sensations, ideas, memory? We do not understand the essence of matter any more than the children who touch its surface.

Who will teach us by what mechanism this grain of wheat that we throw into the ground rises again to produce a pipe laden with an ear of corn, and how the same soil produces an apple at the top of this tree, and a chestnut on its neighbour? Many teachers have said—"What do I not know?" Montaigne used to say—"What do I know?"

Ruthlessly trenchant fellow, wordy pedagogue, meddlesome theorist, you seek the limits of your mind. They are at the end of your nose.

LOCAL CRIMES

Traverse the whole earth, you will find that theft, murder, adultery, calumny are regarded as crimes which society condemns and curbs; but should what is approved in England, and condemned in Italy, be punished in Italy as an outrage against the whole of humanity? That is what I call a local crime. Does not that which is criminal only in the enclosure of some mountains, or between two rivers, demand of judges more indulgence than those outrages which are held in horror in all countries? Should not the judge say to himself: "I should not dare punish at Ragusa what I punish at Loretto"? Should not this reflection soften in his heart the hardness that it is only too easy to contract during the long exercise of his office?

You know the *kermesses* in Flanders; in the last century they were carried to a point of indecency which might revolt eyes unaccustomed to these spectacles. This is how Christmas was celebrated in some towns. First there appeared a young man half naked, with wings on his back; he recited the *Ave Maria* to a young girl who answered him *fiat*, and the angel kissed her on the mouth: then a child enclosed in a great cardboard cock cried, imitating the cock's cry: *Puer natus est nobis.* A big ox bellowed *ubi*, which it pronounced *oubi*; a sheep bleated *Bethlehem*. An ass cried *hihanus*, to signify *eamus*; a long procession, preceded by four fools with baubles and rattles, closed the performance. There remain to-day traces of these popular devotions, which among more educated peoples would be taken for profanations. A bad-tempered Swiss, more drunk maybe than those who played the rôles of ox and ass, came to words with them in Louvain; blows were given; the people wanted to hang the Swiss, who escaped with difficulty.

The same man had a violent quarrel at the Hague in Holland for having stoutly taken Barneveldt's part against an extravagant Gomarist. He was put into prison in Amsterdam for having said that priests are the scourge of humanity and the source of all our misfortunes. "What!" he said. "If one believes that good works make for salvation, one finds oneself in a dungeon; if one laughs at a cock and an ass, one risks being hanged." This adventure, burlesque though it is, makes it quite clear that one can be reprehensible on one or two points in our hemisphere, and be absolutely innocent in the rest of the world.

LOVE

There are so many sorts of love that one does not know to whom to address oneself for a definition of it. The name of "love" is given boldly to a caprice lasting a few days, a sentiment without esteem, gallants' affectations, a frigid habit, a romantic fantasy, relish followed by prompt disrelish: people give this name to a thousand chimeras.

If philosophers want to probe to the bottom this barely philosophical matter, let them meditate on the banquet of Plato, in which Socrates, honourable lover of Alcibiades and Agathon, converses with them on the metaphysics of love.

Lucretius speaks of it more as a natural philosopher: Virgil follows in the steps of Lucretius; *amor omnibus idem.*

129

It is the stuff of nature broidered by nature. Do you want an idea of love? look at the sparrows in your garden; look at your pigeons; look at the bull which is brought to the heifer; look at this proud horse which two of your grooms lead to the quiet mare awaiting him; she draws aside her tail to welcome him; see how her eyes sparkle; hark to the neighing; watch the prancing, the curvetting, the ears pricked, the mouth opening with little convulsions, the swelling nostrils, the flaring breath, the manes rising and floating, the impetuous movement with which he hurls himself on the object which nature has destined for him; but be not jealous of him, and think of the advantages of the human species; in love they compensate for all those that nature has given to the animals—strength, beauty, nimbleness, speed.

There are animals, even, who have no enjoyment in possession. Scale fish are deprived of this delight: the female throws millions of eggs on the mud; the male coming across them passes over them, and fertilizes them with his seed, without troubling about the female to whom they belong.

Most animals that pair, taste pleasure only by a single sense, and as soon as the appetite is satisfied, everything is extinguished. No animal, apart from you, knows what kissing is; the whole of your body is sensitive; your lips especially enjoy a voluptuousness that nothing can tire; and this pleasure belongs to no species but yours: you can give yourself up to love at any time, and the animals have but a fixed time. If you reflect on these superiorities, you will say with the Count of Rochester—"In a country of atheists love would cause the Deity to be worshipped."

As men have received the gift of perfecting all that nature accords them, they have perfected love. Cleanliness, the care of oneself, by rendering the skin more delicate, increase the pleasure of contact; and attention to one's health renders the organs of voluptuousness more sensitive. All the other sentiments that enter into that of love, just like metals which amalgamate with gold: friendship, regard, come to help; the faculties of mind and body are still further chains.

Self-love above all tightens all these bonds. One applauds oneself for one's choice, and a crowd of illusions form the decoration of the building of which nature has laid the foundations.

That is what you have above the animals. But if you taste so many pleasures unknown to them, how many sorrows too of which the beasts have no idea! What is frightful for you is that over three-fourths of the earth nature has poisoned the pleasures of love and the sources of life with an appalling disease to which man alone is subject, and which infects in him the organs of generation alone.

It is in no wise with this plague as with so many other maladies that are the result of our excesses. It was not debauch that introduced it into the world. Phryne, Lais, Flora, Messalina and those like them, were not attacked by it; it was born in some islands where men lived in innocence, and thence spread itself over the ancient world.

If ever one could accuse nature of despising her work, of contradicting her plans, of acting against her designs, it is in this detestable scourge which has soiled the earth with horror and filth. Is that the best of all possible worlds? What! if Cæsar, Antony, Octavius never had this disease, was it not possible for it not to cause the death of François I.? "No," people say, "things were ordered thus for the best." I want to believe it; but it is sad for those to whom Rabelais dedicated his book.

Erotic philosophers have often debated the question of whether Heloïse could still really love Abelard when he was a monk and emasculate? One of these qualities did very great harm to the other.

But console yourself, Abelard, you were loved; the root of the hewn tree still retains a remnant of sap; the imagination aids the heart. One can still be happy at table even though one eats no longer. Is it love? is it simply a memory? is it friendship? All that is composed of something indescribable. It is an obscure feeling resembling the fantastic passions retained by the dead in the Elysian fields. The heroes who, during their lifetime, shone in the chariot races, drove imaginary chariots when they were dead. Heloïse lived with you on illusions and supplements. She kissed you sometimes, and with all the more pleasure that having taken a vow at the Paraclet monastery to love you no longer, her kisses thereby became more precious as more guilty. A woman can barely be seized with a passion for a eunuch: but she can keep her passion for her lover become eunuch, provided that he remains lovable.

It is not the same, ladies, for a lover who has grown old in service; the externals subsist no longer; the wrinkles horrify; the white eyebrows shock; the lost teeth disgust; the infirmities estrange: all that one can do is to have the virtue of being nurse, and of tolerating what one has loved. It is burying a dead man.

LUXURY

People have declaimed against luxury for two thousand years, in verse and in prose, and people have always delighted in it.

What has not been said of the early Romans when these brigands ravaged and pillaged the harvests; when, to enlarge their poor village, they destroyed the poor villages of the Volscians and the Samnites? They were disinterested, virtuous men; they had not yet been able to steal either gold, silver, or precious stones, because there were not any in the little towns they plundered. Their woods and their marshes produced neither pheasants nor partridges, and people praise their temperance.

When gradually they had pillaged everything, stolen everything from the far end of the Adriatic Gulf to the Euphrates, and when they had enough intelligence to enjoy the fruit of their plundering; when they cultivated the arts, when they tasted of all pleasures, and when they even made the vanquished taste of them, they ceased then, people say, to be wise and honest men.

All these declamations reduce themselves to proving that a robber must never either eat the dinner he has taken, or wear the coat he has pilfered, or adorn himself with the ring he has filched. He should throw all that, people say, in the river, so as to live like an honest man. Say rather that he should not have stolen. Condemn brigands when they pillage; but do not treat them as senseless when they enjoy. Honestly, when a large number of English sailors enriched themselves at the taking of Pondicherry and Havana, were they wrong to enjoy themselves later in London, as the price of the trouble they had had in the depths of Asia and America?

The declaimers want one to bury in the ground the wealth one has amassed by the fortune of arms, by agriculture, by commerce and by industry. They cite Lacedæmon; why do they not cite also the republic of San Marino? What good did Sparto to Greece? Did she ever have Demosthenes, Sophocles, Apelles, Phidias? The luxury of Athens produced great men in every sphere; Sparta had a few captains, and in less number even than other towns. But how fine it is that as small a republic as Lacedæmon retains its poverty.[14]

One arrives at death as well by lacking everything as by enjoying what can make life pleasant. The Canadian savage subsists, and comes to old age like the English citizen who has an income of fifty thousand guineas. But who will ever compare the land of the Iroquois to England?

Let the republic of Ragusa and the canton of Zug make sumptuary laws, they are right, the poor man must not spend beyond his powers; but I have read somewhere:

---

[14] Lacedæmon avoided luxury only by preserving the community or equality of property; but she did not preserve either the one or the other save by having the land cultivated by an enslaved people. The existence of the equality or community of property supposes the existence of an enslaved people. The Spartans had virtue, just like highwaymen, inquisitors and all classes of men whom habit has familiarized with a species of crime, to the point of committing them without remorse.

"Learn that luxury enriches a great state, even if it ruins a small."[15]

If by luxury you understand excess, everyone knows that excess in any form is pernicious, in abstinence as in gluttony, in economy as in generosity. I do not know how it has happened that in my village where the land is ungrateful, the taxes heavy, the prohibition against exporting the corn one has sown intolerable, there is nevertheless barely a cultivator who has not a good cloth coat, and who is not well shod and well fed. If this cultivator toiled in his fields in his fine coat, with white linen, his hair curled and powdered, there, certainly, would be the greatest luxury, and the most impertinent; but that a bourgeois of Paris or London should appear at the theatre clad like a peasant, there would be the most vulgar and ridiculous niggardliness.

When scissors, which are certainly not of the remotest antiquity, were invented, what did people not say against the first men who pared their nails, and who cut part of the hair which fell on their noses? They were treated, without a doubt, as fops and prodigals, who bought an instrument of vanity at a high price, in order to spoil the Creator's handiwork. What an enormous sin to cut short the horn which God made to grow at the end of our fingers! It was an outrage against the Deity! It was much worse when shirts and socks were invented. One knows with what fury the aged counsellors who had never worn them cried out against the young magistrates who were addicted to this disastrous luxury.[16]

---

[15] The sumptuary laws are by their nature a violation of the right of property. If in a little state there is not a great inequality of fortune, there will be no luxury; if this inequality exists, luxury is the remedy for it. It is her sumptuary laws that have lost Geneva her liberty.

[16] If by luxury one understands everything that is beyond the necessary, luxury is a natural consequence of the progress of the human species; and to reason consequently every enemy of luxury should believe with Rousseau that the state of happiness and virtue for man is that, not of the savage, but of the orang-outang. One feels that it would be absurd to regard as an evil the comforts which all men would enjoy: also, does one not generally give the name of luxury to the superfluities which only a small number of individuals can enjoy. In this sense, luxury is a necessary consequence of property, without which no society can subsist, and of a great inequality between fortunes which is the consequence, not of the right of property, but of bad laws. Moralists should address their sermons to the legislators, and not to individuals, because it is in the order of possible things that a virtuous and enlightened man may have the power to make reasonable laws, and it is not in human nature for all the rich men of a country to renounce through virtue procuring for themselves for money the enjoyments of pleasure or vanity.

GENERAL REFLECTION ON MAN

It needs twenty years to lead man from the plant state in which he is within his mother's womb, and the pure animal state which is the lot of his early childhood, to the state when the maturity of the reason begins to appear. It has needed thirty centuries to learn a little about his structure. It would need eternity to learn something about his soul. It takes an instant to kill him.

MAN IN THE IRON MASK

The author of the "Siècle de Louis XIV."[17] is the first to speak of the man in the iron mask in an authenticated history. The reason is that he was very well informed about the anecdote which astonishes the present century, which will astonish posterity, and which is only too true. He was deceived about the date of the death of this singularly unfortunate unknown. The date of his burial at St. Paul was March 3rd, 1703, and not 1704. (Note.—According to a certificate reported by Saint-Foix, the date was November 20th, 1703.)

He was imprisoned first of all at Pignerol before being so on St. Margaret's Islands, and later in the Bastille; always under the same man's guard, Saint-Mars, who saw him die. Father Griffet, Jesuit, has communicated to the public the diary of the Bastille, which testifies to the dates. He had this diary without difficulty, for he held the delicate position of confessor of prisoners imprisoned in the Bastille.

The man in the iron mask is a riddle to which everyone wishes to guess the answer. Some say that he was the Duc de Beaufort: but the Duc de Beaufort was killed by the Turks at the defence of Candia, in 1669; and the man in the iron mask was at Pignerol, in 1662. Besides, how would one have arrested the Duc de Beaufort surrounded by his army? how would one have transferred him to France without anybody knowing anything about it? and why should he have been put in prison, and why this mask?

Others have considered the Comte de Vermandois, natural son of Louis XIV., who died publicly of the small-pox in 1683, with the army, and was buried in the town of Arras.

---

[17] Voltaire.

Later it was thought that the Duke of Monmouth, whose head King James II. had cut off publicly in London in 1685, was the man in the iron mask. It would have been necessary for him to be resuscitated, and then for him to change the order of the times, for him to put the year 1662 in place of 1685; for King James who never pardoned anyone, and who on that account deserved all his misfortunes, to have pardoned the Duke of Monmouth, and to have caused the death, in his place, of a man exactly like him. It would have been necessary to find this double who would have been so kind as to have his neck cut off in public in order to save the Duke of Monmouth. It would have been necessary for the whole of England to have been under a misapprehension; for James then to have sent his earnest entreaties to Louis XIV. to be so good as to serve as his constable and gaoler. Then Louis XIV. having done King James this little favour, would not have failed to have the same consideration for King William and for Queen Anne, with whom he was at war; and he would carefully have preserved in these two monarchs' consideration his dignity of gaoler, with which King James had honoured him.

All these illusions being dissipated, it remains to be learned who was this prisoner who was always masked, the age at which he died, and under what name he was buried. It is clear that if he was not allowed to pass into the courtyard of the Bastille, if he was not allowed to speak to his doctor, unless covered by a mask, it was for fear that in his features might be recognized some too striking resemblance. He might show his tongue, and never his face. As regards his age, he himself said to the Bastille apothecary, a few days before his death, that he thought he was about sixty; and Master Marsolan, surgeon to the Maréchal de Richelieu, and later to the Duc d'Orléans, regent, son-in-law of this apothecary, has repeated it to me more than once.

Finally, why give him an Italian name? he was always called Marchiali! He who writes this article knows more about it, maybe, than Father Griffet, and will not say more.

Publishers Note[18]

---

[18] This note, given as a publisher's note in the 1771 edition, passes among many men of letters as being by Voltaire himself. He knew of this edition, and he never contradicted the opinion there advanced on the subject of the man in the iron mask.

He was the first to speak of this man. He always combated all the conjectures made about the mask: he always spoke as though better informed than others on the subject, and as though unwilling to tell all he knew.

There is a letter in circulation from Mlle. de Valois, written to the Duke, afterward Maréchal de Richelieu, where she boasts of having learned from the Duc d'Orléans, her father, under strange conditions, who the man in the iron mask was; this man, she says, was a twin brother of Louis XIV., born a few hours after him.

It is surprising to see so many scholars and so many intelligent and sagacious writers torment themselves with guessing who can have been the famous man in the iron mask, without the simplest, most natural, most probable idea ever presenting itself to them. Once the fact as M. de Voltaire reports it is admitted, with its circumstances; the existence of a prisoner of so singular a species, put in the rank of the best authenticated historical truths; it seems that not only is nothing easier than to imagine who this prisoner was, but that it is even difficult for there to be two opinions on the subject. The author of this article would have communicated his opinion earlier, if he had not believed that this idea must already have come to many others, and if he were not persuaded that it was not worth while giving as a discovery what, according to him, jumps to the eyes of all who read this anecdote.

However, as for some time past this event has divided men's minds, and as quite recently the public has again been given a letter in which it is claimed as proved that this celebrated prisoner was a secretary of the Duke of Mantua (which cannot be reconciled with the great marks of respect shown by M. de Saint-Mars to his prisoner), the author has thought it his duty to tell at last what has been his opinion for many years. Maybe this conjecture will put an end to all other researches, unless the secret be revealed by those who can be its guardians, in such a way as to remove all doubts.

Either this letter, which it was so useless, so indecent, so dangerous to read, is a supposititious letter, or the regent, in giving his daughter the reward she had so nobly acquired, thought to weaken the danger there was in revealing a state secret, by altering the facts, so as to make of this prince a younger son without right to the throne, instead of the heir-apparent to the crown.

But Louis XIV., who had a brother; Louis XIV., whose soul was magnanimous; Louis XIV., who prided himself even on a scrupulous probity, whom history has reproached with no crime, who indeed committed no crime apart from letting himself be too swayed by the counsels of Louvois and the Jesuits; Louis XIV. would never have detained one of his brothers in perpetual prison, in order to forestall the evils announced by an astrologer, in whom he did not believe. He needed more important motives. Eldest son of Louis XIII., acknowledged by this prince, the throne belonged to him; but a son born of Anne of Austria, unknown to her husband, had no rights, and could, nevertheless, try to make himself acknowledged, rend France with a long civil war, win maybe over Louis XIII.'s son, by alleging the right of primogeniture, and substitute a new race for the old race of the Bourbons. These motives, if they did not entirely justify Louis XIV.'s rigour, serve at least to excuse him; and the prisoner, too well-informed of his fate, could be grateful to him for not having listened to more rigorous counsels, counsels which politics have often employed against those who had pretensions to thrones occupied by their competitors.

From his youth Voltaire was connected with the Duc de Richelieu, who was not discreet: if Mlle. de Valois' letter is authentic, he knew of it; but, possessed of a just mind, he felt the error, and sought other information. He was in a position to obtain it; he rectified the truth altered in the letter, as he rectified so many other errors.

He will not amuse himself with refuting those who have imagined that this prisoner could be the Comte de Vermandois, the Duc de Beaufort, or the Duke of Monmouth. The scholarly and very wise author of this last opinion has well refuted the others; but he had based his own opinion essentially merely on the impossibility of finding in Europe some other prince whose detention it would have been of the very highest importance should not be known. M. de Saint-Foix is right, if he means to speak only of princes whose existence was known; but why has nobody yet thought of supposing that the iron mask might have been an unknown prince, brought up in secret, and whose existence it was important should remain unknown?

The Duke of Monmouth was not for France a prince of such great importance; and one does not see even what could have engaged this power, at least after the death of this duke and of James II., to make so great a secret of his detention, if indeed he was the iron mask. It is hardly probable either that M. de Louvois and M. de Saint-Mars would have shown the Duke of Monmouth the profound respect which M. de Voltaire assures they showed the iron mask.

The author conjectures, from the way that M. de Voltaire has told the facts, that this celebrated historian is as persuaded as he is of the suspicion which he is going, he says, to bring to light; but that M. de Voltaire, as a Frenchman, did not wish, he adds, to publish point-blank, particularly as he had said enough for the answer to the riddle not to be difficult to guess. Here it is, he continues, as I see it.

"The iron mask was undoubtedly a brother and an elder brother of Louis XIV., whose mother had that taste for fine linen on which M. de Voltaire lays stress. It was in reading the Memoirs of that time, which report this anecdote about the queen, that, recalling this same taste in the iron mask, I doubted no longer that he was her son: a fact of which all the other circumstances had persuaded me already.

"It is known that Louis XIII. had not lived with the queen for a long time; that the birth of Louis XIV. was due only to a happy chance skilfully induced; a chance which absolutely obliged the king to sleep in the same bed with the queen. This is how I think the thing came to pass.

"The queen may have thought that it was her fault that no heir was born to Louis XIII. The birth of the iron mask will have undeceived her. The cardinal to whom she will have confided the fact will have known, for more than one reason, how to turn the secret to account; he will have thought of making use of this event for his own benefit and for the benefit of the state. Persuaded by this example that the queen could give the king children, the plan which produced the chance of one bed for the king and the queen was arranged in consequence. But the queen and the cardinal, equally impressed with the necessity of hiding from Louis XIII. the iron mask's existence, will have had him brought up in secret. This secret will have been a secret for Louis XIV. until Cardinal Mazarin's death.

"But this monarch learning then that he had a brother, and an elder brother whom his mother could not disacknowledge, who further bore maybe the marked features which betrayed his origin, reflecting that this child born during marriage could not, without great inconvenience and a horrible scandal, be declared illegitimate after Louis XIII.'s death, Louis XIV. will have judged that he could not use a wiser or juster means than the one he employed in order to assure his own tranquillity and the peace of the state; means which relieved him of committing a cruelty which policy would have represented as necessary to a monarch less conscientious and less magnanimous than Louis XIV.

"It seems to me, our author continues, that the more one knows of the history of those times, the more one must be struck by these assembled circumstances which are in favour of such a supposition."

MARRIAGE

I came across a reasoner who said: "Engage your subjects to marry as soon as possible; let them be exempt from taxes the first year, and let their tax be distributed over those who at the same age are celibate.

"The more married men you have, the less crime there will be. Look at the frightful records of your registers of crime; you will find there a hundred bachelors hanged or wheeled for one father of a family.

"Marriage makes man wiser and more virtuous. The father of a family, near to committing a crime, is often stopped by his wife whose blood, less feverish than his, makes her gentler, more compassionate, more fearful of theft and murder, more timorous, more religious.

"The father of a family does not want to blush before his children. He fears to leave them a heritage of shame.

"Marry your soldiers, they will not desert any more. Bound to their families, they will be bound also to their fatherland. A bachelor soldier often is nothing but a vagabond, to whom it is indifferent whether he serves the king of Naples or the king of Morocco."

The Roman warriors were married; they fought for their wives and children; and they enslaved the wives and children of other nations.

A great Italian politician, who further was very learned in oriental languages, a very rare thing among our politicians, said to me in my youth: "*Caro figlio*, remember that the Jews have never had but one good institution, that of having a horror of virginity." If this little race of superstitious intermediaries had not considered marriage as the first law of man, if there had been among them convents of nuns, they were irreparably lost.

MASTER

SECTION I

"Unfortunate that I am to have been born!" said Ardassan Ougli, young page of the great Sultan of the Turks. "If it were only the great Sultan on whom I am dependent; but I am subject to the chief of my oda, to the capigi pasha; and when I receive my pay, I have to bow down to one of the tefterdar's clerks who deducts half of it. Before I was seven years old I had cut off, in spite of myself, in ceremony, the end of my prepuce, and it made me ill for a fortnight. The dervish who prays for us is my master; an iman is still more my master; the mollah is still more my master than the iman. The cadi is another master; the cadi-leskier is master still more; the mufti is much more master than all these together. The grand vizier's kaia can with a word have me thrown into the canal; and the grand vizier, finally, can have my neck wrung at his pleasure, and stuff the skin of my head, without anybody even taking notice.

"How many masters, great God! even if I had as many bodies and as many souls as I have duties to accomplish, I could not attend to everything. Oh, Allah! if only you had made me a screech-owl! I should live free in my hole, and I should eat mice at my ease without masters or servants. That assuredly is man's real destiny; only since he was perverted has he masters. No man was made to serve another man continuously. Each would have charitably aided his fellow, if things were as they should be. The man with eyes would have led the blind man, the active man would have acted as crutch to the cripple. This world would have been the paradise of Mohammed; and it is the hell which is exactly under the pointed bridge."

Thus did Ardassan Ougli speak, after receiving the stirrup-leather from one of his masters.

After a few years Ardassan Ougli became pasha with three tails. He made a prodigious fortune, and he firmly believed that all men, excepting the Great Turk and the Grand Vizier, were born to serve him, and all women to give him pleasure in accordance with his caprice.

139

SECTION II

How has it been possible for one man to become another man's master, and by what species of incomprehensible magic has he been able to become the master of many other men? On this phenomenon a great number of good volumes have been written; but I give the preference to an Indian fable, because it is short, and because the fables have said everything.

Adimo, the father of all the Indians, had two sons and two daughters by his wife Procriti. The elder son was a giant, the younger was a little hunchback, the two daughters were pretty. As soon as the giant was conscious of his strength, he lay with his two sisters, and made the little hunchback serve him. Of his two sisters, one was his cook, the other his gardener. When the giant wanted to sleep, he started by chaining his little hunchback brother to a tree; and when the brother escaped, he caught him in four strides, and gave him twenty strokes with a length of ox sinew.

The hunchback became submissive and the best subject in the world. The giant, satisfied to see him fulfilling his duties as subject, permitted him to lie with one of his sisters for whom he himself had taken a distaste. The children who came of this marriage were not entirely hunchbacked; but they had sufficiently misshapen forms. They were reared in fear of God and the giant. They received an excellent education; they were taught that their great uncle was giant by divine right, that he could do with his family as pleased him; that if he had a pretty niece or great-niece, she was for him alone without a doubt, and that no one could lie with her until he wanted her no longer.

The giant having died, his son, who was not by a long way as strong and as big as he, thought nevertheless that he, like his father, was giant by divine right. He claimed to make all the men work for him, and to lie with all the women. The family leagued itself against him, he was beaten to death, and the others turned themselves into a republic.

The Siamese, on the contrary, maintain that the family had started by being republican, and that the giant did not come until after a great number of years and dissensions; but all the authors of Benares and Siam agree that mankind lived an infinity of centuries before having the intelligence to make laws; and they prove it by an unanswerable reason, which is that even to-day when everyone plumes himself on his intelligence, no way has been found of making a score of passably good laws.

It is indeed still an insoluble question in India whether republics were established before or after monarchies, whether confusion appeared more horrible to mankind than despotism. I do not know what happened in order of time; but in that of nature it must be agreed that all men being born equal, violence and adroitness made the first masters, the laws made the last.

MEN OF LETTERS

In our barbarous times, when the Franks, the Germans, the Bretons, the Lombards, the Spanish Muzarabs, knew not how either to read or write, there were instituted schools, universities, composed almost entirely of ecclesiastics who, knowing nothing but their own jargon, taught this jargon to those who wished to learn it; the academies came only a long time afterwards; they despised the foolishness of the schools, but did not always dare to rise against them, because there are foolishnesses that are respected provided that they concern respectable things.

The men of letters who have rendered the greatest services to the small number of thinking beings spread over the world, are the isolated writers, the true scholars shut in their studies, who have neither argued on the benches of the universities, nor told half-truths in the academies; and almost all of them have been persecuted. Our wretched species is so made that those who walk on the well-trodden path always throw stones at those who are showing a new road.

Montesquieu says that the Scythians rent their slaves' eyes, so that they might be less distracted while they were churning their butter; that is just how the inquisition functions, and in the land where this monster reigns almost everybody is blind. In England people have had two eyes for more than two hundred years; the French are starting to open one eye; but sometimes there are men in power who do not want the people to have even this one eye open.

These poor persons in power are like Doctor Balouard of the Italian Comedy, who does not want to be served by anyone but the dolt Harlequin, and who is afraid of having too shrewd a valet.

Compose some odes in praise of My Lord Superbus Fadus, some madrigals for his mistress; dedicate a book on geography to his door-keeper, you will be well-received; enlighten mankind, you will be exterminated.

Descartes was forced to leave his country, Gassendi was calumniated, Arnauld dragged out his days in exile; every philosopher is treated as the prophets were among the Jews.

Who would believe that in the eighteenth century a philosopher was dragged before the secular tribunals, and treated as impious by the tribunals of arguments, for having said that men could not practise the arts if they had no hands? I do not despair that soon the first person who is so insolent as to say that men could not think if they had no heads will be immediately condemned to the galleys; "for," some young graduate will say to him, "the soul is a pure spirit, the head is only matter; God can put the soul in the heel, as well as in the brain; therefore I denounce you as impious."

The greatest misfortune of a man of letters is not perhaps being the object of his confrères' jealousy, the victim of the cabal, the despised of the men of power; but of being judged by fools. Fools go far sometimes, particularly when bigotry is added to ineptitude, and to ineptitude the spirit of vengeance. The further great misfortune of a man of letters is that ordinarily he is unattached. A bourgeois buys himself a small position, and there he is backed by his colleagues. If he suffers an injustice, he finds defenders at once. The man of letters is unsuccoured; he resembles a flying-fish; if he rises a little, the birds devour him; if he dives, the fish eat him.

Every public man pays tribute to malignity, but he is paid in honours and gold.

METAMORPHOSIS, METEMPSYCHOSIS

Is it not very natural that all the metamorphoses with which the world is covered should have made people imagine in the Orient, where everything has been imagined, that our souls passed from one body to another? An almost imperceptible speck becomes a worm, this worm becomes a butterfly; an acorn transforms itself into an oak; an egg into a bird; water becomes cloud and thunder; wood is changed into fire and ash; everything in nature appears, in fine, metamorphosed. Soon people attributed to souls, which were regarded as light figures, what they saw in more gross bodies. The idea of metempsychosis is perhaps the most ancient dogma of the known universe, and it still reigns in a large part of India and China.

MILTON, ON THE REPROACH OF PLAGIARISM
AGAINST

Some people have accused Milton of having taken his poem from the tragedy of "The Banishment of Adam" by Grotius, and from the "Sarcotis" of the Jesuit Masenius, printed at Cologne in 1654 and in 1661, long before Milton gave his "Paradise Lost."

As regards Grotius, it was well enough known in England that Milton had carried into his epic English poem a few Latin verses from the tragedy of "Adam." It is in no wise to be a plagiarist to enrich one's language with the beauties of a foreign language. No one accused Euripides of plagiarism for having imitated in one of the choruses of "Iphigenia" the second book of the Iliad; on the contrary, people were very grateful to him for this imitation, which they regarded as a homage rendered to Homer on the Athenian stage.

Virgil never suffered a reproach for having happily imitated, in the Æneid, a hundred verses by the first of Greek poets.

Against Milton the accusation was pushed a little further. A Scot, Will Lauder by name, very attached to the memory of Charles I., whom Milton had insulted with the most uncouth animosity, thought himself entitled to dishonour the memory of this monarch's accuser. It was claimed that Milton was guilty of an infamous imposture in robbing Charles I. of the sad glory of being the author of the "Eikon Basilika," a book long dear to the royalists, and which Charles I., it was said, had composed in his prison to serve as consolation for his deplorable adversity.

Lauder, therefore, about the year of 1752, wanted to begin by proving that Milton was only a plagiarist, before proving that he had acted as a forger against the memory of the most unfortunate of kings; he procured some editions of the poem of the "Sarcotis." It seemed evident that Milton had imitated some passages of it, as he had imitated Grotius and Tasso.

But Lauder did not rest content there; he unearthed a bad translation in Latin verse of the "Paradise Lost" of the English poet; and joining several verses of this translation to those by Masenius, he thought thereby to render the accusation more grave, and Milton's shame more complete. It was in that, that he was badly deceived; his fraud was discovered. He wanted to make Milton pass for a forger, and he was himself convicted of forging. No one examined Masenius' poem of which at that time there were only a few copies in Europe. All England, convinced of the Scot's poor trick, asked no more about it. The accuser, confounded, was obliged to disavow his manœuvre, and ask pardon for it.

Since then a new edition of Masenius was printed in 1757. The literary public was surprised at the large number of very beautiful verses with which the Sarcotis was sprinkled. It is in truth nothing but a long declamation of the schools on the fall of man: but the exordium, the invocation, the description of the garden of Eden, the portrait of Eve, that of the devil, are precisely the same as in Milton. Further, it is the same subject, the same plot, the same catastrophe. If the devil wishes, in Milton, to be revenged on man for the harm which God has done him, he has precisely the same plan in the work of the Jesuit Masenius; and he manifests it in verses worthy maybe of the century of Augustus. ("Sarcotis," I., 271 *et seq.*)

One finds in both Masenius and Milton little episodes, trifling digressions which are absolutely alike; both speak of Xerxes who covered the sea with his ships. Both speak in the same tone of the Tower of Babel; both give the same description of luxury, of pride, of avarice, of gluttony.

What most persuaded the generality of readers of Milton's plagiarism was the perfect resemblance of the beginning of the two poems. Many foreigners, after reading the exordium, had no doubt but that the rest of Milton's poem was taken from Masenius. It is a very great error and easy to recognize.

I do not think that the English poet imitated in all more than two hundred of the Jesuit of Cologne's verses; and I dare say that he imitated only what was worthy of being imitated. These two hundred verses are very beautiful; so are Milton's; and the total of Masenius' poem, despite these two hundred beautiful verses, is not worth anything at all.

Molière took two whole scenes from the ridiculous comedy of the "Pédant Joué" by Cyrano de Bergerac. "These two scenes are good," he said as he was jesting with his friends. "They belong to me by right: I recover my property." After that anyone who treated the author of "Tartufe" and "Le Misanthrope" as a plagiarist would have been very badly received.

It is certain that generally Milton, in his "Paradise", has in imitating flown on his own wings; and it must be agreed that if he borrowed so many traits from Grotius and from the Jesuit of Cologne, they are blended in the crowd of original things which are his; in England he is always regarded as a very great poet.

It is true that he should have avowed having translated two hundred of a Jesuit's verses; but in his time, at the court of Charles II., people did not worry themselves with either the Jesuits, or Milton, or "Paradise

Lost", or "Paradise Regained". All those things were either scoffed at, or unknown.

MOHAMMEDANS

I tell you again, ignorant imbeciles, whom other ignoramuses have made believe that the Mohammedan religion is voluptuous and sensual, there is not a word of truth in it; you have been deceived on this point as on so many others.

Canons, monks, vicars even, if a law were imposed on you not to eat or drink from four in the morning till ten at night, during the month of July, when Lent came at this period; if you were forbidden to play at any game of chance under pain of damnation; if wine were forbidden you under the same pain; if you had to make a pilgrimage into the burning desert; if it were enjoined on you to give at least two and a half per cent. of your income to the poor; if, accustomed to enjoy possession of eighteen women, the number were cut down suddenly by fourteen; honestly, would you dare call that religion sensual?

The Latin Christians have so many advantages over the Mussulmans, I do not say in the matter of war, but in the matter of doctrines; the Greek Christians have so beaten them latterly from 1769 to 1773, that it is not worth the trouble to indulge in unjust reproaches against Islam.

Try to retake from the Mohammedans all that they usurped; but it is easier to calumniate them.

I hate calumny so much that I do not want even to impute foolishness to the Turks, although I detest them as tyrants over women and enemies of the arts.

I do not know why the historian of the Lower Empire maintains that Mohammed speaks in his Koran of his journey into the sky: Mohammed does not say a word about it; we have proved it.

One must combat ceaselessly. When one has destroyed an error, there is always someone who resuscitates it.

145

MOUNTAIN

It is a very old, very universal fable that tells of the mountain which, having frightened all the countryside by its outcry that it was in labour, was hissed by all present when it brought into the world a mere mouse. The people in the pit were not philosophers. Those who hissed should have admired. It was as fine for the mountain to give birth to a mouse, as for the mouse to give birth to a mountain. A rock which produces a rat is a very prodigious thing; and never has the world seen anything approaching this miracle. All the globes of the universe could not call a fly into existence. Where the vulgar laugh, the philosopher admires; and he laughs where the vulgar open their big, stupid eyes in astonishment.

NAKEDNESS

Why should one lock up a man or a woman who walked stark naked in the street? and why is no one shocked by absolutely nude statues, by pictures of the Madonna and of Jesus that may be seen in some churches?

It is probably that the human species lived long without being clothed.

People unacquainted with clothing have been found in more than one island and in the American continent.

The most civilized hide the organs of generation with leaves, woven rushes, feathers.

Whence comes this form of modesty? is it the instinct for lighting desires by hiding what it gives pleasure to discover?

Is it really true that among slightly more civilized nations, such as the Jews and half-Jews, there have been entire sects who would not worship God save by stripping themselves of all their clothes? such were, it is said, the Adamites and the Abelians. They gathered quite naked to sing the praises of God: St. Epiphanius and St. Augustine say so. It is true that they were not contemporary, and that they were very far from these people's country. But at all events this madness is possible: it is not even more extraordinary, more mad than a hundred other madnesses which have been round the world one after the other.

We have said elsewhere that to-day even the Mohammedans still have saints who are madmen, and who go naked like monkeys. It is very possible that some fanatics thought it was better to present themselves

146

to the Deity in the state in which He formed them, than in the disguise invented by man. It is possible that they showed everything out of piety. There are so few well-made persons of both sexes, that nakedness might have inspired chastity, or rather disgust, instead of increasing desire.

It is said particularly that the Abelians renounced marriage. If there were any fine lads and pretty lasses among them, they were at least comparable to St. Adhelme and to blessed Robert d'Arbrisselle, who slept with the prettiest persons, that their continence might triumph all the more.

But I avow that it would have been very comic to see a hundred Helens and Parises singing anthems, giving each other the kiss of peace, and making agapæ.

All of which shows that there is no singularity, no extravagance, no superstition which has not passed through the heads of mankind. Happy the day when these superstitions do not trouble society and make of it a scene of disorder, hatred and fury! It is better without doubt to pray God stark naked, than to stain His altars and the public places with human blood.

NATURAL LAW

B: What is natural law?

A: The instinct which makes us feel justice.

B: What do you call just and unjust?

A: What appears such to the entire universe.

B: The universe is composed of many heads. It is said that in Lacedæmon were applauded thefts for which people in Athens were condemned to the mines.

A: Abuse of words, logomachy, equivocation; theft could not be committed at Sparta, when everything was common property. What you call "theft" was the punishment for avarice.

B: It was forbidden to marry one's sister in Rome. It was allowed among the Egyptians, the Athenians and even among the Jews, to marry one's sister on the father's side. It is but with regret that I cite that wretched little Jewish people, who should assuredly not serve as a rule for anyone, and who (putting religion aside) was never anything but

147

a race of ignorant and fanatic brigands. But still, according to their books, the young Thamar, before being ravished by her brother Amnon, says to him:—"Nay, my brother, do not thou this folly, but speak unto the king; for he will not withhold me from thee." (2 Samuel xiii. 12, 13.)

A: Conventional law all that, arbitrary customs, fashions that pass: the essential remains always. Show me a country where it was honourable to rob me of the fruit of my toil, to break one's promise, to lie in order to hurt, to calumniate, to assassinate, to poison, to be ungrateful towards a benefactor, to beat one's father and one's mother when they offer you food.

B: Have you forgotten that Jean-Jacques, one of the fathers of the modern Church, has said that "the first man who dared enclose and cultivate a piece of land" was the enemy "of the human race," that he should have been exterminated, and that "the fruits of the earth are for all, and that the land belongs to none"? Have we not already examined together this lovely proposition which is so useful to society (Discourse on Inequality, second part)?

A: Who is this Jean-Jacques? he is certainly not either John the Baptist, nor John the Evangelist, nor James the Greater, nor James the Less[19]; it must be some Hunnish wit who wrote that abominable impertinence or some poor joker *bufo magro* who wanted to laugh at what the entire world regards as most serious. For instead of going to spoil the land of a wise and industrious neighbour, he had only to imitate him; and every father of a family having followed this example, behold soon a very pretty village formed. The author of this passage seems to me a very unsociable animal.

B: You think then that by outraging and robbing the good man who has surrounded his garden and chicken-run with a live hedge, he has been wanting in respect towards the duties of natural law?

A: Yes, yes, once again, there is a natural law, and it does not consist either in doing harm to others, or in rejoicing thereat.

B: I imagine that man likes and does harm only for his own advantage. But so many people are led to look for their own interest in the misfortune of others, vengeance is so violent a passion, there are such disastrous examples of it; ambition, still more fatal, has inundated the world with so much blood, that when I retrace for myself the horrible picture, I am tempted to avow that man is a very devil. In vain have I in my heart the notion of justice and injustice; an Attila courted by St. Leo, a Phocas flattered by St. Gregory with the most cowardly

---

[19] Jean=John: Jacques=James.

baseness, an Alexander VI. sullied with so many incests, so many murders, so many poisonings, with whom the weak Louis XII., who is called "the good," makes the most infamous and intimate alliance; a Cromwell whose protection Cardinal Mazarin seeks, and for whom he drives out of France the heirs of Charles I., Louis XIV.'s first cousins, etc., etc.; a hundred like examples set my ideas in disorder, and I know no longer where I am.

A: Well, do storms stop our enjoyment of to-day's beautiful sun? Did the earthquake which destroyed half the city of Lisbon stop your making the voyage to Madrid very comfortably? If Attila was a brigand and Cardinal Mazarin a rogue, are there not princes and ministers who are honest people? Has it not been remarked that in the war of 1701, Louis XIV.'s council was composed of the most virtuous men? The Duc de Beauvilliers, the Marquis de Torci, the Maréchal de Villars, Chamillart lastly who passed for being incapable, but never for dishonest. Does not the idea of justice subsist always? It is upon that idea that all laws are founded. The Greeks called them "daughters of heaven," which only means daughters of nature. Have you no laws in your country?

B: Yes, some good, some bad.

A: Where, if it was not in the notions of natural law, did you get the idea that every man has within himself when his mind is properly made? You must have obtained it there, or nowhere.

B: You are right, there is a natural law; but it is still more natural to many people to forget it.

A: It is natural also to be one-eyed, hump-backed, lame, deformed, unhealthy; but one prefers people who are well made and healthy.

B: Why are there so many one-eyed and deformed minds?

A: Peace! But go to the article on "Power."

NATURE

Dialogue between the Philosopher and Nature

THE PHILOSOPHER:

Who are you, Nature? I live in you; for fifty years have I been seeking you, and I have not found you yet.

NATURE:

The ancient Egyptians, who lived, it is said, some twelve hundred years, made me the same reproach. They called me Isis; they put a great veil on my head, and they said that nobody could lift it.

THE PHILOSOPHER:

That is what makes me address myself to you. I have been able to measure some of your globes, know their paths, assign the laws of motion; but I have not been able to learn who you are.

Are you always active? are you always passive? did your elements arrange themselves, as water deposits itself on sand, oil on water, air on oil? have you a mind which directs all your operations, as councils are inspired as soon as they are assembled, although their members are sometimes ignoramuses? I pray you tell me the answer to your riddle.

NATURE:

I am the great everything. I know no more about it. I am not a mathematician; and everything is arranged in my world according to mathematical laws. Guess if you can how it is all done.

THE PHILOSOPHER:

Certainly, since your great everything does not know mathematics, and since all your laws are most profoundly geometrical, there must be an eternal geometer who directs you, a supreme intelligence who presides over your operations.

NATURE:

You are right; I am water, earth, fire, atmosphere, metal, mineral, stone, vegetable, animal. I feel indeed that there is in me an intelligence; you have an intelligence, you do not see it. I do not see mine either; I feel this invisible power; I cannot know it: why should you, who are but a small part of me, want to know what I do not know?

THE PHILOSOPHER:

We are curious. I want to know how being so crude in your mountains, in your deserts, in your seas, you appear nevertheless so industrious in your animals, in your vegetables?

NATURE:

My poor child do you want me to tell you the truth? It is that I have been given a name which does not suit me; my name is "Nature", and I am all art.

150

THE PHILOSOPHER:

That word upsets all my ideas. What! nature is only art?

NATURE:

Yes, without any doubt. Do you not know that there is an infinite art in those seas and those mountains that you find so crude? do you not know that all those waters gravitate towards the centre of the earth, and mount only by immutable laws; that those mountains which crown the earth are the immense reservoirs of the eternal snows which produce unceasingly those fountains, lakes and rivers without which my animal species and my vegetable species would perish? And as for what are called my animal kingdom, my vegetable kingdom and my mineral kingdom, you see here only three; learn that I have millions of kingdoms. But if you consider only the formation of an insect, of an ear of corn, of gold, of copper, everything will appear as marvels of art.

THE PHILOSOPHER:

It is true. The more I think about it, the more I see that you are only the art of I know not what most potent and industrious great being, who hides himself and who makes you appear. All reasoners since Thales, and probably long before him, have played at blind man's buff with you; they have said: "I have you!" and they had nothing. We all resemble Ixion; he thought he was kissing Juno, and all that he possessed was a cloud.

NATURE:

Since I am all that is, how can a being such as you, so small a part of myself, seize me? Be content, atoms my children, with seeing a few atoms that surround you, with drinking a few drops of my milk, with vegetating for a few moments on my breast, and with dying without having known your mother and your nurse.

THE PHILOSOPHER:

My dear mother, tell me something of why you exist, of why there is anything.

NATURE:

I will answer you as I have answered for so many centuries all those who have interrogated me about first principles: I KNOW NOTHING ABOUT THEM.

THE PHILOSOPHER:

Would not non-existence be better than this multitude of existences made in order to be continually dissolved, this crowd of animals born and reproduced in order to devour others and to be devoured, this crowd of sentient beings formed for so many painful sensations, that other crowd of intelligences which so rarely hear reason. What is the good of all that, Nature?

NATURE:

Oh! go and ask Him who made me.

NECESSARY

OSMIN:

Do you not say that everything is necessary?

SELIM:

If everything were not necessary, it would follow that God had made useless things.

OSMIN:

That is to say that it was necessary to the divine nature to make all that it has made?

SELIM:

I think so, or at least I suspect it; there are people who think otherwise; I do not understand them; maybe they are right. I am afraid of disputes on this subject.

OSMIN:

It is also of another necessary that I want to talk to you.

SELIM:

What! of what is necessary to an honest man that he may live? of the misfortune to which one is reduced when one lacks the necessary?

OSMIN:

No; for what is necessary to one is not always necessary to the other: it is necessary for an Indian to have rice, for an Englishman to have meat; a fur is necessary to a Russian, and a gauzy stuff to an African; this man thinks that twelve coach-horses are necessary to him, that man limits himself to a pair of shoes, a third walks gaily barefoot: I want to talk to you of what is necessary to all men.

SELIM:

It seems to me that God has given all that is necessary to this species: eyes to see with, feet for walking, a mouth for eating, an œsophagus for swallowing, a stomach for digesting, a brain for reasoning, organs for producing one's fellow creature.

OSMIN:

How does it happen then that men are born lacking a part of these necessary things?

SELIM:

It is because the general laws of nature have brought about some accidents which have made monsters to be born; but generally man is provided with everything that is necessary to him in order to live in society.

OSMIN:

Are there notions common to all men which serve to make them live in society?

SELIM:

Yes. I have travelled with Paul Lucas, and wherever I went, I saw that people respected their father and their mother, that people believed themselves to be obliged to keep their promises, that people pitied oppressed innocents, that they hated persecution, that they regarded liberty of thought as a rule of nature, and the enemies of this liberty as enemies of the human race; those who think differently seemed to me badly organized creatures, monsters like those who are born without eyes and hands.

OSMIN:

Are these necessary things in all time and in all places?

SELIM:

Yes, if they were not they would not be necessary to the human species.

OSMIN:

So a belief which is new is not necessary to this species. Men could very well live in society and accomplish their duty to God, before believing that Mahomet had frequent interviews with the angel Gabriel.

SELIM:

Nothing is clearer; it would be ridiculous to think that man could not accomplish his duty to God before Mahomet came into the world; it was not at all necessary for the human species to believe in the Alcoran: the world went along before Mahomet just as it goes along to-day. If Mahometanism had been necessary to the world, it would have existed in all places; God who has given us all two eyes to see the sun, would have given us all an intelligence to see the truth of the Mussulman religion. This sect is therefore only like the positive laws that change according to time and place, like the fashions, like the opinions of the natural philosophers which follow one after the other.

The Mussulman sect could not be essentially necessary to mankind.

OSMIN:

But since it exists, God has permitted it?

SELIM:

Yes, as he permits the world to be filled with foolishness, error and calamity; that is not to say that men are all essentially made to be fools and miscreants. He permits that some men be eaten by snakes; but one cannot say—"God made man to be eaten by snakes."

OSMIN:

What do you mean when you say "God permits"? can nothing happen without His order? permit, will and do, are they not the same thing for Him?

SELIM:

He permits crime, but He does not commit it.

OSMIN:

Committing a crime is acting against divine justice, it is disobeying God. Well, God cannot disobey Himself, He cannot commit crime; but He has made man in such a way that man may commit many crimes: where does that come from?

SELIM:

There are people who know, but I do not; all that I know is that the Alcoran is ridiculous, although from time to time it has some tolerably good things; certainly the Alcoran was not at all necessary to man; I stick by that: I see clearly what is false, and I know very little that is true.

OSMIN:

I thought you would instruct me, and you teach me nothing.

SELIM:

Is it not a great deal to recognize people who deceive you, and the gross and dangerous errors which they retail to you?

OSMIN:

I should have ground for complaint against a doctor who showed me all the harmful plants, and who did not show me one salutary plant.

SELIM:

I am not a doctor, and you are not ill; but it seems to me I should be giving you a very good prescription if I said to you: "Put not your trust in all the inventions of charlatans, worship God, be an honest man, and believe that two and two make four."

NEW NOVELTIES

It seems that the first words of Ovid's "Metamorphoses," *In nova fert animus*, are the motto of the human race. Nobody is touched by the admirable spectacle of the sun which rises, or rather seems to rise, every day; everybody runs to see the smallest little meteor which appears for an instant in that accumulation of vapours, called the sky, that surround the earth.

An itinerant bookseller does not burden himself with a Virgil, with a Horace, but with a new book, even though it be detestable. He draws you aside and says to you: "Sir, do you want some books from Holland?"

From the beginning of the world women have complained of the fickleness that is imputed to them in favour of the first new object which

155

presents itself, and whose novelty is often its only merit. Many ladies (it must be confessed, despite the infinite respect we have for them) have treated men as they complain they have themselves been treated; and the story of Gioconda is much older than Ariosto.

Perhaps this universal taste for novelty is one of nature's favours. People cry to us: "Be content with what you have, desire nothing that is beyond your estate, restrain your curiosity, tame your intellectual disquiet." These are very good maxims; but if we had always followed them, we should still be eating acorns, we should be sleeping in the open air, and we should not have had Corneille, Racine, Molière, Poussin, Lebrun, Lemoine or Pigalle.

PHILOSOPHER

Philosopher, *lover of wisdom*, that is to say, *of truth*. All philosophers have had this dual character; there is not one in antiquity who has not given mankind examples of virtue and lessons in moral truths. They have all contrived to be deceived about natural philosophy; but natural philosophy is so little necessary for the conduct of life, that the philosophers had no need of it. It has taken centuries to learn a part of nature's laws. One day was sufficient for a wise man to learn the duties of man.

The philosopher is not enthusiastic; he does not set himself up as a prophet; he does not say that he is inspired by the gods. Thus I shall not put in the rank of philosophers either the ancient Zarathustra, or Hermes, or the ancient Orpheus, or any of those legislators of whom the nations of Chaldea, Persia, Syria, Egypt and Greece boasted. Those who styled themselves children of the gods were the fathers of imposture; and if they used lies for the teaching of truths, they were unworthy of teaching them; they were not philosophers; they were at best very prudent liars.

By what fatality, shameful maybe for the Western peoples, is it necessary to go to the far Orient to find a wise man who is simple, unostentatious, free from imposture, who taught men to live happily six hundred years before our vulgar era, at a time when the whole of the North was ignorant of the usage of letters, and when the Greeks were barely beginning to distinguish themselves by their wisdom?

This wise man is Confucius, who being legislator never wanted to deceive men. What more beautiful rule of conduct has ever been given since him in the whole world?

"Rule a state as you rule a family; one can only govern one's family well by setting the example.

"Virtue should be common to both husbandman and monarch.

"Apply thyself to the trouble of preventing crimes in order to lessen the trouble of punishing them.

"Under the good kings Yao and Xu the Chinese were good; under the bad kings Kie and Chu they were wicked.

"Do to others as to thyself.

"Love all men; but cherish honest people. Forget injuries, and never kindnesses.

"I have seen men incapable of study; I have never seen them incapable of virtue."

Let us admit that there is no legislator who has proclaimed truths more useful to the human race.

A host of Greek philosophers have since taught an equally pure moral philosophy. If they had limited themselves to their empty systems of natural philosophy, their names would be pronounced to-day in mockery only. If they are still respected, it is because they were just and that they taught men to be so.

One cannot read certain passages of Plato, and notably the admirable exordium of the laws of Zaleucus, without feeling in one's heart the love of honourable and generous actions. The Romans have their Cicero, who alone is worth perhaps all the philosophers of Greece. After him come men still more worthy of respect, but whom one almost despairs of imitating; Epictetus in bondage, the Antonines and the Julians on the throne.

Which is the citizen among us who would deprive himself, like Julian, Antoninus and Marcus Aurelius, of all the delicacies of our flabby and effeminate lives? who would sleep as they did on the ground? who would impose on himself their frugality? who, as they did, would march barefoot and bareheaded at the head of the armies, exposed now to the heat of the sun, now to the hoar-frost? who would command all their passions as they did? There are pious men among us; but where are the wise men? where are the resolute, just and tolerant souls?

There have been philosophers of the study in France; and all, except Montaigne, have been persecuted. It is, I think, the last degree of the malignity of our nature, to wish to oppress these very philosophers who would correct it.

157

I quite understand that the fanatics of one sect slaughter the enthusiasts of another sect, that the Franciscans hate the Dominicans, and that a bad artist intrigues to ruin one who surpasses him; but that the wise Charron should have been threatened with the loss of his life, that the learned and generous Ramus should have been assassinated, that Descartes should have been forced to flee to Holland to escape the fury of the ignorant, that Gassendi should have been obliged to withdraw several times to Digne, far from the calumnies of Paris; these things are a nation's eternal shame.

POWER, OMNIPOTENCE

I suppose that the man who reads this article is convinced that this world is formed with intelligence, and that a little astronomy and anatomy suffices to make this universal and supreme intelligence admired.

Can he know by himself if this intelligence is omnipotent, that is to say, infinitely powerful? Has he the least notion of the infinite, to understand what is an infinite power?

The celebrated historian philosopher, David Hume, says in "Particular Providence": "A weight of ten ounces is lifted in a balance by another weight; therefore this other weight is of more than ten ounces; but one can adduce no reason why it should weigh a hundred ounces."

One can say likewise: You recognize a supreme intelligence strong enough to form you, to preserve you for a limited time, to reward you, to punish you. Do you know enough of this power to demonstrate that it can do still more?

How can you prove by your reason that this being can do more than he has done?

The life of all animals is short. Could he make it longer?

All animals are the prey of each other: everything is born to be devoured. Could he form without destroying?

You do not know what nature is. You cannot therefore know if nature has not forced him to do only the things he has done.

This globe is only a vast field of destruction and carnage. Either the great Being has been able to make of it an eternal abode of delight for all sentient beings, or He has not been able. If He has been able and if He has not done so, fear to regard him as malevolent; but if He has not

158

been able, fear not to look on Him as a very great power, circumscribed by nature in His limits.

Whether or no His power is infinite does not regard you. It is a matter of indifference to a subject whether his master possesses five hundred leagues of land or five thousand; he is subject neither more nor less.

Which would be the greater insult to this ineffable Being, to say: "He has made miserable men without being able to dispense with them, or He has made them for His pleasure?"

Many sects represent Him as cruel; others, for fear of admitting a wicked God, have the audacity to deny His existence. Is it not better to say that probably the necessity of His nature and the necessity of things have determined everything?

The world is the theatre of moral ill and physical ill; one is only too aware of it: and the "All is good" of Shaftesbury, Bolingbroke and Pope, is only a witty paradox, a poor joke.

The two principles of Zarathustra and Manes, so carefully scrutinized by Bayle, are a still poorer joke. They are, as has been observed already, Molière's two doctors, one of whom says to the other: "Grant me the emetic, and I will grant you the bleeding." Manichæism is absurd; and that is why it has had so many supporters.

I admit that I have not been enlightened by all that Bayle says about the Manichæans and the Paulicians. That is controversy; I would have preferred pure philosophy. Why discuss our mysteries beside Zarathustra's? As soon as you dare to treat of our mysteries, which need only faith and no reasoning, you open precipices for yourself.

The trash in our scholastic theology has nothing to do with the trash in Zarathustra's reveries.

Why debate original sin with Zarathustra? There was never any question of it save in St. Augustine's time. Neither Zarathustra nor any legislator of antiquity had ever heard speak of it.

If you dispute with Zarathustra, put under lock and key the old and the new Testaments which he did not know, and which one must revere without desiring to explain them.

What then should I have said to Zarathustra? My reason cannot admit two gods who fight, that is good only in a poem where Minerva quarrels with Mars. My feeble reason is much more content with a single great Being, whose essence was to make, and who has made all that nature has permitted Him, than it is satisfied with two great Beings, one of whom spoils the works of the other. Your bad principle Ahriman, has not been able to upset a single one of the astronomical and physical laws of

159

the good principle Ormuzd; everything progresses in the heavens with the greatest regularity. Why should the wicked Ahriman have had power over this little globe of the world?

If I had been Ahriman, I should have attacked Ormuzd in his fine grand provinces of so many suns and stars. I should not have limited myself to making war on him in a little village.

There is much evil in this village: but whence have you the knowledge that this evil is not inevitable?

You are forced to admit an intelligence diffused over the universe; but (1) do you know, for instance, if this power reaches right to foreseeing the future? You have asserted it a thousand times; but you have never been able either to prove it, or to understand it. You cannot know how any being whatever sees what is not. Well, the future is not; therefore no being can see it. You are reduced to saying that He foresees it; but foreseeing is conjecturing. This is the opinion of the Socinians.

Well, a God who, according to you, conjectures, can be mistaken. In your system He is really mistaken; for if He had foreseen that His enemy would poison all His works here below, He would not have produced them; He would not have prepared for Himself the shame of being continually vanquished.

(2) Do I not do Him much more honour by saying that He has made everything by the necessity of His nature, than you do Him by raising an enemy who disfigures, who soils, who destroys all His works here below?

(3) It is not to have an unworthy idea of God to say that, having formed thousands of millions of worlds where death and evil do not dwell, it was necessary that evil and death should dwell in this world.

(4) It is not to disparage God to say that He could not form man without giving him self-esteem; that this self-esteem could not lead him without misguiding him almost always; that his passions are necessary, but that they are disastrous; that propagation cannot be executed without desire; that desire cannot animate man without quarrels; that these quarrels necessarily bring wars in their train, etc.

(5) When he sees part of the combinations of the animal, vegetable and mineral kingdoms, and this globe pierced everywhere like a sieve, from which escape in crowds so many exhalations, what philosopher will be bold enough, what scholastic foolish enough to see clearly that nature could stop the effects of volcanoes, the inclemencies of the atmosphere, the violence of the winds, the plagues, and all the destructive scourges?

160

(6) One must be very powerful, very strong, very industrious, to have formed lions which devour bulls, and to have produced men who invent arms to kill at one blow, not only bulls and lions, but even each other. One must be very powerful to have caused to be born spiders which spin webs to catch flies; but that is not to be omnipotent, infinitely powerful.

(7) If the great Being had been infinitely powerful, there is no reason why He should not have made sentient animals infinitely happy; He has not done so, therefore He was not able.

(8) All the sects of the philosophers have stranded on the reef of moral and physical ill. It only remains to avow that God having acted for the best has not been able to act better.

(9) This necessity settles all the difficulties and finishes all the disputes. We have not the impudence to say—"All is good." We say—"All is the least bad that is possible."

(10) Why does a child often die in its mother's womb? Why is another who has had the misfortune to be born, reserved for torments as long as his life, terminated by a frightful death?

Why has the source of life been poisoned all over the world since the discovery of America? why since the seventh century of our era does smallpox carry off the eighth part of the human race? why since all time have bladders been subject to being stone quarries? why the plague, war, famine, the inquisition? Turn in every direction, you will find no other solution than that everything has been necessary.

I speak here to philosophers only and not to theologians. We know well that faith is the thread in the labyrinth. We know that the fall of Adam and Eve, original sin, the immense power given to the devil, the predilection accorded by the great Being to the Jewish people, and the baptism substituted for the amputation of the prepuce, are the answers which explain everything. We have argued only against Zarathustra and not against the university of Conimbre or Coïmbre, to which we submit in our articles.

PRAYERS

We do not know any religion without prayers, even the Jews had some, although there was not among them any public form, until the time when they sang canticles in their synagogues, which happened very late.

161

All men, in their desires and their fears, invoked the aid of a deity. Some philosophers, more respectful to the Supreme Being, and less condescending to human frailty, for all prayer desired only resignation. It is indeed what seems proper as between creature and creator. But philosophy is not made to govern the world; she rises above the common herd; she speaks a language that the crowd cannot understand. It would be suggesting to fishwives that they should study conic sections.

Even among the philosophers, I do not believe that anyone apart from Maximus of Tyre has treated of this matter; this is the substance of Maximus' ideas.

The Eternal has His intentions from all eternity. If prayer accords with His immutable wishes, it is quite useless to ask of Him what He has resolved to do. If one prays Him to do the contrary of what He has resolved, it is praying Him to be weak, frivolous, inconstant; it is believing that He is thus, it is to mock Him. Either you ask Him a just thing; in this case He must do it, and the thing will be done without your praying Him for it; entreating Him is even to distrust Him: or the thing is unjust, and then you outrage Him. You are worthy or unworthy of the grace you implore: if worthy, He knows it better than you; if unworthy, you commit a crime the more in asking for what you do not deserve.

In a word, we pray to God only because we have made Him in our own image. We treat Him like a pasha, like a sultan whom one may provoke and appease.

In short, all nations pray to God: wise men resign themselves and obey Him.

Let us pray with the people, and resign ourselves with the wise men.

PRÉCIS OF ANCIENT PHILOSOPHY

I have spent nearly forty years of my pilgrimage in two or three corners of this world seeking the philosopher's stone that is called Truth. I have consulted all the adepts of antiquity, Epicurus and Augustine, Plato and Malebranche, and I have remained in my poverty. Maybe in all these philosophers' crucibles there are one or two ounces of gold; but all the rest is residue, dull mud, from which nothing can be born.

It seems to me that the Greeks our masters wrote much more to show their intelligence than that they used their intelligence in order to learn. I do not see a single author of antiquity who had a coherent system, a clear, methodical system progressing from consequence to consequence.

When I wanted to compare and combine the systems of Plato, of the preceptor of Alexander, of Pythagoras and of the Orientals, here, more or less, is what I was able to gather:

Chance is a word empty of sense; nothing can exist without a cause. The world is arranged according to mathematical laws; it is therefore arranged by an intelligence.

It is not an intelligent being such as I am, who directed the formation of this world, for I cannot form a mite; therefore this world is the work of a prodigiously superior intelligence.

Does this being, who possesses intelligence and power in so high a degree, exist necessarily? It must be so, for either the being received existence from another, or from its own nature. If the being received existence from another, which is very difficult to imagine, I must have recourse to this other, and this other will be the prime author. To whichever side I turn I have to admit a prime author, potent and intelligent, who is such necessarily by his own nature.

Did this prime author produce things out of nothing? that is not imaginable; to create out of nothing is to change nothing into something. I must not admit such a production unless I find invincible reasons which force me to admit what my intelligence can never comprehend.

All that exists appears to exist necessarily, since it exists. For if to-day there is a reason for the existence of things, there was one yesterday, there was one in all time; and this cause must always have had its effect, without which it would have been during eternity a useless cause.

But how shall things have always existed, being visibly under the hand of the prime author? This power therefore must always have acted; in the same way, nearly, that there is no sun without light, so there is no movement without a being that passes from one point of space to another point.

There is therefore a potent and intelligent being who has always acted; and if this being had never acted, of what use would his existence have been to him?

All things are therefore eternal emanations of this prime author.

But how imagine that stone and mud are emanations of the eternal Being, potent and intelligent?

Of two things one, either the matter of this stone and this mud exist necessarily by themselves, or they exist necessarily through this prime author; there is no middle course.

Thus, therefore, there are only two choices to make, admit either matter eternal by itself, or matter issuing eternally from the potent, intelligent eternal Being.

But, either subsisting by its own nature, or emanated from the producing Being, it exists from all eternity, because it exists, and there is no reason why it should not have existed before.

If matter is eternally necessary, it is therefore impossible, it is therefore contradictory that it does not exist; but what man can affirm that it is impossible, that it is contradictory that this pebble and this fly have not existence? One is, nevertheless, forced to suppress this difficulty which astonishes the imagination more than it contradicts the principles of reasoning.

In fact, as soon as you have imagined that everything has emanated from the supreme and intelligent Being, that nothing has emanated from the Being without reason, that this Being existing always, must always have acted, that consequently all things must have eternally issued from the womb of His existence, you should no more refuse to believe in the matter of which this pebble and this fly, an eternal production, are formed, than you refuse to imagine light as an eternal emanation from the omnipotent Being.

Since I am a being with extension and thought, my extension and my thought are therefore necessary productions of this Being. It is evident to me that I cannot give myself either extension or thought. I have therefore received both from this necessary Being.

Can He give me what He has not? I have intelligence and I am in space; therefore He is intelligent, and He is in space.

To say that this eternal Being, this omnipotent God, has from all time necessarily filled the universe with His productions, is not to deprive Him of His liberty; on the contrary, for liberty is only the power of acting. God has always acted to the full; therefore God has always made use of the fullness of His liberty.

The liberty that is called *liberty of indifference* is a phrase without idea, an absurdity; for it would be determination without reason; it would be an effect without a cause. Therefore, God cannot have this so-called liberty which is a contradiction in terms. He has therefore always acted through this same necessity which makes His existence.

It is therefore impossible for the world to be without God, it is impossible for God to be without the world.

This world is filled with beings who succeed each other, therefore God has always produced beings who succeed each other.

These preliminary assertions are the basis of the ancient Oriental philosophy and of that of the Greeks. One must except Democritus and Epicurus, whose corpuscular philosophy combated these dogmas. But let us remark that the Epicureans relied on an entirely erroneous natural philosophy, and that the metaphysical system of all the other philosophers holds good with all the systems of natural philosophy. The whole of nature, excepting the vacuum, contradicts Epicurus; and no phenomenon contradicts the philosophy which I have just explained. Well, is not a philosophy which is in accord with all that passes in nature, and which contents the most careful minds, superior to all other non-revealed systems?

After the assertions of the ancient philosophers, which I have reconciled as far as has been possible for me, what is left to us? a chaos of doubts and chimeras. I do not think that there has ever been a philosopher with a system who did not at the end of his life avow that he had wasted his time. It must be admitted that the inventors of the mechanical arts have been much more useful to mankind than the inventors of syllogisms: the man who invented the shuttle surpasses with a vengeance the man who imagined innate ideas.

PREJUDICES

Prejudice is an opinion without judgment. Thus all over the world do people inspire children with all the opinions they desire, before the children can judge.

There are some universal, necessary prejudices, which even make virtue. In all countries children are taught to recognize a rewarding and revenging God; to respect and love their father and their mother; to look on theft as a crime, selfish lying as a vice before they can guess what is a vice and what a virtue.

There are then some very good prejudices; they are those which are ratified by judgment when one reasons.

Sentiment is not a simple prejudice; it is something much stronger. A mother does not love her son because she has been told she must love him; she cherishes him happily in spite of herself. It is not through prejudice that you run to the help of an unknown child about to fall into a precipice, or be eaten by a beast.

But it is through prejudice that you will respect a man clad in certain clothes, walking gravely, speaking likewise. Your parents have told you that you should bow before this man; you respect him before knowing whether he merits your respect; you grow in years and in knowledge; you perceive that this man is a charlatan steeped in arrogance, self-interest and artifice; you despise what you revered, and the prejudice cedes to judgment. Through prejudice you have believed the fables with which your childhood was cradled; you have been told that the Titans made war on the gods, and Venus was amorous of Adonis; when you are twelve you accept these fables as truths; when you are twenty you look on them as ingenious allegories.

Let us examine briefly the different sorts of prejudices, so as to set our affairs in order. We shall be perhaps like those who, at the time of Law's system, perceived that they had calculated imaginary riches.

Prejudices of the Senses

Is it not strange that our eyes always deceive us, even when we have very good sight, and that on the contrary our ears do not deceive us? Let your well-informed ear hear "You are beautiful, I love you"; it is quite certain that someone has not said "I hate you, you are ugly": but you see a smooth mirror; it is demonstrated that you are mistaken, it has a very uneven surface. You see the sun as about two feet in diameter; it is demonstrated that it is a million times bigger than the earth.

It seems that God has put truth in your ears, and error in your eyes; but study optics, and you will see that God has not deceived you, and that it is impossible for objects to appear to you otherwise than you see them in the present state of things.

Physical Prejudices

The sun rises, the moon also, the earth is motionless: these are natural physical prejudices. But that lobsters are good for the blood, because when cooked they are red; that eels cure paralysis because they wriggle; that the moon affects our maladies because one day someone observed that a sick man had an increase of fever during the waning of the moon; these ideas and a thousand others are the errors of ancient charlatans who judged without reasoning, and who, being deceived, deceived others.

166

Historical Prejudices

Most historical stories have been believed without examination, and this belief is a prejudice. Fabius Pictor relates that many centuries before him, a vestal of the town of Alba, going to draw water in her pitcher, was ravished, that she gave birth to Romulus and Remus, that they were fed by a she-wolf, etc. The Roman people believed this fable; they did not examine whether at that time there were vestals in Latium, whether it were probable that a king's daughter would leave her convent with her pitcher, whether it were likely that a she-wolf would suckle two children instead of eating them; the prejudice established itself.

A monk writes that Clovis, being in great danger at the battle of Tolbiac, made a vow to turn Christian if he escaped; but is it natural to address oneself to a foreign god on such an occasion? is it not then that the religion in which one was born acts most potently? Which is the Christian who, in a battle against the Turks, will not address himself to the Holy Virgin rather than to Mohammed? It is added that a pigeon brought the holy phial in its beak to anoint Clovis, and that an angel brought the oriflamme to lead him; prejudice believed all the little stories of this kind. Those who understand human nature know well that Clovis the usurper and Rolon (or Rol) the usurper turned Christian in order to govern the Christians more surely, just as the Turkish usurpers turned Mussulman in order to govern the Mussulmans more surely.

Religious Prejudices

If your nurse has told you that Ceres rules over the crops, or that Vistnou and Xaca made themselves men several times, or that Sammonocodom came to cut down a forest, or that Odin awaits you in his hall near Jutland, or that Mohammed or somebody else made a journey into the sky; if lastly your tutor comes to drive into your brain what your nurse has imprinted on it you keep it for life. If your judgment wishes to rise against these prejudices, your neighbours and, above all, your neighbours' wives cry out "Impious reprobate," and dismay you; your dervish, fearing to see his income diminish, accuses you to the cadi, and this cadi has you impaled if he can, because he likes ruling over fools, and thinks that fools obey better than others: and that will last until your neighbours and the dervish and the cadi begin to understand that foolishness is good for nothing, and that persecution is abominable.

RARE

Rare in natural philosophy is the opposite of dense. In moral philosophy, it is the opposite of common.

This last variety of rare is what excites admiration. One never admires what is common, one enjoys it.

An eccentric thinks himself above the rest of wretched mortals when he has in his study a rare medal that is good for nothing, a rare book that nobody has the courage to read, an old engraving by Albrecht Durer, badly designed and badly printed: he triumphs if he has in his garden a stunted tree from America. This eccentric has no taste; he has only vanity. He has heard say that the beautiful is rare; but he should know that all that is rare is not beautiful.

Beauty is rare in all nature's works, and in all works of art.

Whatever ill things have been said of women, I maintain that it is rarer to find women perfectly beautiful than passibly good.

You will meet in the country ten thousand women attached to their homes, laborious, sober, feeding, rearing, teaching their children; and you will find barely one whom you could show at the theatres of Paris, London, Naples, or in the public gardens, and who would be looked on as a beauty.

Likewise, in works of art, you have ten thousand daubs and scrawls to one masterpiece.

If everything were beautiful and good, it is clear that one would no longer admire anything; one would enjoy. But would one have pleasure in enjoying? that is a big question.

Why have the beautiful passages in "The Cid," "The Horaces," "Cinna," had such a prodigious success? Because in the profound night in which people were plunged, they suddenly saw shine a new light that they did not expect. It was because this beauty was the rarest thing in the world.

The groves of Versailles were a beauty unique in the world, as were then certain passages of Corneille. St. Peter's, Rome, is unique.

But let us suppose that all the churches of Europe were equal to St. Peter's, Rome, that all statues were Venus dei Medici, that all tragedies were as beautiful as Racine's "Iphigénie", all works of poetry as well written as Boileau's "Art Poétique", all comedies as good as "Tartufe", and thus in every sphere; would you then have as much pleasure in enjoying masterpieces become common as they made you taste when they were rare? I say boldly "No!"; and I believe that the ancient school, which so rarely was right, was right when it said: *Ab assuetis non fit passio*, habit does not make passion.

But, my dear reader, will it be the same with the works of nature? Will you be disgusted if all the maids are so beautiful as Helen; and you, ladies, if all the lads are like Paris? Let us suppose that all wines are excellent, will you have less desire to drink? if the partridges, pheasants, pullets are common at all times, will you have less appetite? I say boldly again "No!", despite the axiom of the schools, "Habit does not make passion": and the reason, you know it, is that all the pleasures which nature gives us are always recurring needs, necessary enjoyments, and that the pleasures of the arts are not necessary. It is not necessary for a man to have groves where water gushes to a height of a hundred feet from the mouth of a marble face, and on leaving these groves to go to see a fine tragedy. But the two sexes are always necessary to each other. The table and the bed are necessities. The habit of being alternately on these two thrones will never disgust you.

In Paris a few years ago people admired a rhinoceros. If there were in one province ten thousand rhinoceroses, men would run after them only to kill them. But let there be a hundred thousand beautiful women men will always run after them to ... honour them.

REASON

At the time when all France was mad about Law's system, and Law was controller-general, there came to him in the presence of a great assembly a man who was always right, who always had reason on his side. Said he to Law:

"Sir, you are the biggest madman, the biggest fool, or the biggest rogue who has yet appeared among us; and that is saying a great deal: this is how I prove it. You have imagined that a state's wealth can be increased tenfold with paper; but as this paper can represent only the money that is representative of true wealth, the products of the land and industry, you should have begun by giving us ten times more corn, wine, cloth, canvas, etc. That is not enough, you must be sure of your market. But you make ten times as many notes as we have of silver and commodities, therefore you are ten times more extravagant, or more inept, or more of a rogue than all the comptrollers who have preceded you. This is how I prove my major."

Hardly had he started his major than he was conducted to Saint-Lazare.

169

When he came out of Saint-Lazare, where he studied much and strengthened his reason, he went to Rome; he asked for a public audience of the Pope, on condition that he was not interrupted in his harangue; and he spoke to the Pope in these terms:

"Holy Father, you are an antichrist and this is how I prove it to Your Holiness. I call antichrist the man who does the contrary to what Christ did and commanded. Now Christ was poor, and you are very rich; he paid tribute, and you exact tribute; he submitted to the powers that were, and you have become a power; he walked on foot, and you go to Castel-Gandolfo in a sumptuous equipage; he ate all that one was so good as to give him, and you want us to eat fish on Friday and Saturday, when we live far from sea and river; he forbade Simon Barjona to use a sword, and you have swords in your service, etc., etc., etc. Therefore in this sense Your Holiness is antichrist. In every other sense I hold you in great veneration, and I ask you for an indulgence *in articulo mortis.*"

My man was put in the Castello St. Angelo.

When he came out of the Castello St. Angelo, he rushed to Venice, and asked to speak to the doge.

"Your Serenity," he said, "must be a scatter-brain to marry the sea every year: for firstly, one only marries the same person once; secondly, your marriage resembles Harlequin's which was half made, seeing that it lacked but the consent of the bride; thirdly, who has told you that one day other maritime powers will not declare you incapable of consummating the marriage?"

He spoke, and was shut up in the Tower of St. Mark's.

When he came out of the Tower of St. Mark's, he went to Constantinople; he had audience of the mufti; and spoke to him in these terms:

"Your religion, although it has some good points, such as worship of the great Being, and the necessity of being just and charitable, is otherwise nothing but a rehash of Judaism and a tedious collection of fairy tales. If the archangel Gabriel had brought the leaves of the Koran to Mahomet from some planet, all Arabia would have seen Gabriel come down: nobody saw him; therefore Mahomet was a brazen impostor who deceived imbeciles."

Hardly had he pronounced these words than he was impaled. Nevertheless he had always been right, and had always had reason on his side.

RELIGION

I meditated last night; I was absorbed in the contemplation of nature; I admired the immensity, the course, the harmony of these infinite globes which the vulgar do not know how to admire.

I admired still more the intelligence which directs these vast forces. I said to myself: "One must be blind not to be dazzled by this spectacle; one must be stupid not to recognize the author of it; one must be mad not to worship Him. What tribute of worship should I render Him? Should not this tribute be the same in the whole of space, since it is the same supreme power which reigns equally in all space? Should not a thinking being who dwells in a star in the Milky Way offer Him the same homage as the thinking being on this little globe where we are? Light is uniform for the star Sirius and for us; moral philosophy must be uniform. If a sentient, thinking animal in Sirius is born of a tender father and mother who have been occupied with his happiness, he owes them as much love and care as we owe to our parents. If someone in the Milky Way sees a needy cripple, if he can relieve him and if he does not do it, he is guilty toward all globes. Everywhere the heart has the same duties: on the steps of the throne of God, if He has a throne; and in the depth of the abyss, if He is an abyss."

I was plunged in these ideas when one of those genii who fill the intermundane spaces came down to me. I recognized this same aerial creature who had appeared to me on another occasion to teach me how different God's judgments were from our own, and how a good action is preferable to a controversy.

He transported me into a desert all covered with piled up bones; and between these heaps of dead men there were walks of ever-green trees, and at the end of each walk a tall man of august mien, who regarded these sad remains with pity.

"Alas! my archangel," said I, "where have you brought me?"

"To desolation," he answered.

"And who are these fine patriarchs whom I see sad and motionless at the end of these green walks? they seem to be weeping over this countless crowd of dead."

"You shall know, poor human creature," answered the genius from the intermundane spaces; "but first of all you must weep."

He began with the first pile. "These," he said, "are the twenty-three thousand Jews who danced before a calf, with the twenty-four thousand who were killed while lying with Midianitish women. The number of those massacred for such errors and offences amounts to nearly three hundred thousand.

"In the other walks are the bones of the Christians slaughtered by each other for metaphysical disputes. They are divided into several heaps of four centuries each. One heap would have mounted right to the sky; they had to be divided."

"What!" I cried, "brothers have treated their brothers like this, and I have the misfortune to be of this brotherhood!"

"Here," said the spirit, "are the twelve million Americans killed in their fatherland because they had not been baptized."

"My God! why did you not leave these frightful bones to dry in the hemisphere where their bodies were born, and where they were consigned to so many different deaths? Why assemble here all these abominable monuments to barbarism and fanaticism?"

"To instruct you."

"Since you wish to instruct me," I said to the genius, "tell me if there have been peoples other than the Christians and the Jews in whom zeal and religion wretchedly transformed into fanaticism, have inspired so many horrible cruelties."

"Yes," he said. "The Mohammedans were sullied with the same inhumanities, but rarely; and when one asked *amman*, pity, of them and offered them tribute, they pardoned. As for the other nations there has not been one right from the existence of the world which has ever made a purely religious war. Follow me now." I followed him.

A little beyond these piles of dead men we found other piles; they were composed of sacks of gold and silver, and each had its label: *Substance of the heretics massacred in the eighteenth century, the seventeenth and the sixteenth.* And so on in going back: *Gold and silver of Americans slaughtered*, etc., etc. And all these piles were surmounted with crosses, mitres, croziers, triple crowns studded with precious stones.

"What, my genius! it was then to have these riches that these dead were piled up?"

"Yes, my son."

I wept; and when by my grief I had merited to be led to the end of the green walks, he led me there.

"Contemplate," he said, "the heroes of humanity who were the world's benefactors, and who were all united in banishing from the world, as far as they were able, violence and rapine. Question them."

I ran to the first of the band; he had a crown on his head, and a little censer in his hand; I humbly asked him his name. "I am Numa Pompilius," he said to me. "I succeeded a brigand, and I had brigands to govern: I taught them virtue and the worship of God; after me they forgot both more than once; I forbade that in the temples there should be any image, because the Deity which animates nature cannot be represented. During my reign the Romans had neither wars nor seditions, and my religion did nothing but good. All the neighbouring peoples came to honour me at my funeral: that happened to no one but me."

I kissed his hand, and I went to the second. He was a fine old man about a hundred years old, clad in a white robe. He put his middle-finger on his mouth, and with the other hand he cast some beans behind him. I recognized Pythagoras. He assured me he had never had a golden thigh, and that he had never been a cock; but that he had governed the Crotoniates with as much justice as Numa governed the Romans, almost at the same time; and that this justice was the rarest and most necessary thing in the world. I learned that the Pythagoreans examined their consciences twice a day. The honest people! how far we are from them! But we who have been nothing but assassins for thirteen hundred years, we say that these wise men were arrogant.

In order to please Pythagoras, I did not say a word to him and I passed to Zarathustra, who was occupied in concentrating the celestial fire in the focus of a concave mirror, in the middle of a hall with a hundred doors which all led to wisdom. (Zarathustra's precepts are called *doors*, and are a hundred in number.) Over the principal door I read these words which are the précis of all moral philosophy, and which cut short all the disputes of the casuists: "When in doubt if an action is good or bad, refrain."

"Certainly," I said to my genius, "the barbarians who immolated all these victims had never read these beautiful words."

We then saw the Zaleucus, the Thales, the Aniximanders, and all the sages who had sought truth and practised virtue.

When we came to Socrates, I recognized him very quickly by his flat nose. "Well," I said to him, "here you are then among the number of the Almighty's confidants! All the inhabitants of Europe, except the Turks and the Tartars of the Crimea, who know nothing, pronounce your name with respect. It is revered, loved, this great name, to the point that people have wanted to know those of your persecutors. Melitus and Anitus are known because of you, just as Ravaillac is known because of Henry IV.; but I know only this name of Anitus. I do not know precisely

173

who was the scoundrel who calumniated you, and who succeeded in having you condemned to take hemlock."

"Since my adventure," replied Socrates, "I have never thought about that man; but seeing that you make me remember it, I have much pity for him. He was a wicked priest who secretly conducted a business in hides, a trade reputed shameful among us. He sent his two children to my school. The other disciples taunted them with having a father who was a currier; they were obliged to leave. The irritated father had no rest until he had stirred up all the priests and all the sophists against me. They persuaded the counsel of the five hundred that I was an impious fellow who did not believe that the Moon, Mercury and Mars were gods. Indeed, I used to think, as I think now, that there is only one God, master of all nature. The judges handed me over to the poisoner of the republic; he cut short my life by a few days: I died peacefully at the age of seventy; and since that time I pass a happy life with all these great men whom you see, and of whom I am the least."

After enjoying some time in conversation with Socrates, I went forward with my guide into a grove situated above the thickets where all the sages of antiquity seemed to be tasting sweet repose.

I saw a man of gentle, simple countenance, who seemed to me to be about thirty-five years old. From afar he cast compassionate glances on these piles of whitened bones, across which I had had to pass to reach the sages' abode. I was astonished to find his feet swollen and bleeding, his hands likewise, his side pierced, and his ribs flayed with whip cuts. "Good Heavens!" I said to him, "is it possible for a just man, a sage, to be in this state? I have just seen one who was treated in a very hateful way, but there is no comparison between his torture and yours. Wicked priests and wicked judges poisoned him; is it by priests and judges that you have been so cruelly assassinated?"

He answered with much courtesy—"*Yes.*"

"And who were these monsters?"

"They were hypocrites."

"Ah! that says everything; I understand by this single word that they must have condemned you to death. Had you then proved to them, as Socrates did, that the Moon was not a goddess, and that Mercury was not a god?"

"No, these planets were not in question. My compatriots did not know at all what a planet is; they were all arrant ignoramuses. Their superstitions were quite different from those of the Greeks."

"You wanted to teach them a new religion, then?"

174

"Not at all; I said to them simply—'Love God with all your heart and your fellow-creature as yourself, for that is man's whole duty.' Judge if this precept is not as old as the universe; judge if I brought them a new religion. I did not stop telling them that I had come not to destroy the law but to fulfil it; I had observed all their rites; circumcised as they all were, baptized as were the most zealous among them, like them I paid the Corban; I observed the Passover as they did, eating standing up a lamb cooked with lettuces. I and my friends went to pray in the temple; my friends even frequented this temple after my death; in a word, I fulfilled all their laws without a single exception."

"What! these wretches could not even reproach you with swerving from their laws?"

"No, without a doubt."

"Why then did they put you in the condition in which I now see you?"

"What do you expect me to say! they were very arrogant and selfish. They saw that I knew them; they knew that I was making the citizens acquainted with them; they were the stronger; they took away my life: and people like them will always do as much, if they can, to whoever does them too much justice."

"But did you say nothing, do nothing that could serve them as a pretext?"

"To the wicked everything serves as pretext.

""Did you not say once that you were come not to send peace, but a sword?"

"It is a copyist's error; I told them that I sent peace and not a sword. I have never written anything; what I said can have been changed without evil intention."

"You therefore contributed in no way by your speeches, badly reported, badly interpreted, to these frightful piles of bones which I saw on my road in coming to consult you?"

"It is with horror only that I have seen those who have made themselves guilty of these murders."

"And these monuments of power and wealth, of pride and avarice, these treasures, these ornaments, these signs of grandeur, which I have seen piled up on the road while I was seeking wisdom, do they come from you?"

"That is impossible; I and my people lived in poverty and meanness: my grandeur was in virtue only."

175

I was about to beg him to be so good as to tell me just who he was. My guide warned me to do nothing of the sort. He told me that I was not made to understand these sublime mysteries. Only did I conjure him to tell me in what true religion consisted.

"Have I not already told you? Love God and your fellow-creature as yourself."

"What! if one loves God, one can eat meat on Friday?"

"I always ate what was given me; for I was too poor to give anyone food."

"In loving God, in being just, should one not be rather cautious not to confide all the adventures of one's life to an unknown man?"

"That was always my practice."

"Can I not, by doing good, dispense with making a pilgrimage to St. James of Compostella?"

"I have never been in that country."

"Is it necessary for me to imprison myself in a retreat with fools?"

"As for me, I always made little journeys from town to town."

"Is it necessary for me to take sides either for the Greek Church or the Latin?"

"When I was in the world I never made any difference between the Jew and the Samaritan."

"Well, if that is so, I take you for my only master." Then he made me a sign with his head which filled me with consolation. The vision disappeared, and a clear conscience stayed with me.

SECT

SECTION I

Every sect, in whatever sphere, is the rallying-point of doubt and error. Scotist, Thomist, Realist, Nominalist, Papist, Calvinist, Molinist, Jansenist, are only pseudonyms.

There are no sects in geometry; one does not speak of a Euclidian, an Archimedean.

When the truth is evident, it is impossible for parties and factions to arise. Never has there been a dispute as to whether there is daylight at noon.

The branch of astronomy which determines the course of the stars and the return of eclipses being once known, there is no more dispute among astronomers.

In England one does not say—"I am a Newtonian, a Lockian, a Halleyan." Why? Those who have read cannot refuse their assent to the truths taught by these three great men. The more Newton is revered, the less do people style themselves Newtonians; this word supposes that there are anti-Newtonians in England. Maybe we still have a few Cartesians in France; that is solely because Descartes' system is a tissue of erroneous and ridiculous imaginings.

It is likewise with the small number of truths of fact which are well established. The records of the Tower of London having been authentically gathered by Rymer, there are no Rymerians, because it occurs to no one to combat this collection. In it one finds neither contradictions, absurdities nor prodigies; nothing which revolts the reason, nothing, consequently, which sectarians strive to maintain or upset by absurd arguments. Everyone agrees, therefore, that Rymer's records are worthy of belief.

You are Mohammedan, therefore there are people who are not, therefore you might well be wrong.

What would be the true religion if Christianity did not exist? the religion in which there were no sects; the religion in which all minds were necessarily in agreement.

Well, to what dogma do all minds agree? to the worship of a God and to integrity. All the philosophers of the world who have had a religion have said in all time—"There is a God, and one must be just." There, then, is the universal religion established in all time and throughout mankind.

The point in which they all agree is therefore true, and the systems through which they differ are therefore false.

"My sect is the best," says a Brahmin to me. But, my friend, if your sect is good, it is necessary; for if it were not absolutely necessary you would admit to me that it was useless: if it is absolutely necessary, it is for all men; how then can it be that all men have not what is absolutely necessary to them? How is it possible for the rest of the world to laugh at you and your Brahma?

When Zarathustra, Hermes, Orpheus, Minos and all the great men say—"Let us worship God, and let us be just," nobody laughs; but everyone hisses the man who claims that one cannot please God unless when one dies one is holding a cow's tail, and the man who wants one to have the end of one's prepuce cut off, and the man who consecrates crocodiles and onions, and the man who attaches eternal salvation to the dead men's bones one carries under one's shirt, or to a plenary indulgence which one buys at Rome for two and a half sous.

Whence comes this universal competition in hisses and derision from one end of the world to the other? It is clear that the things at which everyone sneers are not of a very evident truth. What shall we say of one of Sejan's secretaries who dedicated to Petronius a bombastic book entitled—"The Truths of the Sibylline Oracles, Proved by the Facts"?

This secretary proves to you first that it was necessary for God to send on earth several sibyls one after the other; for He had no other means of teaching mankind. It is demonstrated that God spoke to these sibyls, for the word *sibyl* signifies *God's counsel*. They had to live a long time, for it is the very least that persons to whom God speaks should have this privilege. They were twelve in number, for this number is sacred. They had certainly predicted all the events in the world, for Tarquinius Superbus bought three of their Books from an old woman for a hundred crowns. "What incredulous fellow," adds the secretary, "will dare deny all these evident facts which happened in a corner before the whole world? Who can deny the fulfilment of their prophecies? Has not Virgil himself quoted the predictions of the sibyls? If we have not the first examples of the Sibylline Books, written at a time when people did not know how to read or write, have we not authentic copies? Impiety must be silent before such proofs." Thus did Houttevillus speak to Sejan. He hoped to have a position as augur which would be worth an income of fifty thousand francs, and he had nothing.[20]

"What my sect teaches is obscure, I admit it," says a fanatic; "and it is because of this obscurity that it must be believed; for the sect itself says it is full of obscurities. My sect is extravagant, therefore it is divine; for how should what appears so mad have been embraced by so many peoples, if it were not divine?" It is precisely like the Alcoran which the Sonnites say has an angel's face and an animal's snout; be not scandalized by the animal's snout, and worship the angel's face. Thus

---

[20] Reference to the Abbé Houtteville, author of a book entitled—"The Truth of the Christian Religion, Proved by the Facts."

speaks this insensate fellow. But a fanatic of another sect answers—"It is you who are the animal, and I who am the angel."

Well, who shall judge the suit? who shall decide between these two fanatics? The reasonable, impartial man learned in a knowledge that is not that of words; the man free from prejudice and lover of truth and justice; in short, the man who is not the foolish animal, and who does not think he is the angel.

SECTION II

Sect and *error* are synonymous. You are Peripatetic and I Platonician; we are therefore both wrong; for you combat Plato only because his fantasies have revolted you, and I am alienated from Aristotle only because it seems to me that he does not know what he is talking about. If one or the other had demonstrated the truth, there would be a sect no longer. To declare oneself for the opinion of the one or the other is to take sides in a civil war. There are no sects in mathematics, in experimental physics. A man who examines the relations between a cone and a sphere is not of the sect of Archimedes: he who sees that the square of the hypotenuse of a right-angled triangle is equal to the square of the two other sides is not of the sect of Pythagoras.

When you say that the blood circulates, that the air is heavy, that the sun's rays are pencils of seven refrangible rays, you are not either of the sect of Harvey, or the sect of Torricelli, or the sect of Newton; you agree merely with the truth demonstrated by them, and the entire universe will ever be of your opinion.

This is the character of truth; it is of all time; it is for all men; it has only to show itself to be recognized; one cannot argue against it. A long dispute signifies—"Both parties are wrong."

SELF-ESTEEM

Nicole in his "Essais de Morale," written after two or three thousand volumes of ethics ("Treatise on Charity," Chap. II), says that "by means of the wheels and gibbets which people establish in common are repressed the tyrannous thoughts and designs of each individual's self-esteem."

I shall not examine whether people have gibbets in common, as they have meadows and woods in common, and a common purse, and if one represses ideas with wheels; but it seems very strange to me that Nicole should take highway robbery and assassination for self-esteem. One should distinguish shades of difference a little better. The man who said that Nero had his mother assassinated through self-esteem, that Cartouche had much self-esteem, would not be expressing himself very correctly. Self-esteem is not wickedness, it is a sentiment that is natural to all men; it is much nearer vanity than crime.

A beggar in the suburbs of Madrid nobly begged charity; a passer-by says to him: "Are you not ashamed to practise this infamous calling when you are able to work?"

"Sir," answered the beggar, "I ask for money, not advice." And he turned on his heel with full Castillian dignity.

This gentleman was a proud beggar, his vanity was wounded by a trifle. He asked charity out of love for himself, and could not tolerate the reprimand out of further love for himself.

A missionary travelling in India met a fakir laden with chains, naked as a monkey, lying on his stomach, and having himself whipped for the sins of his compatriots, the Indians, who gave him a few farthings.

"What self-denial!" said one of the lookers-on.

"Self-denial!" answered the fakir. "Learn that I have myself flogged in this world in order to return it in another, when you will be horses and I horseman."

Those who have said that love of ourselves is the basis of all our opinions and all our actions, have therefore been quite right in India, Spain, and all the habitable world: and as one does not write to prove to men that they have faces, it is not necessary to prove to them that they have self-esteem. Self-esteem is the instrument of our conservation; it resembles the instrument of the perpetuity of the species: it is necessary, it is dear to us, it gives us pleasure, and it has to be hidden.

SOUL

SECTION I

This is a vague, indeterminate term, which expresses an unknown principle of known effects that we feel in us. The word *soul* corresponds to the Latin *anima*, to the Greek πνεῦμα, to the term of which all nations have made use to express what they did not understand any better than we do.

In the proper and literal sense of the Latin and the languages derived from Latin, it signifies *that which animates*. Thus people have spoken of the soul of men, of animals, sometimes of plants, to signify their principal of vegetation and life. In pronouncing this word, people have never had other than a confused idea, as when it is said in Genesis— "And the Lord God formed man of the dust of the ground, and breathed into his nostrils the breath of life; and man became a living soul; and the soul of animals is in the blood; and kill not my soul, etc."

Thus the soul was generally taken for the origin and the cause of life, for life itself. That is why all known nations long imagined that everything died with the body. If one can disentangle anything in the chaos of ancient histories, it seems that the Egyptians at least were the first to distinguish between the intelligence and the soul: and the Greeks learned from them to distinguish their νοῦς, their πνεῦμα, their σκιὰ. The Latins, following their example, distinguish *animus* and *anima*; and we, finally, have also had our *soul* and our *understanding*. But is that which is the principle of our life different from that which is the principle of our thoughts? is it the same being? Does that which directs us and gives us sensation and memory resemble that which is in animals the cause of digestion and the cause of their sensations and of their memory?

There is the eternal object of the disputes of mankind; I say eternal object; for not having any first notion from which we can descend in this examination, we can only rest for ever in a labyrinth of doubt and feeble conjecture.

We have not the smallest step where we may place a foot in order to reach the most superficial knowledge of what makes us live and of what makes us think. How should we have? we should have had to see life and thought enter a body. Does a father know how he has produced his son? does a mother how she conceived him? Has anyone ever been able to divine how he acts, how he wakes, how he sleeps? Does anyone know how his limbs obey his will? has anyone discovered by what art ideas are marked out in his brain and issue from it at his command? Frail automatons moved by the invisible hand which directs us on this stage of the world, which of us has been able to detect the wire which guides us?

We dare question whether the soul is "spirit" or "matter"; if it is created before us, if it issues from non-existence at our birth, if after animating us for one day on earth, it lives after us into eternity. These questions appear sublime; what are they? questions of blind men saying to other blind men—"What is light?"

When we want to learn something roughly about a piece of metal, we put it in a crucible in the fire. But have we a crucible in which to put the soul? "The soul is *spirit*," says one. But what is spirit? Assuredly no one has any idea; it is a word that is so void of sense that one is obliged to say what spirit is not, not being able to say what it is. "The soul is matter," says another. But what is matter? We know merely some of its appearances and some of its properties; and not one of these properties, not one of these appearances, seems to have the slightest connection with thought.

"Thought is something distinct from matter," say you. But what proof of it have you? Is it because matter is divisible and figurable, and thought is not? But who has told you that the first principles of matter are divisible and figurable? It is very probable that they are not; entire sects of philosophers maintain that the elements of matter have neither form nor extension. With a triumphant air you cry—"Thought is neither wood, nor stone, nor sand, nor metal, therefore thought does not belong to matter." Weak, reckless reasoners! gravitation is neither wood, nor sand, nor metal, nor stone; movement, vegetation, life are not these things either, and yet life, vegetation, movement, gravitation, are given to matter. To say that God cannot make matter think is to say the most insolently absurd thing that anyone has ever dared utter in the privileged schools of lunacy. We are not certain that God has treated matter like this; we are only certain that He can. But what matters all that has been said and all that will be said about the soul? what does it matter that it has been called entelechy, quintessence, flame, ether? that it has been thought universal, uncreated, transmigrant, etc.?

In these matters that are inaccessible to the reason, what do these romances of our uncertain imaginations matter? What does it matter that the Fathers of the first four centuries thought the soul corporeal? What does it matter that Tertullian, by a contradiction frequent in him, has decided that it is simultaneously corporeal, formed and simple? We have a thousand witnesses to ignorance, and not one that gives a glimmer of probability.

How then are we so bold as to assert what the soul is? We know certainly that we exist, that we feel, that we think. Do we want to take a step beyond? we fall into a shadowy abyss; and in this abyss we are still so madly reckless as to dispute whether this soul, of which we have not the least idea, was made before us or with us, and whether it perishes or is immortal.

The article SOUL, and all the articles of the nature of metaphysics, must start by a sincere submission to the incontrovertible dogmas of the Church. Revelation is worth more, without doubt, than the whole of philosophy. Systems exercise the mind, but faith illumines and guides it.

Do we not often pronounce words of which we have only a very confused idea, or even of which we have none at all? Is not the word *soul* an instance? When the clapper or valve of a bellows is out of order, and when air which is in the bellows leaves it by some unexpected opening in this valve, so that it is no longer compressed against the two blades, and is not thrust violently towards the hearth which it has to light, French servants say—"The soul of the bellows has burst." They know no more about it than that; and this question in no wise disturbs their peace of mind.

The gardener utters the phrase "the soul of the plants," and cultivates them very well without knowing what he means by this term.

The violin-maker poses, draws forward or back the "soul of a violin" beneath the bridge in the belly of the instrument; a puny piece of wood more or less gives the violin or takes away from it a harmonious soul.

We have many industries in which the workmen give the qualification of "soul" to their machines. Never does one hear them dispute about this word. Such is not the case with philosophers.

For us the word "soul" signifies generally that which animates. Our ancestors the Celts gave to their soul the name of *seel*, from which the English *soul*, and the German *seel*; and probably the ancient Teutons and the ancient Britons had no quarrels in their universities over this expression.

The Greeks distinguished three sorts of souls—ψυχὴ, which signified the sensitive soul, the soul of the senses; and that is why Love, child of Aphrodite, had so much passion for Psyche, and why Psyche loved him so tenderly: πνεῦμα, the breath which gives life and movement to the whole machine, and which we have translated by *spiritus*, spirit; vague word to which have been given a thousand different meanings: and finally voῦς, the intelligence.

We possessed therefore three souls, without having the least notion of any of them. St. Thomas Aquinas (Summation of St. Thomas. Lyons edition, 1738) admits these three souls as a peripatetic, and distinguishes each of these three souls in three parts. ψυχὴ was in the breast, πνεῦμα was distributed throughout the body, and voῦς was in the head. There has been no other philosophy in our schools up to our day, and woe betide any man who took one of these souls for the other.

In this chaos of ideas there was, nevertheless, a foundation. Men had noticed that in their passions of love, hate, anger, fear, their internal organs were stimulated to movement. The liver and the heart were the seat of the passions. If one thought deeply, one felt a strife in the organs of the head; therefore the intellectual soul was in the head. Without respiration no vegetation, no life; therefore the vegetative soul was in the breast which receives the breath of air.

When men saw in dreams their dead relatives or friends, they had to seek what had appeared to them. It was not the body which had been consumed on a funeral pyre, or swallowed up in the sea and eaten by

183

the fishes. It was, however, something, so they maintained; for they had seen it; the dead man had spoken; the dreamer had questioned him. Was it ψυχὴ, was it πνεῦμα, was it νοῦς, with whom one had conversed in the dream? One imagined a phantom, an airy figure: it was σκιὰ, it was δαίμων, a ghost from the shades, a little soul of air and fire, very unrestricted, which wandered I know not where.

Eventually, when one wanted to sift the matter, it became a constant that this soul was corporeal; and the whole of antiquity never had any other idea. At last came Plato who so subtilized this soul that it was doubtful if he did not separate it entirely from matter; but that was a problem that was never solved until faith came to enlighten us.

In vain do the materialists quote some of the fathers of the Church who did not express themselves with precision. St. Irenæus says (liv. v. chaps. vi and vii) that the soul is only the breath of life, that it is incorporeal only by comparison with the mortal body, and that it preserves the form of man so that it may be recognized.

In vain does Tertullian express himself like this—"The corporeality of the soul shines bright in the Gospel." (*Corporalitas animæ in ipso Evangelio relucescit*, De Anima, cap. vii.) For if the soul did not have a body, the image of the soul would not have the image of the body.

In vain does he record the vision of a holy woman who had seen a very shining soul, of the colour of air.

In vain does Tatien say expressly (*Oratio ad Græcos*, c. xxiii.)—"The soul of man is composed of many parts."

In vain is St. Hilarius quoted as saying in later times (St. Hilarius on St. Matthew)—"There is nothing created which is not corporeal, either in heaven, or on earth, or among the visible, or among the invisible: everything is formed of elements; and souls, whether they inhabit a body, or issue from it, have always a corporeal substance."

In vain does St. Ambrose, in the sixth century, say (On Abraham, liv. ii., ch. viii.)—"We recognize nothing but the material, except the venerable Trinity alone."

The body of the entire Church has decided that the soul is immaterial. These saints fell into an error at that time universal; they were men; but they were not mistaken over immortality, because that is clearly announced in the Gospels.

We have so evident a need of the decision of the infallible Church on these points of philosophy, that we have not indeed by ourselves any sufficient notion of what is called "pure spirit," and of what is named "matter." Pure spirit is an expression which gives us no idea; and we know matter only by a few phenomena. We know it so little that we call it "substance"; well, the word substance means "that which is under"; but what is under will be eternally hidden from us. What is *under* is the Creator's secret; and this secret of the Creator is everywhere. We do not know either how we receive life, or how we give it, or how we grow, or how we digest, or how we sleep, or how we think, or how we feel.

The great difficulty is to understand how a being, whoever he be, has thoughts.

SECTION II

The author of the article SOUL in the "Encyclopedia" (the Abbé Yvon) followed Jaquelot scrupulously; but Jaquelot teaches us nothing. He sets himself also against Locke, because the modest Locke said (liv. iv, ch. iii, para. vi.)—"We possibly shall never be able to know whether any mere material being thinks or no; it being impossible for us, by the contemplation of our own ideas without revelation, to discover whether Omnipotency has not given to some systems of matter, fitly disposed, a power to perceive and think, or else joined and fixed to matter, so disposed, a thinking immaterial substance: it being, in respect of our notions, not much more remote from our comprehension to conceive that God can, if he pleases, superadd to matter a faculty of thinking, than that he should superadd to it another substance with a faculty of thinking; since we know not wherein thinking consists, nor to what sort of substances the Almighty has been pleased to give that power which cannot be in any created being but merely by the good pleasure and bounty of the Creator, for I see no contradiction in it, that the first eternal thinking Being should, if he pleased, give to certain systems of created senseless matter, put together as he thinks fit, some degrees of sense, perception and thought."

Those are the words of a profound, religious and modest man.

We know what quarrels he had to undergo on account of this opinion which appeared bold, but which was in fact in him only a consequence of his conviction of the omnipotence of God and the weakness of man. He did not say that matter thought; but he said that we have not enough knowledge to demonstrate that it is impossible for God to add the gift of thought to the unknown being called "matter", after according it the gift of gravitation and the gift of movement, both of which are equally incomprehensible.

185

Locke was not assuredly the only one who had advanced this opinion; it was the opinion of all antiquity, who, regarding the soul as very unrestricted matter, affirmed consequently that matter could feel and think.

It was Gassendi's opinion, as may be seen in his objections to Descartes. "It is true," says Gassendi, "that you know what you think; but you are ignorant of what species of substance you are, you who think. Thus although the operation of thought is known to you, the principle of your essence is hidden from you; and you do not know what is the nature of this substance, one of the operations of which is to think. You are like a blind man who, feeling the heat of the sun and being informed that it is caused by the heat of the sun, thinks he has a clear and distinct idea of this luminary; because if he were asked what the sun was, he could reply that it is a thing which heats, etc."

The same Gassendi, in his "Epicurean Philosophy," repeats several times that there is no mathematical evidence of the pure spirituality of the soul.

Descartes, in one of his letters to the Palatine Princess Elisabeth, says to her—"I confess that by the natural reason alone we can make many conjectures on the soul, and have gratifying hopes, but no certainty." And in that sentence Descartes combats in his letters what he puts forward in his works; a too ordinary contradiction.

In fine we have seen that all the Fathers of the first centuries of the Church, while believing the soul immortal, believed it at the same time material; they thought that it is as easy for God to conserve as to create. They said—"God made the soul thinking, He will preserve it thinking."

Malebranche has proved very well that we have no idea by ourselves, and that objects are incapable of giving us ideas: from that he concludes that we see everything in God. That is at the bottom the same thing as making God the author of all our ideas; for with what should we see in Him, if we had not instruments for seeing? and these instruments, it is He alone who holds them and guides them. This system is a labyrinth, one lane of which would lead you to Spinozism, another to Stoicism, another to chaos.

When one has had a good argument about spirit and matter, one always finishes by not understanding each other. No philosopher has been able with his own strength to lift this veil stretched by nature over all the first principles of things. Men argue, nature acts.

SECTION III

Of the Soul of Animals, and of some Empty Ideas

Before the strange system which supposes animals to be pure machines without any sensation, men had never thought that the beasts possessed an immaterial soul; and nobody had pushed recklessness to the point of saying that an oyster has a spiritual soul. Everyone concurred peaceably in agreeing that the beasts had received from God feeling, memory, ideas, and no pure spirit. Nobody had abused the gift of reason to the point of saying that nature had given the beasts all the organs of feeling so that they might not feel anything. Nobody had said that they cry when they are wounded, and that they fly when pursued, without experiencing pain or fear.

At that time people did not deny the omnipotence of God; He had been able to communicate to the organized matter of animals pleasure, pain, remembrance, the combination of a few ideas; He had been able to give to several of them, such as the monkey, the elephant, the hunting-dog, the talent of perfecting themselves in the arts which were taught to them; not only had He been able to endow nearly all carnivorous animals with the talent of warring better in their experienced old age than in their too trustful youth; not only, I say, had He been able to do these things, but He had done them: the universe bore witness thereto.

Pereira and Descartes maintained that the universe was mistaken, that God was a juggler, that He had given animals all the instruments of life and sensation, so that they might have neither life nor sensation, properly speaking. But I do not know what so-called philosophers, in order to answer Descartes' chimera, leaped into the opposite chimera; they gave liberally of pure spirit to the toads and the insects.

Between these two madnesses, the one refusing feeling to the organs of feeling, the other lodging a pure spirit in a bug, somebody thought of a middle path. It was instinct. And what is instinct? Oh, oh, it is a substantial form; it is a plastic form; it is I do not know what! it is instinct. I shall be of your opinion so long as you will call the majority of things, "I do not know what"; so long as your philosophy begins and ends with "I do not know what", I shall quote Prior to you in his poem on the vanity of the world.

The author of the article SOUL in the "Encyclopedia" explains himself like this:—"I picture the animals' soul as an immaterial and intelligent substance, but of what species? It must, it seems to me, be an active principle which has sensations, and which has only that.... If we reflect on the nature of the soul of animals, it supplies us with groundwork which might lead us to think that its spirituality will save it from annihilation."

I do not know how one pictures an immaterial substance. To picture something is to make an image of it; and up till now nobody has been able to paint the spirit. For the word "picture", I want the author to understand "I conceive"; speaking for myself, I confess I do not conceive it. I confess still less that a spiritual soul may be annihilated, because I do not conceive either creation or non-existence; because I have never been present at God's council; because I know nothing at all about the principle of things.

If I wish to prove that the soul is a real being, someone stops me by telling me that it is a faculty. If I assert that it is a faculty, and that I have the faculty of thinking, I am told that I am mistaken; that God, the eternal master of all nature, does everything in me, and directs all my actions and all my thoughts; that if I produced my thoughts, I should know the thought I will have in a minute; that I never know it; that I am only an automaton with sensations and ideas, necessarily dependent, and in the hands of the Supreme Being, infinitely more compliant to Him than clay is to the potter.

I confess my ignorance, therefore; I avow that four thousand tomes of metaphysics will not teach us what our soul is.

An orthodox philosopher said to a heterodox philosopher—"How have you been able to come to the point of imagining that the soul is mortal by nature, and eternal only by the pure wish of God?"

"By my own experience," said the other.

"How! are you dead?"

"Yes, very often. I suffered from epilepsy in my youth, and I assure you that I was completely dead for several hours. No sensation, no remembrance even of the moment that I fell ill. The same thing happens to me now nearly every night. I never feel the precise moment that I go to sleep; my sleep is absolutely dreamless. I cannot imagine by conjecture how long I have slept. I am dead regularly six hours out of the twenty-four. That is a quarter of my life."

The orthodox then asserted that he always thought during his sleep without knowing anything about it. The heterodox answered him—"I believe through revelation that I shall always think in the other life; but I assure you I think rarely in this one."

The orthodox was not mistaken in asserting the immortality of the soul, for faith and reason demonstrate this truth; but he might be mistaken in asserting that a sleeping man always thinks.

Locke admitted frankly that he did not always think while he was asleep: another philosopher has said—"Thought is characteristic of man; but it is not his essence."

Let us leave to each man the liberty and consolation of seeking himself, and of losing himself in his ideas.

It is good, however, to know, that in 1730 a philosopher[21] suffered a severe enough persecution for having confessed, with Locke, that his understanding was not exercised at every moment of the day and night, just as he did not use his arms and his legs at all moments. Not only did court ignorance persecute him, but the malignant influence of a few so-called men of letters was let loose against him. What in England had produced merely a few philosophical disputes, produced in France the most cowardly atrocities; a Frenchman suffered by Locke.

There have always been in the mud of our literature more than one of these miscreants who have sold their pens, and intrigued against their benefactors even. This remark is rather foreign to the article SOUL; but should one miss an opportunity of dismaying those who make themselves unworthy of the name of men of letters, who prostitute the little mind and conscience they have to a vile self-interest, to a fantastic policy, who betray their friends to flatter fools, who in secret powder the hemlock which the powerful and malicious ignoramus wants to make useful citizens drink?

In short, while we worship God with all our soul, let us confess always our profound ignorance of this soul, of this faculty of feeling and thinking which we possess from His infinite goodness. Let us avow that our feeble reasonings can take nothing away from, or add anything to revelation and faith. Let us conclude in fine that we should use this intelligence, the nature of which is unknown, for perfecting the sciences which are the object of the "Encyclopedia"; just as watchmakers use springs in their watches, without knowing what a spring is.

SECTION IV

About the Soul, and About our Little Knowledge

On the testimony of our acquired knowledge, we have dared question whether the soul is created before us, whether it comes from non-existence into our body? at what age it came to settle between a bladder and the intestines *cæcum* and *rectum*? if it brought ideas with it or received them there, and what are these ideas? if after animating us for a few moments, its essence is to live after us into eternity without the intervention of God Himself? if being spirit, and God being spirit,

---

[21] Voltaire himself.

they are both of like nature? These questions seem sublime; what are they? questions about light by men born blind.

What have all the philosophers, ancient and modern, taught us? a child is wiser than they are; he does not think about things of which he can form no conception.

You will say that it is sad for our insatiable curiosity, for our inexhaustible thirst for happiness, to be thus ignorant of ourselves! I agree, and there are still sadder things; but I shall answer you:

Sors tua mortalis, non est mortale quod optas.
—Ovid, Met. II. 56

"You have a man's fate, and a god's desires."

Once again, it seems that the nature of every principle of things is the Creator's secret. How does the air carry sound? how are animals formed? how do some of our limbs constantly obey our wills? what hand puts ideas in our memory, keeps them there as in a register, and pulls them out sometimes when we want them and sometimes in spite of ourselves? Our nature, the nature of the universe, the nature of the least plant, everything for us is sunk in a shadowy pit.

Man is an acting, feeling, thinking being: that is all we know of him: it is not given to us to know what makes us feel and think, or what makes us act, or what makes us exist. The acting faculty is as incomprehensible for us as the thinking faculty. The difficulty is less to conceive how a body of mud has feelings and ideas, than to conceive how a being, whatever it be, has ideas and feelings.

Here on one side the soul of Archimedes, on the other the soul of an idiot; are they of the same nature? If their essence is to think, they think always, and independently of the body which cannot act without them. If they think by their own nature, can the species of a soul which cannot do a sum in arithmetic be the same as that which measured the heavens? If it is the organs of the body which made Archimedes think, why is it that my idiot, who has a stronger constitution than Archimedes, who is more vigorous, digests better and performs all his functions better, does not think at all? It is, you say, because his brain is not so good. But you are making a supposition; you do not know at all. No difference has ever been found between healthy brains that have been dissected. It is even very probable that a fool's cerebellum will be in better condition than Archimedes', which has worked prodigiously, and which might be worn out and shrivelled.

Let us conclude therefore what we have already concluded, that we are ignoramuses about all first principles. As regards ignoramuses who pride themselves on their knowledge, they are far inferior to monkeys.

Now dispute, choleric arguers: present your petitions against each other; proffer your insults, pronounce your sentences, you who do not know one word about the matter.

SECTION V

Of Warburton's Paradox on the Immortality of the Soul

Warburton, editor and commentator of Shakespeare and Bishop of Gloucester, making use of English freedom, and abuse of the custom of hurling insults at one's adversaries, has composed four volumes to prove that the immortality of the soul was never announced in the Pentateuch, and to conclude from this same proof that Moses' mission is divine. Here is the précis of his book, which he himself gives, pages 7 and 8 of the first volume.

"1. The doctrine of a life to come, of rewards and punishments after death, is necessary to all civil society.

"2. The whole human race (*and this is where he is mistaken*), and especially the wisest and most learned nations of antiquity, concurred in believing and teaching this doctrine.

"3. It cannot be found in any passage of the law of Moses; therefore the law of Moses is of divine origin. Which I am going to prove by the two following syllogisms:

First Syllogism

"Every religion, every society that has not the immortality of the soul for its basis, can be maintained only by an extraordinary providence; the Jewish religion had not the immortality of the soul for basis; therefore the Jewish religion was maintained by an extraordinary providence.

Second Syllogism

"All the ancient legislators have said that a religion which did not teach the immortality of the soul could not be maintained but by an extraordinary providence; Moses founded a religion which is not founded on the immortality of the soul; therefore Moses believed his religion maintained by an extraordinary providence."

What is much more extraordinary is this assertion of Warburton's, which he has put in big letters at the beginning of his book. He has

191

often been reproached with the extreme rashness and bad faith with which he dares to say that all the ancient legislators believed that a religion which is not founded on pains and recompenses after death, can be maintained only by an extraordinary providence; not one of them ever said it. He does not undertake even to give any example in his huge book stuffed with a vast number of quotations, all of which are foreign to his subject. He has buried himself beneath a pile of Greek and Latin authors, ancient and modern, for fear one might see through him on the other side of a horrible multitude of envelopes. When criticism finally probed to the bottom, he was resurrected from among all these dead men in order to load all his adversaries with insults.

It is true that towards the end of his fourth volume, after having walked through a hundred labyrinths, and having fought with everybody he met on the road, he comes at last to his great question which he had left there. He lays all the blame on the Book of Job which passes among scholars for an Arab work, and he tries to prove that Job did not believe in the immortality of the soul. Later he explains in his own way all the texts of Holy Writ by which people have tried to combat this opinion.

All one can say about it is that, if he was right, it was not for a bishop to be right in such a way. He should have felt that one might draw dangerous inferences; but everything in this world is a mass of contradiction. This man, who became accuser and persecutor, was not made bishop by a minister of state's patronage until immediately after he had written his book.

At Salamanca, Coimbre or Rome, he would have been obliged to recant and to ask pardon. In England he became a peer of the realm with an income of a hundred thousand *livres*; it was enough to modify his methods.

SECTION VI

Of the Need of Revelation

The greatest benefit we owe to the New Testament is that it has revealed to us the immortality of the soul. It is in vain, therefore, that this fellow Warburton tried to cloud over this important truth, by continually representing in his legation of Moses that "the ancient Jews knew nothing of this necessary dogma, and that the Sadducees did not admit it in the time of our Lord Jesus."

He interprets in his own way the very words that have been put into Jesus Christ's mouth: "... have ye not read that which was spoken unto you by God, saying, I am the God of Abraham, and the God of Isaac, and the God of Jacob? God is not the God of the dead, but of the living"

(St. Matt. xxii. 31, 32). He gives to the parable of the wicked rich man a sense contrary to that of all the Churches. Sherlock, Bishop of London, and twenty other scholars refuted him. English philosophers even reproached him with the scandal of an Anglican bishop manifesting an opinion so contrary to the Anglican Church; and after that, this man takes it into his head to treat these persons as impious: like the character of *Arlequin* in the comedy of the *Dévaliseur de maisons*, who, after throwing the furniture out of the window, sees a man carrying some of it off, and cries with all his might "Stop thief!"

One should bless the revelation of the immortality of the soul, and of rewards and punishments after death, all the more that mankind's vain philosophy has always been sceptical of it. The great Cæsar did not believe in it at all, he made himself quite clear in full senate when, in order to stop Catalina being put to death, he represented that death left man without sensation, that everything died with him; and nobody refuted this view.

The Roman Empire was divided between two principal sects: that of Epicurus which asserted that deity was useless to the world, and that the soul perished with the body: and that of the Stoics who regarded the soul as part of the Deity, which after death was joined again to its origin, to the great everything from which it emanated. Thus, whether one believed the soul mortal, or whether one believed it immortal, all the sects were agreed in laughing at pains and punishments after death.

We still have a hundred monuments of this belief of the Romans. It is by virtue of this opinion graved profoundly in their hearts, that so many simple Roman citizens killed themselves without the least scruple; they did not wait for a tyrant to hand them over to the executioners.

The most virtuous men even, and those most persuaded of the existence of a God, hoped for no reward, and feared no punishment. Clement, who later was Pope and saint, began by himself doubting what the early Christians said of another life, and consulted St. Peter at Cæsarea. We are far from believing that St. Clement wrote the history that is attributed to him; but this history makes evident the need the human race had of a precise revelation. All that can surprise us is that so repressive and salutary a doctrine has left a prey to so many horrible crimes men who have so little time to live, and who see themselves squeezed between two eternities.

SECTION VII

Souls of Fools and Monsters

A deformed child is born absolutely imbecile, it has no ideas and lives without ideas; we have seen examples of this. How shall this animal be defined? doctors have said that it is something between man and beast; others have said that it had a sensitive soul, but not an intellectual soul. It eats, drinks, sleeps, wakes, has sensations; but it does not think.

Is there another life for this creature, or is there none? The question has been posed, and has not yet been completely answered.

Some say that this creature must have a soul, because its father and mother had one. But by this reasoning one would prove that if it came into the world without a nose it would be deemed to have one, because its father and its mother had noses.

A woman gives birth to child with no chin, its forehead is receding and rather black, its nose is slim and pointed, its eyes are round, it bears not a bad resemblance to a swallow; the rest of its body, nevertheless, is made like ours. The parents have it baptised; by a plurality of votes it is considered a man and possessor of an immortal soul. But if this ridiculous little figure has pointed nails and beak-like mouth, it is declared a monster, it has no soul, and is not baptised.

It is well known that in London in 1726 there was a woman who gave birth every week to a rabbit. No difficulty was made about refusing baptism to this child, despite the epidemic mania there was for three weeks in London for believing that this poor rogue was making wild rabbits. The surgeon who attended her, St. André by name, swore that nothing was more true, and people believed him. But what reason did the credulous have for refusing a soul to this woman's children? she had a soul, her children should be provided with souls also; whether they had hands, whether they had paws, whether they were born with a little snout or with a face; cannot the Supreme Being bestow the gift of thought and sensation on a little I know not what, born of a woman, shaped like a rabbit, as well as to a little I know not what, shaped like a man? Shall the soul that was ready to lodge in this woman's fœtus go back again into space?

Locke makes the sound observation, about monsters, that one must not attribute immortality to the exterior of a body; that the form has nothing to do with it. This immortality, he says, is no more attached to the form of his face or his chest, than to the way his beard is dressed or his coat cut.

He asks what is the exact measure of deformity by which you can recognize whether or no a child has a soul? What is the precise degree at which it must be declared a monster and deprived of a soul?

One asks still further what would be a soul which never has any but fantastic ideas? there are some which never escape from them. Are they worthy or unworthy? what is to be done with their pure spirit?

What is one to think of a child with two heads? without deformity apart from this? Some say that it has two souls because it is provided with two pineal glands, with two *corpus callosum*, with two *sensorium commune*. Others reply that one cannot have two souls when one has only one chest and one navel.[22]

In fine, so many questions have been asked about this poor human soul, that if it were necessary to answer them all, this examination of its own person would cause it the most intolerable boredom. There would happen to it what happened to Cardinal de Polignac at a conclave. His steward, tired of never being able to make him settle his accounts, made the journey from Rome, and came to the little window of his cell burdened with an immense bundle of papers. He read for nearly two hours. At last, seeing that no reply was forthcoming, he put his head forward. The cardinal had departed nearly two hours before. Our souls will depart before their stewards have acquainted them with the facts: but let us be exact before God, whatever sort of ignoramuses we are, we and our stewards.

STATES, GOVERNMENTS

The ins and outs of all governments have been closely examined recently. Tell me then, you who have travelled, in what state, under what sort of government you would choose to be born. I imagine that a great land-owning lord in France would not be vexed to be born in Germany; he would be sovereign instead of subject. A peer of France would be very glad to have the privileges of the English peerage; he would be legislator. The lawyer and the financier would be better off in France than elsewhere.

---

[22] The Chevalier d'Angos, learned astronomer, has carefully observed a two-headed lizard for several days; and he has assured himself that the lizard had two independent wills, each of which had an almost equal power over the body. When the lizard was given a piece of bread, in such a way that it could see it with only one head, this head wanted to go after the bread, and the other wanted the body to remain at rest.

But what country would a wise, free man, a man with a moderate fortune, and without prejudices, choose?

A member of the government of Pondicherry, a learned man enough, returned to Europe by land with a Brahmin better educated than the ordinary Brahmin. "What do you think of the government of the Great Mogul?" asked the councillor.

"I think it abominable," answered the Brahmin. "How can you expect a state to be happily governed by the Tartars? Our rajahs, our omrahs, our nabobs, are very content, but the citizens are hardly so; and millions of citizens are something."

Reasoning, the councillor and the Brahmin traversed the whole of Upper Asia. "I make the observation," said the Brahmin, "that there is not one republic in all this vast part of the world."

"Formerly there was the republic of Tyre," said the councillor, "but it did not last long; there was still another one in the direction of Arabia Petrea, in a little corner called Palestine, if one can honour with the name of republic a horde of thieves and usurers sometimes governed by judges, sometimes by a species of kings, sometimes by grand-pontiffs, become slave seven or eight times, and finally driven out of the country which it had usurped."

"I imagine," said the Brahmin, "that one ought to find very few republics on the earth. Men are rarely worthy of governing themselves. This happiness should belong only to little peoples who hide themselves in islands, or among the mountains, like rabbits who shun carnivorous beasts; but in the long run they are discovered and devoured."

When the two travellers reached Asia Minor, the councillor said to the Brahmin: "Would you believe that a republic was formed in a corner of Italy, which lasted more than five hundred years, and which owned Asia Minor, Asia, Africa, Greece, Gaul, Spain and the whole of Italy?"

"She soon became a monarchy, then," said the Brahmin.

"You have guessed right," said the other. "But this monarchy fell, and every day we compose beautiful dissertations in order to find the cause of its decadence and downfall."

"You take a deal of trouble," said the Indian. "This empire fell because it existed. Everything has to fall. I hope as much will happen to the Grand Mogul's empire."

"By the way," said the European, "do you consider that there should be more honour in a despotic state, and more virtue in a republic?"

The Indian, having had explained to him what we mean by honour, answered that honour was more necessary in a republic, and that one had more need of virtue in a monarchical state. "For," said he, "a man who claims to be elected by the people, will not be if he is dishonoured; whereas at the court he could easily obtain a place, in accordance with a great prince's maxim, that in order to succeed a courtier should have neither honour nor character. As regards virtue, one must be prodigiously virtuous to dare to say the truth. The virtuous man is much more at his ease in a republic; he has no one to flatter."

"Do you think," said the man from Europe, "that laws and religions are made for climates, just as one has to have furs in Moscow, and gauzy stuffs in Delhi?"

"Without a doubt," answered the Brahmin. "All the laws which concern material things are calculated for the meridian one lives in. A German needs only one wife, and a Persian three or four.

"The rites of religion are of the same nature. How, if I were Christian, should I say mass in my province where there is neither bread nor wine? As regards dogmas, that is another matter; the climate has nothing to do with them. Did not your religion begin in Asia, whence it was driven out? does it not exist near the Baltic Sea, where it was unknown?"

"In what state, under what domination, would you like best to live?" asked the councillor.

"Anywhere but where I do live," answered his companion. "And I have met many Siamese, Tonkinese, Persians and Turks who said as much."

"But, once again," persisted the European, "what state would you choose?"

The Brahmin answered: "The state where only the laws are obeyed."

"That is an old answer," said the councillor.

"It is none the worse for that," said the Brahmin.

"Where is that country?" asked the councillor.

"We must look for it," answered the Brahmin.

SUPERSTITION

The superstitious man is to the rogue what the slave is to the tyrant. Further, the superstitious man is governed by the fanatic and becomes fanatic. Superstition born in Paganism, adopted by Judaism, infested the Christian Church from the earliest times. All the fathers of the Church, without exception, believed in the power of magic. The Church always condemned magic, but she always believed in it: she did not excommunicate sorcerers as madmen who were mistaken, but as men who were really in communication with the devil.

To-day one half of Europe thinks that the other half has long been and still is superstitious. The Protestants regard the relics, the indulgences, the mortifications, the prayers for the dead, the holy water, and almost all the rites of the Roman Church, as a superstitious dementia. Superstition, according to them, consists in taking useless practices for necessary practices. Among the Roman Catholics there are some more enlightened than their ancestors, who have renounced many of these usages formerly considered sacred; and they defend themselves against the others who have retained them, by saying: "They are indifferent, and what is merely indifferent cannot be an evil."

It is difficult to mark the limits of superstition. A Frenchman travelling in Italy finds almost everything superstitious, and is hardly mistaken. The Archbishop of Canterbury maintains that the Archbishop of Paris is superstitious; the Presbyterians make the same reproach against His Grace of Canterbury, and are in their turn treated as superstitious by the Quakers, who are the most superstitious of all in the eyes of other Christians.

In Christian societies, therefore, no one agrees as to what superstition is. The sect which seems to be the least attacked by this malady of the intelligence is that which has the fewest rites. But if with few ceremonies it is still strongly attached to an absurd belief, this absurd belief is equivalent alone to all the superstitious practices observed from the time of Simon the magician to that of Father Gauffridi.

It is therefore clear that it is the fundamentals of the religion of one sect which is considered as superstition by another sect.

The Moslems accuse all Christian societies of it, and are themselves accused. Who will judge this great matter? Will it be reason? But each sect claims to have reason on its side. It will therefore be force which will judge, while awaiting the time when reason will penetrate a sufficient number of heads to disarm force.

Up to what point does statecraft permit superstition to be destroyed? This is a very thorny question; it is like asking up to what point one should make an incision in a dropsical person, who may die under the operation. It is a matter for the doctor's discretion.

Can there exist a people free from all superstitious prejudices? That is to ask—Can there exist a nation of philosophers? It is said that there is no superstition in the magistrature of China. It is probable that none will remain in the magistrature of a few towns of Europe.

Then the magistrates will stop the superstition of the people from being dangerous. These magistrates' example will not enlighten the mob, but the principal persons of the middle-classes will hold the mob in check. There is not perhaps a single riot, a single religious outrage in which the middle-classes were not formerly imbrued, because these middle classes were then the mob; but reason and time will have changed them. Their softened manners will soften those of the lowest and most savage populace; it is a thing of which we have striking examples in more than one country. In a word, less superstition, less fanaticism; and less fanaticism, less misery.

TEARS

Tears are the mute language of sorrow. But why? What connection is there between a sad idea and this limpid, salt liquid, filtered through a little gland at the external corner of the eye, which moistens the conjunctiva and the small lachrymal points, whence it descends into the nose and mouth through the reservoir called the lachrymal sack and its ducts?

Why in women and children, whose organs are part of a frail and delicate network, are tears more easily excited by sorrow than in grown men, whose tissue is firmer?

Did nature wish compassion to be born in us at sight of these tears which soften us, and lead us to help those who shed them? The woman of a savage race is as firmly determined to help the child that cries as would be a woman of the court, and maybe more, because she has fewer distractions and passions.

In the animal body everything has an object without a doubt. The eyes especially bear such evident, such proven, such admirable relation to the rays of light; this mechanism is so divine, that I should be tempted to take for a delirium of burning fever the audacity which denies the final causes of the structure of our eyes.

The use of tears does not seem to have so well determined and striking an object; but it would be beautiful that nature made them flow in order to stir us to pity.

There are women who are accused of weeping when they wish. I am not at all surprised at their talent. A live, sensitive, tender imagination can fix itself on some object, on some sorrowful memory, and picture it in such dominating colours that they wring tears from it. It is what happens to many actors, and principally to actresses, on the stage.

The women who imitate them in their own homes add to this talent the petty fraud of appearing to weep for their husbands, whereas in fact they are weeping for their lovers. Their tears are true, but the object of them is false.

One asks why the same man who has watched the most atrocious events dry-eyed, who even has committed cold-blooded crimes, will weep at the theatre at the representation of these events and crimes? It is that he does not see them with the same eyes, he sees them with the eyes of the author and the actor. He is no longer the same man; he was a barbarian, he was agitated by furious passions when he saw an innocent woman killed, when he stained himself with his friend's blood. His soul was filled with stormy tumult; it is tranquil, it is empty; nature returns to it; he sheds virtuous tears. That is the true merit, the great good of the theatres; there is achieved what can never be achieved by the frigid declamations of an orator paid to bore the whole of an audience for an hour.

David the capitoul, who, without emotion, caused and saw the death of innocent Calas on the wheel, would have shed tears at the sight of his own crime in a well-written and well-spoken tragedy.

It is thus that Pope has said in the prologue to Addison's Cato:—

"Tyrants no more their savage nature kept;
And foes to virtue wondered how they wept."

THEIST

The theist is a man firmly persuaded of the existence of a Supreme Being as good as He is powerful, who has formed all beings with extension, vegetating, sentient and reflecting; who perpetuates their species, who punishes crimes without cruelty, and rewards virtuous actions with kindness.

The theist does not know how God punishes, how he protects, how he pardons, for he is not reckless enough to flatter himself that he knows how God acts, but he knows that God acts and that He is just. Difficulties against Providence do not shake him in his faith, because they are merely great difficulties, and not proofs. He submits to this Providence, although he perceives but a few effects and a few signs of this Providence: and, judging of the things he does not see by the things he sees, he considers that this Providence reaches all places and all centuries.

Reconciled in this principle with the rest of the universe, he does not embrace any of the sects, all of which contradict each other; his religion is the most ancient and the most widespread; for the simple worship of a God has preceded all the systems of the world. He speaks a language that all peoples understand, while they do not understand one another. He has brothers from Pekin to Cayenne, and he counts all wise men as his brethren. He believes that religion does not consist either in the opinions of an unintelligible metaphysic, or in vain display, but in worship and justice. The doing of good, there is his service; being submissive to God, there is his doctrine. The Mahometan cries to him— "Have a care if you do not make the pilgrimage to Mecca!" "Woe unto you," says a Recollet, "if you do not make a journey to Notre-Dame de Lorette!" He laughs at Lorette and at Mecca; but he succours the needy and defends the oppressed.

TOLERANCE

What is tolerance? it is the consequence of humanity. We are all formed of frailty and error; let us pardon reciprocally each other's folly— that is the first law of nature.

It is clear that the individual who persecutes a man, his brother, because he is not of the same opinion, is a monster. That admits of no difficulty. But the government! but the magistrates! but the princes! how do they treat those who have another worship than theirs? If they are powerful strangers, it is certain that a prince will make an alliance with them. François I., very Christian, will unite with Mussulmans against Charles V., very Catholic. François I. will give money to the Lutherans of Germany to support them in their revolt against the emperor; but, in accordance with custom, he will start by having Lutherans burned at home. For political reasons he pays them in Saxony; for political reasons he burns them in Paris. But what will happen? Persecutions make proselytes? Soon France will be full of new Protestants. At first they will let themselves be hanged, later they in their turn will hang. There will be civil wars, then will come the St.

Bartholomew; and this corner of the world will be worse than all that the ancients and moderns have ever told of hell.

Madmen, who have never been able to give worship to the God who made you! Miscreants, whom the example of the Noachides, the learned Chinese, the Parsees and all the sages, has never been able to lead! Monsters, who need superstitions as crows' gizzards need carrion! you have been told it already, and there is nothing else to tell you—if you have two religions in your countries, they will cut each other's throat; if you have thirty religions, they will dwell in peace. Look at the great Turk, he governs Guebres, Banians, Greek Christians, Nestorians, Romans. The first who tried to stir up tumult would be impaled; and everyone is tranquil.

Of all religions, the Christian is without doubt the one which should inspire tolerance most, although up to now the Christians have been the most intolerant of all men. The Christian Church was divided in its cradle, and was divided even in the persecutions which under the first emperors it sometimes endured. Often the martyr was regarded as an apostate by his brethren, and the Carpocratian Christian expired beneath the sword of the Roman executioners, excommunicated by the Ebionite Christian, the which Ebionite was anathema to the Sabellian.

This horrible discord, which has lasted for so many centuries, is a very striking lesson that we should pardon each other's errors; discord is the great ill of mankind; and tolerance is the only remedy for it.

There is nobody who is not in agreement with this truth, whether he meditates soberly in his study, or peaceably examines the truth with his friends. Why then do the same men who admit in private indulgence, kindness, justice, rise in public with so much fury against these virtues? Why? it is that their own interest is their god, and that they sacrifice everything to this monster that they worship.

I possess a dignity and a power founded on ignorance and credulity; I walk on the heads of the men who lie prostrate at my feet; if they should rise and look me in the face, I am lost; I must bind them to the ground, therefore, with iron chains.

Thus have reasoned the men whom centuries of bigotry have made powerful. They have other powerful men beneath them, and these have still others, who all enrich themselves with the spoils of the poor, grow fat on their blood, and laugh at their stupidity. They all detest tolerance, as partisans grown rich at the public expense fear to render their accounts, and as tyrants dread the word liberty. And then, to crown everything, they hire fanatics to cry at the top of their voices: "Respect my master's absurdities, tremble, pay, and keep your mouths shut."

It is thus that a great part of the world long was treated; but to-day when so many sects make a balance of power, what course to take with them? Every sect, as one knows, is a ground of error; there are no sects of geometers, algebraists, arithmeticians, because all the propositions of geometry, algebra and arithmetic are true. In every other science one may be deceived. What Thomist or Scotist theologian would dare say seriously that he is sure of his case?

If it were permitted to reason consistently in religious matters, it is clear that we all ought to become Jews, because Jesus Christ our Saviour was born a Jew, lived a Jew, died a Jew, and that he said expressly that he was accomplishing, that he was fulfilling the Jewish religion. But it is clearer still that we ought to be tolerant of one another, because we are all weak, inconsistent, liable to fickleness and error. Shall a reed laid low in the mud by the wind say to a fellow reed fallen in the opposite direction: "Crawl as I crawl, wretch, or I shall petition that you be torn up by the roots and burned?"

TRUTH

"Pilate therefore said unto him, Art thou a king then? Jesus answered, Thou sayest that I am a king. To this end was I born, and for this cause came I into the world, that I should bear witness unto the truth. Everyone that is of the truth heareth my voice.

"Pilate saith unto Him, What is truth? And when he had said this he went out, etc." (St. John xviii. 37.)

It is a sad thing for the human race that Pilate went out without waiting for the answer; we should know what truth is. Pilate had very little curiosity. The accused led before him, says he is king, that he was to be king; and Pilate does not inquire how that can be. He is supreme judge in Cæsar's name, he has power of life and death; his duty was to probe the sense of these words. He ought to say—"Tell me what you understand by being king. How were you born to be king and to bear witness to the truth? It is maintained that truth reaches but with difficulty to the ear of kings. I am judge, I have always had great trouble in finding it. While your enemies are howling against you without, give me some information on the point; you will be doing me the greatest service that has ever been done a judge; and I much prefer to learn to recognize truth, than to accede to the Jews' clamorous demand to have you hanged."

We shall not dare, to be sure, seek what the author of all truth would have been able to reply to Pilate.

Would he have said: "Truth is an abstract word which most men use indifferently in their books and judgments, for error and falsehood?"

This definition would have been marvellously appropriate to all makers of systems. Similarly is the word "wisdom" taken often for folly, and "wit" for nonsense.

Humanly speaking, let us define truth, while waiting for a better definition, as—"a statement of the facts as they are."

I suppose that if one had given only six months to teaching Pilate the truths of logic, he would assuredly have made this conclusive syllogism. One must not take away the life of a man who has only preached good morality: well, the man who has been impeached has, on the showing of his enemies even, often preached excellent morality; therefore he should not be punished with death.

He might have drawn this further argument.

My duty is to disperse the riotous assemblage of a seditious people who demand a man's death, unreasonably and without legal form; well, that is the position of the Jews in this instance; therefore I must drive them away and break up their meeting.

We suppose that Pilate knew arithmetic; hence we will not speak of those forms of truth.

As regards mathematical truths, I think it would have taken at least three years before he could have learned higher geometry. The truths of physics combined with those of geometry would have demanded more than four years. We spend six, ordinarily, in studying theology; I ask twelve for Pilate, seeing that he was pagan, and that six years would not have been too much for eradicating all his old errors, and six years more for making him fit to receive a doctor's hood.

If Pilate had had a well-balanced mind, I should have asked only two years to teach him metaphysical truth; and as metaphysical truth is necessarily allied to moral truth, I flatter myself that in less than nine years he would have become a real scholar and a perfectly honest man.

I should then have said to Pilate:—Historical truths are merely probabilities. If you had fought at the battle of Philippi, that is for you a truth which you know by intuition, by perception. But for us who dwell near the Syrian desert, it is merely a very probable thing, which we know by hearsay. How much hearsay is necessary to form a conviction equal to that of a man who, having seen the thing, can flatter himself that he has a sort of certainty?

He who has heard the thing told by twelve thousand eyewitnesses, has only twelve thousand probabilities, equal to one strong probability, which is not equal to certainty.

If you have the thing from only one of these witnesses, you know nothing; you should be sceptical. If the witness is dead, you should be still more sceptical, for you cannot enlighten yourself. If from several witnesses who are dead, you are in the same plight. If from those to whom the witnesses have spoken, your scepticism should increase still more.

From generation to generation scepticism increases, and probability diminishes; and soon probability is reduced to zero.

TYRANNY

One gives the name of tyrant to the sovereign who knows no laws but those of his caprice, who takes his subjects' property, and who afterwards enrols them to go to take the property of his neighbours. There are none of these tyrants in Europe.

One distinguishes between the tyranny of one man and that of many. The tyranny of many would be that of a body which invaded the rights of other bodies, and which exercised despotism in favour of the laws corrupted by it. Nor are there any tyrants of this sort in Europe.

Under which tyranny would you like to live? Under neither; but if I had to choose, I should detest the tyranny of one man less than that of many. A despot always has his good moments; an assembly of despots never. If a tyrant does me an injustice, I can disarm him through his mistress, his confessor or his page; but a company of grave tyrants is inaccessible to all seductions. When it is not unjust, it is at the least hard, and never does it bestow favours.

If I have only one despot, I am quit of him by drawing myself up against a wall when I see him pass, or by bowing low, or by striking the ground with my forehead, according to the custom of the country; but if there is a company of a hundred despots, I am exposed to repeating this ceremony a hundred times a day, which in the long run is very annoying if one's hocks are not supple. If I have a farm in the neighbourhood of one of our lords, I am crushed; if I plead against a relation of the relations of one of our lords, I am ruined. What is to be done? I fear that in this world one is reduced to being either hammer or anvil; lucky the man who escapes these alternatives!

VIRTUE

SECTION I

It is said of Marcus Brutus that, before killing himself, he uttered these words: "O virtue! I thought you were something; but you are only an empty phantom!"

You were right, Brutus, if you considered virtue as being head of a faction, and assassin of your benefactor; but if you had considered virtue as consisting only of doing good to those dependent on you, you would not have called it a phantom, and you would not have killed yourself in despair.

I am very virtuous says this excrement of theology, for I have the four cardinal virtues, and the three divine. An honest man asks him—"What is the cardinal virtue?" The other answers—"Strength, prudence, temperance and justice."

THE HONEST MAN:

If you are just, you have said everything; your strength, your prudence, your temperance, are useful qualities. If you have them, so much the better for you; but if you are just, so much the better for the others. But it is not enough to be just, you must do good; that is what is really cardinal. And your divine virtues, which are they?

THE EXCREMENT:

Faith, hope, charity.

THE HONEST MAN:

Is it a virtue to believe? either what you believe seems true to you, and in this case there is no merit in believing; or it seems false to you, and then it is impossible for you to believe.

Hope cannot be a virtue any more than fear; one fears and one hopes, according as one receives a promise or a threat. As for charity, is it not what the Greeks and the Romans understood by humanity, love of one's neighbour? this love is nothing if it be not active; doing good, therefore, is the sole true virtue.

THE EXCREMENT:

One would be a fool! Really, I am to give myself a deal of torment in order to serve mankind, and I shall get no return! all work deserves payment. I do not mean to do the least honest action, unless I am certain of paradise.

THE HONEST MAN:

Ah, master! that is to say that, if you did not hope for paradise, and if you did not fear hell, you would never do any good action. Believe me, master, there are two things worthy of being loved for themselves, God and virtue.

THE EXCREMENT:

I see, sir, you are a disciple of Fénélon.

THE HONEST MAN:

Yes, master.

THE EXCREMENT:

I shall denounce you to the judge of the ecclesiastical court at Meaux.

THE HONEST MAN:

Go along, denounce!

SECTION II

What is virtue? Beneficence towards the fellow-creature. Can I call virtue things other than those which do me good? I am needy, you are generous. I am in danger, you help me. I am deceived, you tell me the truth. I am neglected, you console me. I am ignorant, you teach me. Without difficulty I shall call you virtuous. But what will become of the cardinal and divine virtues? Some of them will remain in the schools.

What does it matter to me that you are temperate? you observe a precept of health; you will have better health, and I am happy to hear it. You have faith and hope, and I am happy still; they will procure you eternal life. Your divine virtues are celestial gifts; your cardinal virtues are excellent qualities which serve to guide you: but they are not virtues as regards your fellow-creature. The prudent man does good to himself,

207

the virtuous man does good to mankind. St. Paul was right to tell you that charity prevails over faith and hope.

But shall only those that are useful to one's fellow-creature be admitted as virtues? How can I admit any others? We live in society; really, therefore, the only things that are good for us are those that are good for society. A recluse will be sober, pious; he will be clad in hair-cloth; he will be a saint: but I shall not call him virtuous until he has done some act of virtue by which other men have profited. So long as he is alone, he is doing neither good nor evil; for us he is nothing. If St. Bruno brought peace to families, if he succoured want, he was virtuous; if he fasted, prayed in solitude, he was a saint. Virtue among men is an interchange of kindness; he who has no part in this interchange should not be counted. If this saint were in the world, he would doubtless do good; but so long as he is not in the world, the world will be right in refusing him the title of virtuous; he will be good for himself and not for us.

But, you say to me, if a recluse is a glutton, a drunkard, given to secret debauches with himself, he is vicious; he is virtuous, therefore, if he has the opposite qualities. That is what I cannot agree: he is a very disagreeable fellow if he has the faults you mention; but he is not vicious, wicked, punishable as regards society to whom these infamies do no harm. It is to be presumed that were he to return to society he would do harm there, that he would be very vicious; and it is even more probable that he would be a wicked man, than it is sure that the other temperate and chaste recluse would be a virtuous man, for in society faults increase, and good qualities diminish.

A much stronger objection is made; Nero, Pope Alexander VI., and other monsters of this species, have bestowed kindnesses; I answer hardily that on that day they were virtuous.

A few theologians say that the divine emperor Antonine was not virtuous; that he was a stubborn Stoic who, not content with commanding men, wished further to be esteemed by them; that he attributed to himself the good he did to the human race; that all his life he was just, laborious, beneficent through vanity, and that he only deceived men through his virtues. "My God!" I exclaim. "Give us often rogues like him!"

WHY?

Why does one hardly ever do the tenth part of the good one might do?

Why in half Europe do girls pray to God in Latin, which they do not understand?

Why in antiquity was there never a theological quarrel, and why were no people ever distinguished by the name of a sect? The Egyptians were not called Isiacs or Osiriacs; the peoples of Syria did not have the name of Cybelians. The Cretans had a particular devotion to Jupiter, and were never entitled Jupiterians. The ancient Latins were very attached to Saturn; there was not a village in Latium called Saturnian: on the contrary, the disciples of the God of truth taking their master's title, and calling themselves "anointed" like Him, declared, as soon as they could, an eternal war on all the peoples who were not anointed, and made war among themselves for fourteen hundred years, taking the names of Arians, Manicheans, Donatists, Hussites, Papists, Lutherans, Calvinists. And lastly, the Jansenists and the Molinists have had no more poignant mortification than that of not having been able to slaughter each other in pitched battle. Whence does this come?

Why is the great number of hard-working, innocent men who till the land every day of the year that you may eat all its fruits, scorned, vilified, oppressed, robbed; and why is it that the useless and often very wicked man who lives only by their work, and who is rich only through their poverty, is on the contrary respected, courted, considered?

Why is it that, the fruits of the earth being so necessary for the conservation of men and animals, one yet sees so many years and so many countries where there is entire lack of these fruits?

Why is the half of Africa and America covered with poisons?

Why is there no land where insects are not far in excess of men?

Why does a little whitish, evil-smelling secretion form a being which has hard bones, desires and thoughts? and why do these beings always persecute each other?

Why does so much evil exist, seeing that everything is formed by a God whom all theists are agreed in naming "good?"

Why, since we complain ceaselessly of our ills, do we spend all our time in increasing them?

Why, as we are so miserable, have we imagined that not to be is a great ill, when it is clear that it was not an ill not to be before we were born?

Why and how does one have dreams during sleep, if one has no soul; and how is it that these dreams are always so incoherent, so extravagant, if one has a soul?

Why do the stars move from west to east rather than from east to west?

Why do we exist? why is there anything?

DECLARATION OF THE ADMIRERS, QUESTIONERS AND DOUBTERS WHO HAVE AMUSED THEMSELVES BY PROPOUNDING TO THE SCHOLARS THE ABOVE QUESTIONS IN NINE VOLUMES.[23]

We declare to the scholars that, being like them prodigiously ignorant about the first principles of all things, and about the natural, typical, mystic, allegorical sense of many things, we refer these things to the infallible judgment of the Holy Inquisition of Rome, Florence, Madrid, Lisbon, and to the decrees of the Sorbonne of Paris, perpetual council of the Gauls.

Our errors springing in no wise from malice, but being the natural consequence of human frailty, we hope that they will be pardoned to us in this world and the other.

We beseech the small number of heavenly spirits who are still shut up in France in mortal bodies, and who, from there, enlighten the universe at *thirty sous* the sheet, to communicate their luminousness to us for the tenth volume which we reckon on publishing at the end of Lent

---

[23] The Philosophical Dictionary was first published as "Questions on the Encyclopedia," then reprinted as "Reason by Alphabet," and then finally, with many additions, became the "Philosophical Dictionary."

210

1772, or in Advent 1773; and for their luminousness we will pay *forty sous*.

This tenth volume will contain some very curious articles, which, if God favours us, will give new point to the salt which we shall endeavour to bestow in the thanks we shall give to these gentlemen.